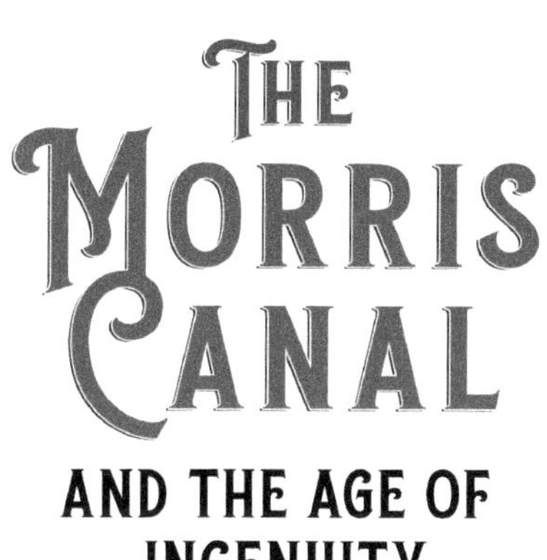

THE MORRIS CANAL

AND THE AGE OF INGENUITY

THE MORRIS CANAL

AND THE AGE OF INGENUITY

CLIMBING MOUNTAINS TO SOLVE AMERICA'S FIRST ENERGY CRISIS

KEVIN W. WRIGHT

AMERICA THROUGH TIME

America Through Time®
An imprint of Sutton Publishing Inc
www.through-time.com

This edition published in the United States of America 2025

ISBN 978-1-62545-164-4 (paperback)

Typeset in 10pt on 13pt Sabon
Printed and bound in the United States of America

Contents

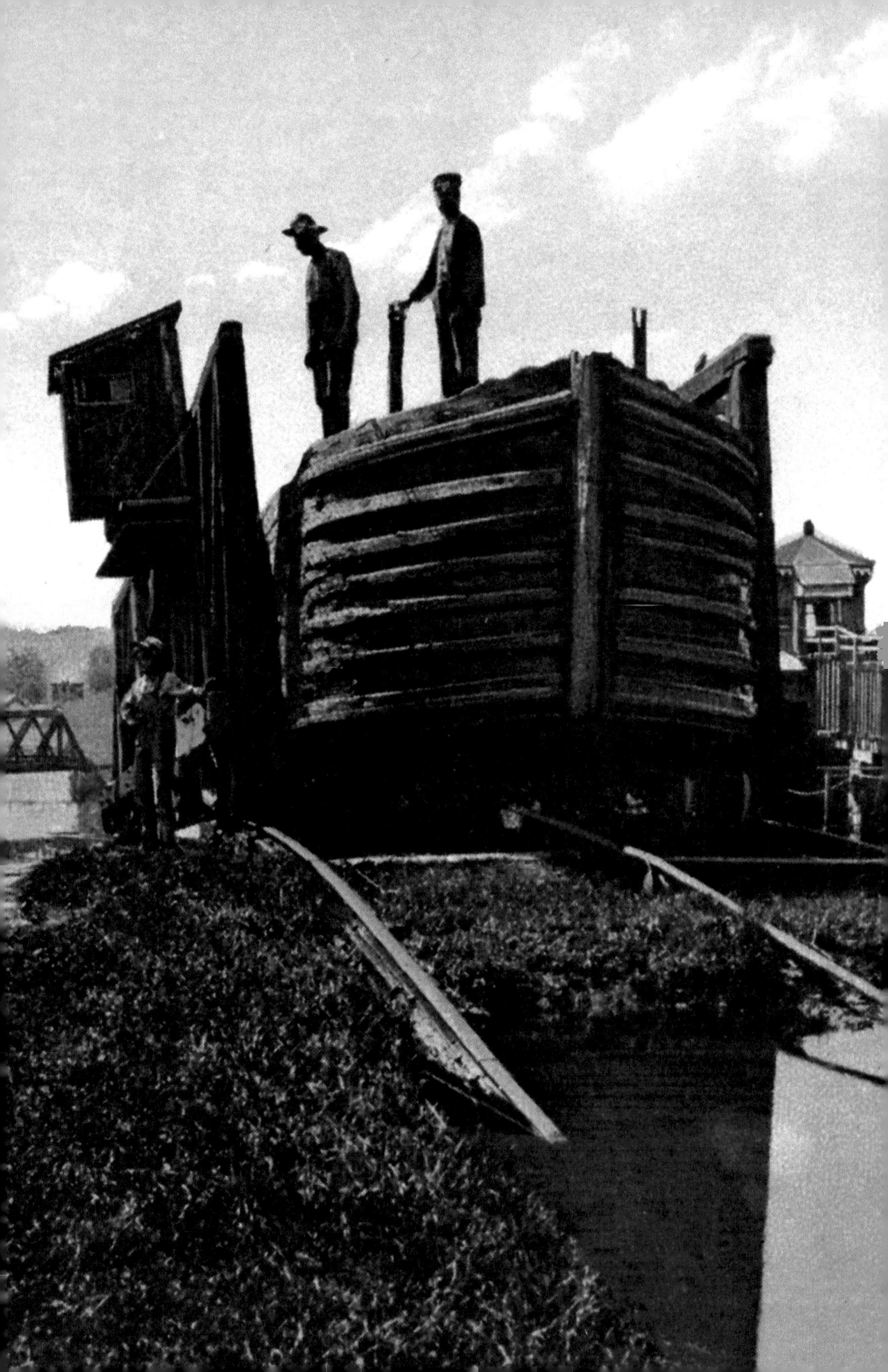

Acknowledgments

In 1870, census takers listed my great-great-grandfather Samuel Wright as a boatman on the Morris Canal in Washington, New Jersey. Despite this connection, the Morris Canal did not capture my interest until 1978, when I worked at the restored canal village of Waterloo. I soon made the pilgrimage to Plane No. 9 West at Stewartsville, where Jim and Mary Lee, residing in the old plane-tender's house, tenderly nourished the memory of towpath days. There I first met and marveled at an age of mechanical ingenuity that never afterwards lost its fascination. James Lee authored the groundbreaking *The Morris Canal, A Photographic History* (1973) and *Tales the Boatmen Told* (1977).

Friendly luminaries of the Canal Society of New Jersey, such as Clayton F. Smith, William Moss and Robert R. Goller, fostered my curiosity. Barbara Kalata compiled the comprehensive *A Hundred Years, A Hundred Miles* (1983). Robert Goller published the equally popular *The Morris Canal—Across New Jersey by Water and Rail* and regularly contributes to *Reflections on the Morris Canal*, published by the Canal Society. I am grateful to friend and scholar Robert Goller for his thoughtful review of my manuscript, providing many corrections, revisions and helpful suggestions.

I also acknowledge the full partnership of my wife Deborah Powell and our children, Ivan, Benjamin and Anna. I also thank those who gave me a love of history at an early age.

Introduction

How did America ascend from a colonial backwater to a global economic powerhouse in a single century? Determination, powered by muscle and genius, is the easy answer. And we need look no farther than our own neighborhoods for important evidence. For, in recesses of the Jersey Highlands as well as along well-trodden urban avenues, the towpath of the old Morris Canal exhibits the handiwork of nineteenth-century Americans, who resolutely laid the groundwork with shovel and wheelbarrow for a future we inhabit. Cut across a thinly settled countryside, the canal gave birth or nourishment to a string of hamlets and cities across northern New Jersey, between Phillipsburg on the Delaware River and Jersey City on the Hudson River.

This is the story of America's first energy crisis. As the primeval forest receded steadily inland from the populating seaboard, city-dwellers and manufacturers paid ever more dearly for cordwood. Anthracite coal, embedded in the high hills of north-eastern Pennsylvania, promised a solution, if only it could be brought to market at a reasonable price. This challenged engineers, bankers and politicians to design and build an extensive system of water and rail transport to ensure a dependable coal supply to consumers. In the lofty estimation of Joseph C. Potts, who published *The New Jersey Register* in 1837, the Morris Canal and Banking Company was chartered in 1824 'to undertake a most bold, original and adventurous enterprise.' Its objective 'was no less than to open a canal navigation between the Delaware and Hudson, a distance of one hundred and two miles, over hills at least nine hundred feet high.' That task proved more daunting than anticipated. American civil engineers, trained largely at West Point, struggled to substitute a system of water-powered inclined planes for traditional lockage, for 1,400 feet of ascent and descent along the mountainous route. Since perfecting a reliable system of inclined planes for the Morris Canal was more tedious and expensive than envisioned, financing it proved as tricky as mechanical engineering. So this too is a tale of high finance. Shortly after its birth, the

Morris Canal and Banking Company became embroiled in intrigue, scandal and embarrassment on Wall Street.

Seven years of technological experimentation and backbreaking labor tried the patience of mechanics, engineers and anxious investors, but pushed innovation and talent beyond the comfortable boundaries of accepted theory and traditional thinking. In truth, even though a greatly improved model of an inclined plane—employing an iron turbine and wire rope—was installed at Port Colden in 1847, it wasn't until the last inclined plane on the Eastern Division of the Morris Canal was upgraded in 1860 that boats of 70 gross tons could finally pass between the coal regions and tidewater. In 1866, its peak year, the Morris Canal carried 889,220 tons of freight. Within a decade, the canal was competing against three railroads which operated the year round, each with a carrying capacity of 10 million tons annually. But before the Morris Canal succumbed to obsolescence, it forever altered the economic landscape through which it passed. Most importantly, it married iron ore to anthracite coal, giving birth to the age of American railroads.

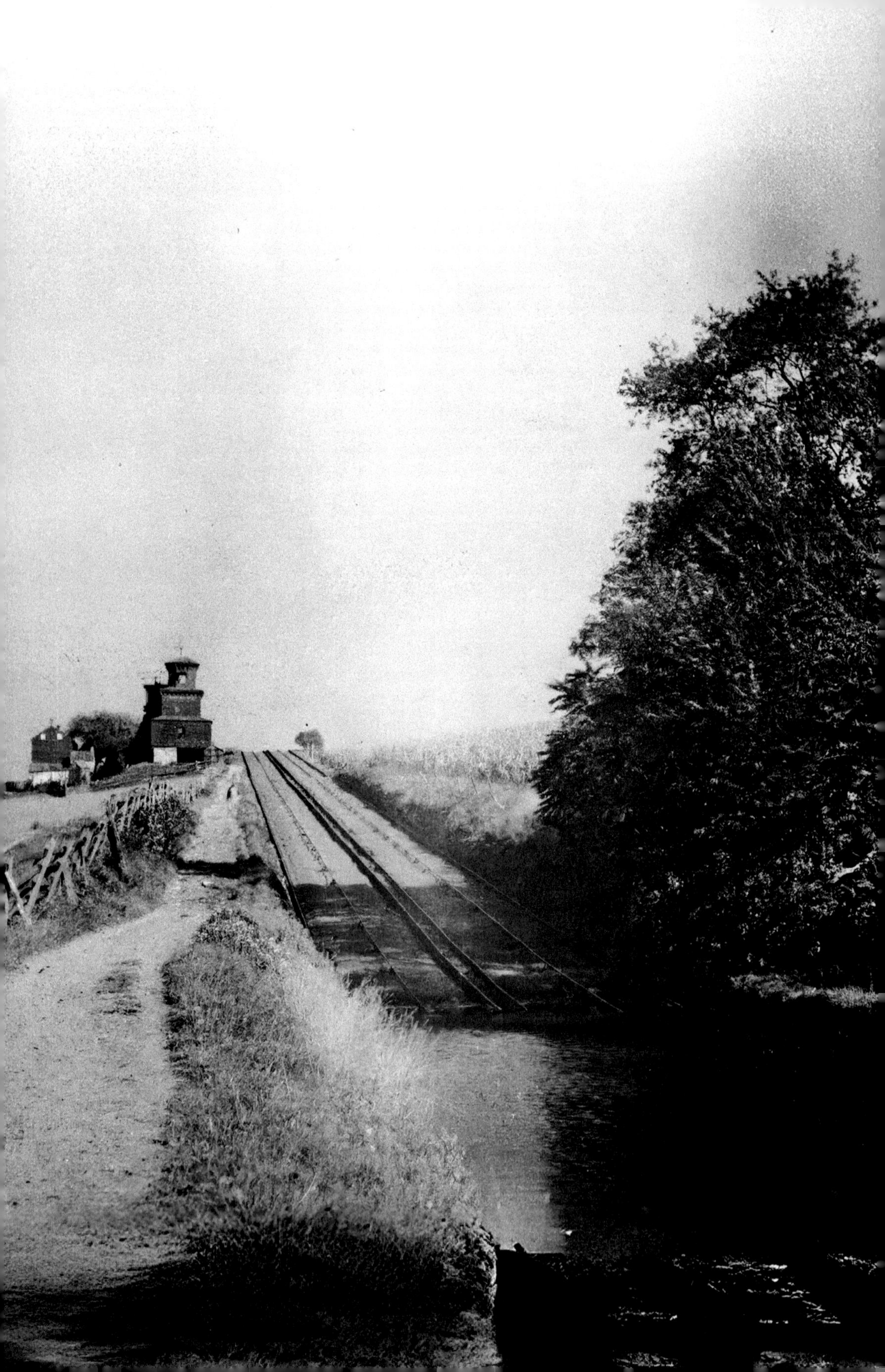

1

The Coal Rush

As one encyclopedist noted in 1840, 'Before the discovery of coal mines, or the invention of cheap means of working them, wood was the general fuel of the earth.'[1] The average eighteenth-century American household annually consumed 35 cords of firewood, representing the clear cutting of approximately 2 acres of woodland.[2] Even more devouring, Highland blast furnaces each consumed 6,000 bushels of charcoal weekly in the production of 20 tons of pig iron.[3] Watching 16,000 cords of wood annually go up in smoke in his two furnaces and forge, one New Jersey ironmaker complained that 20,000 acres of woodland were hardly sufficient to supply a single furnace.[4] Almost inevitably, the iron industry languished once adjacent woodlands were denuded.

As seaport villages grew from colonial footholds into manufacturing cities, their populations exhausted woodlots within carting range. *Niles' Weekly Register* commented in 1815 on the great advance in firewood prices over the previous thirty years, noting, 'as the number of the inhabitants of our towns increase and manufactures that require fuel are introduced, the woods of the neighborhood diminish and the expense of transportation is increased.'[5] Frozen rivers and deep snow reduced supply in the season of greatest demand. Consequently, Philadelphians paid a high price, $10 to $15 per cord, for wood in the winter of 1820.[6]

Fuel economy invited city dwellers and mechanics to import bituminous coal from Virginia or Great Britain. When a British blockade cut off supplies during the War of 1812, Americans were forced to take a hard look at 'stone coal'. Finding it difficult to ignite in a fireplace, they remained prejudiced against its use until 1808 when Judge Jesse Fell, of Wilkes-Barre, first burnt anthracite in a crudely made hearth-grate of his own invention.[7] Once ablaze, anthracite supplied greater heat than even hickory wood and without the trouble of constant attendance.[8] Blacksmiths were among the first to recognize its value.[9] In 1807, John and Obadiah Smith shipped 55 tons of coal down the

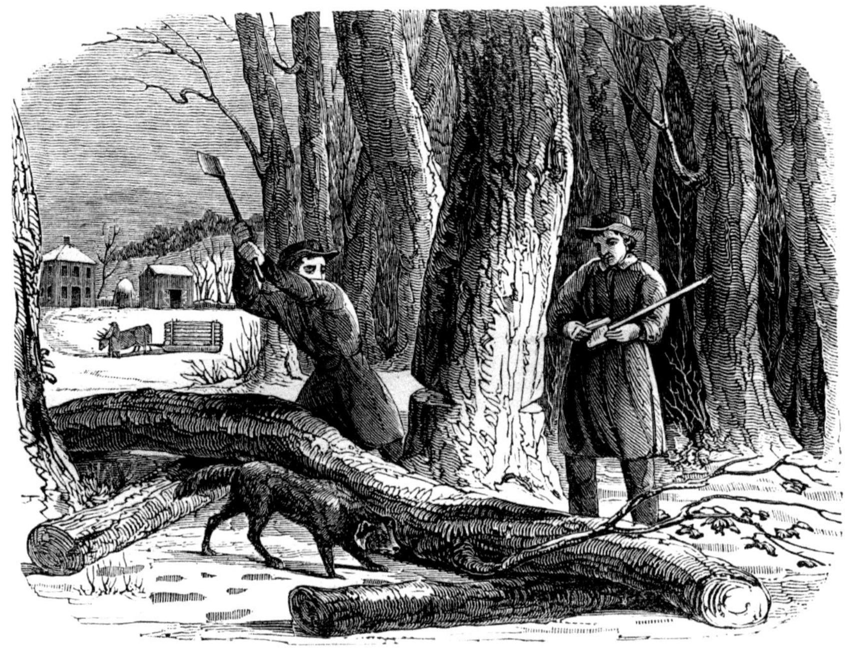

One woodcutter whets his axe as another chops. Oxen haul timber on a sledge. Farmers' almanacs and encyclopedias depicted woodcutting as a winter occupation. (*The American Magazine of Useful and Entertaining Knowledge*)

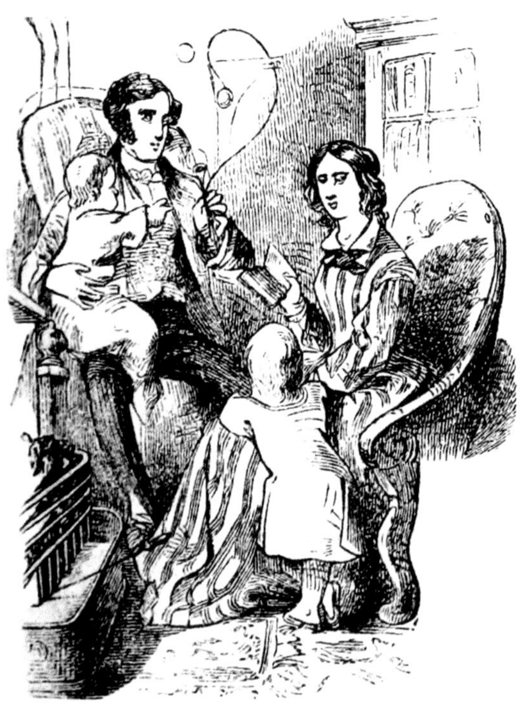

Family enjoys heat from coal grate. (*Harper's New Monthly Magazine*)

Susquehanna River from Plymouth, Pennsylvania, to Columbia. Over the next five years, shipments increased to 500 tons annually with anthracite selling at $10 per ton in Baltimore and $12 per ton in New York. To increase sales, the Smiths demonstrated the use of coal grates in public houses.[10]

So near and yet so far! A vast anthracite formation covers 470 square miles of north-eastern Pennsylvania, residing in mountains at the head of the Schuylkill, Lehigh and Lackawaxen Rivers. According to tradition, lumberman Nicho Allen, while out hunting in 1790, lit a campfire that accidently ignited an outcrop of anthracite on Broad Mountain in Schuylkill County.[11] Another hunter, Philip Ginter, discovered coal on Summit Hill at Mauch Chunk in 1791. A year later, financiers John Nicholson and Robert Morris founded the Lehigh Coal Mine Company, acquiring 10,000 acres on Mauch Chunk Mountain, where they were first to mine stone coal, poling small quantities on arks downstream to Philadelphia.[12] Impeached but acquitted on charges of diverting public funds to his own advantage, John Nicholson resigned as comptroller general of Pennsylvania in 1794. He and Robert Morris partnered to grab 3,700,000 acres of Pennsylvania real estate on speculation. Learning of coal deposits at the headwaters of the Schuylkill,

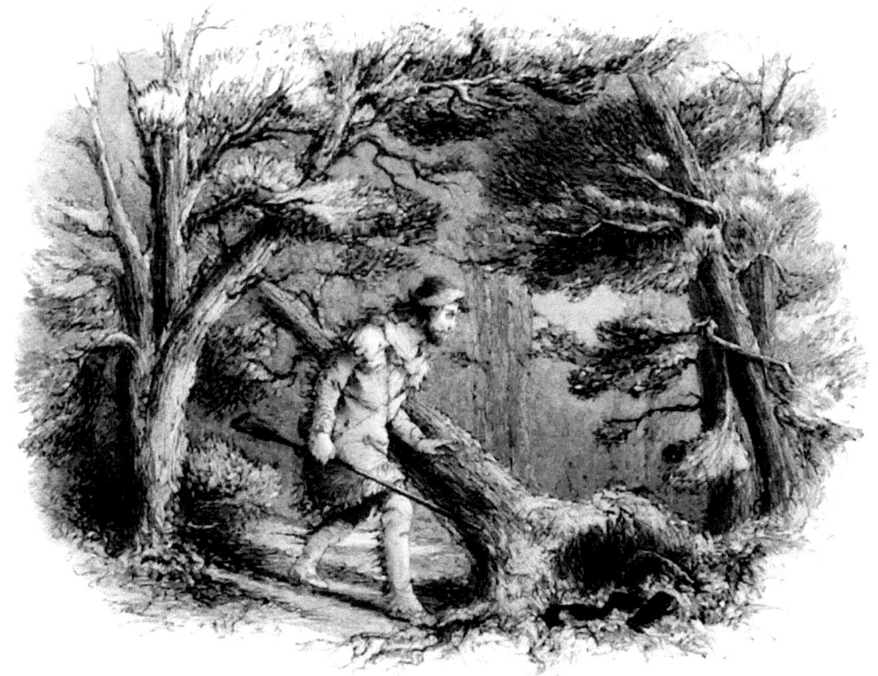

Out hunting, Philip Ginter finds 'stone coal' under the roots of a blown-down tree on Summit Hill, above Mauch Chunk, in 1791. (*Harper's New Monthly Magazine*)

Nicholson purchased 21,649 acres from Isaac Snowden, of Philadelphia, by a mortgage deed dated 22 January 1795. Like many others, Snowden was left holding the bag when Nicholson's overextended financial empire collapsed and the former comptroller general died in a debtors' prison on December 5, 1800.

Trained for the Presbyterian ministry at Princeton, Isaac Snowden's son Charles veered into a career in journalism in New York City, becoming editor of the Federalist *Daily-Advertiser* in 1798.[13] Two years later, following Nicholson's financial disgrace and death, Charles Jeffry Snowden looked to recover ownership of his father's coal lands at the headwaters of the Schuylkill and so returned to his native Pennsylvania.[14] By this time, Isaac Snowden had on behalf of his son Nathaniel brought suit against John Nicholson's widow and heirs to recover the debt owed on the Schuylkill coalfields, but Isaac died on 26 December 1809. According to testimony offered in 1837 to settle a subsequent dispute over title to these lands, Major Charles Snowden dissuaded others from bidding when this valuable property was sold at sheriff's sale in August 1810.[15] Claiming he acted on behalf of his brother, Reverend Nathaniel R. Snowden (a poor preacher who supposedly "did not understand anything about business"), Charles successfully bid $100. However, as the deed was being recorded, he reputedly persuaded a clerk to fraudulently erase his brother's name and substitute his own.

Reacting to the opportunity created when President Jefferson embargoed foreign imports, Josiah White and Erskine Hazard opened the Fairmount Nail and Wire Works at the falls of the Schuylkill, above Philadelphia, in 1810. Shortly after the outbreak of war in 1812, they experimented with a wagonload of anthracite, purchased from Colonel George Shoemaker of Pottsville.[16] Sensing its enormous potential, White and Hazard applied for a charter to improve navigation on the Schuylkill, but were frustrated when the senator from Schuylkill County asserted the 'black stone' found at its headwaters would not burn and therefore was not coal.[17] Undeterred, they incorporated the Schuylkill Navigation Company in 1815.

A decade of embargo and blockade stimulated American manufacturing. When Congress doubled tariff duties as a wartime measure, domestic manufacturers such as Josiah White and Erskine Hazard enjoyed a profitable respite from foreign competition. National credit was exhausted, however, by the time the Treaty of Ghent ended hostilities in December 1814. Facing rampant inflation, many state banks suspended specie payments. As American farmers slumped into recession, Free Traders regained ascendancy in 1816, allowing British merchants to 'dump' goods on the American market at ruinous prices. The duty on imported coal was 5 cents per bushel from 1794 to 1812; it doubled during the War of 1812, but was again reduced to 5 cents in 1816.[18] As a sign of hard times, a soup kitchen on Franklin Street, New York,

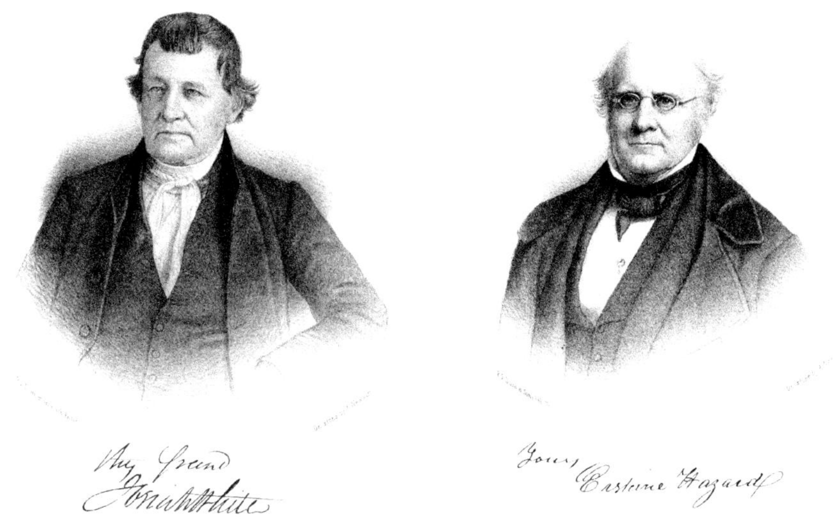

Above left: Josiah White. (*History of the Lehigh Valley*)

Above right: Erskine Hazard. (*History of the Lehigh Valley*)

fed 3,853 persons in February 1817.[19] Firewood and imported coal became so expensive that many skimped on heat. Those who promoted American agriculture and industry understood cheap and reliable transportation was key to tapping the nation's immense resources.

While only a few feet of gravelly loam blanketed coal beds in Pennsylvania, these seams were situated in hills ranging 300 to 600 feet above the level of adjacent rivers, complicating its transport. Given the strain and expense of hauling bulk materials over rough roads, canals offered an attractive alternative. To reduce costs and make anthracite the common fuel, speculators would have to create an extensive system of water carriage, improving or connecting the Hudson, Delaware, Lehigh, Schuylkill and Susquehanna Rivers to feed and fuel growing seaboard markets. But where would the young nation find capital sufficient to fund internal improvements on such a grand scale or the engineering skill to build them?

For its part, the New Jersey legislature appointed John Rutherfurd, John N. Simpson and George Holcombe in 1816 to ascertain the best route and probable cost of a canal to connect the Delaware and Raritan Rivers.[20] These canal commissioners reconsidered a plan, originally proposed in 1804, to canalize the Raritan and Millstone Rivers by building locks in milldams, continuing in this fashion up Stony Brook to the Great Meadows in Lawrence Township. Here the canal would cross its summit level, using locks to ascend and descend the divide between Stony Brook and Shipetaukin Creek, a tributary of the

Assunpink. By also canalizing Assunpink Creek to the Delaware River, the proposed canal would open 40 miles of inland navigation. Objections included the prohibitive expense of clearing obstructions from sandstone riverbeds and diverting sufficient water, especially in summer, to operate a canal without adversely effecting waterpowers. Narrow ravines along the projected route would not readily admit the construction of towpaths, so the commissioners instead recommended excavating a canal across the sandy inner coastal plain with locks overcoming changes in elevation of 136 feet along a 29-mile route. The estimated cost was $836,824. There remained unresolved, however, 'the almost insuperable difficulty of procuring a sufficient supply of water at the crown to answer the demand at the locks, for the passage of every boat to or from the summit, and from thence to tidewater.'[21]

Elsewhere more ambitious hands were already at work. Contractor John Richardson officially broke ground near Rome, NY, on 4 July 1817, for the Erie Canal, boldly planned to connect Lake Erie and the Hudson River over a distance of 362 miles. The faltering post-war economy raised concerns about such an expensive undertaking, especially when the Second Bank of the United States called in loans and foreclosed mortgages in 1819, feeding a financial storm.[22] Bank closures, currency depreciation, a collapse in prices and high unemployment wracked the nation. Some attributed economic distress, a persistent drought and even outbreaks of whooping cough and yellow fever to the appearance of a long-tailed comet in July 1819; yet work proceeded apace on Governor DeWitt Clinton's 'Big Ditch'. Finally, on 26 October 1825, cannon salutes marked the progress of the first boat to travel between New York and Buffalo. Since Lake Erie stands 564 feet above the Hudson, 80 locks were needed to overcome a total rise and fall of 662 feet. Built 40 feet wide at water level, 28 feet wide at bottom and 4 feet deep, the Erie Canal accommodated boats of 40 to 100 tons, drawn by horses at a rate not exceeding 5 miles per hour. Packet boats could travel nearly 100 miles in 24 hours, charging passengers 3 or 4 cents per mile. A wonder of its time, the Erie Canal halved the cost of transporting goods between the Ohio and Hudson Valleys. Flour manufactured on the shores of Lake Erie suddenly sold at New Bern, North Carolina, for $5.50 per barrel. Yet it cost $2.00 to transport a barrel of flour only 120 miles overland from Raleigh to New Bern, a much larger sum than was paid for freight from Lake Erie to New Bern over a distance of 1,200 miles.

The lesson was not lost on others. Having leased coal mines above Mauch Chunk for twenty years, Josiah White and Erskine Hazard formed the Lehigh Navigation Company and the Lehigh Coal Company in 1818.[23] They built an 8-mile road between the summit mine and the Lehigh River for oxen to pull carts capable of carrying 9 tons of stone coal.[24] They also erected a saw mill with 25 saws, including a circular saw, to cut 20,000 feet of lumber

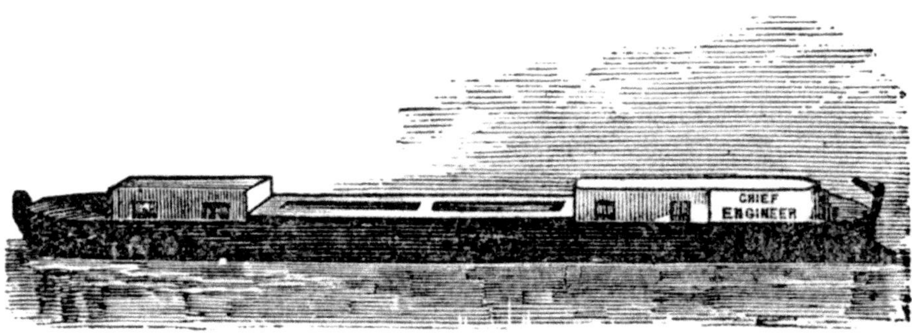

FIRST CANAL BOAT.

Built by Canvass White, the first canal boat to pass the Erie Canal on 22 October 1819, measured 61 feet long, 7½ feet wide and was named the *Chief Engineer* in honor of Benjamin Wright. (Stuart, *Lives and Works of Civil and Military Engineers of America*)

daily, floating planks downstream to construct 50 dams and 13 locks. This enabled them to wash 365 tons of coal on arks to Philadelphia on a sequence of artificial freshets in 1819, their first year of operation. Consequently, both Lehigh and Liverpool coal sold for $14 per chaldron ($4.73 per ton) in Philadelphia in January 1824.[25]

A boat from Mauch Chunk bearing 325 barrels of flour, manufactured on the north-east branch of the Susquehanna, and 20 tons of Lehigh coal, arrived in Philadelphia on 19 July 1824. Costing 13 cents per barrel to transport the flour over a distance of 140 miles, this shipment was hailed as the first experiment in bringing the trade of the Susquehanna River to Philadelphia by means of improved navigation on the Lehigh River.[26] The *Philadelphia National Gazette* also found it 'gratifying to state that the Lehigh Company have sent down to this city the present season, 150 boats, carrying 250,000 bushels of Coal—and that the regular shipments from Mauch Chunk now amount to 2,000 bushels per day.'

Six-and-a-half thousand tons of Lehigh anthracite sold for $3.08 per ton in Philadelphia in 1825. Coal shipments from the Schuylkill basin commenced in 1825 with delivery of 6,500 tons. By 1830, combined shipments grew to 90,000 tons, dropping the price to $2.52 per ton.[27] Between 1825 and 1835, coal outstripped every other type of fuel in the three largest Atlantic seaboard cities, not only for manufacturing purposes, but also for domestic heating and cooking. It was a startling revolution: for the first fifteen years after anthracite was introduced in 1820, the market grew by 33 percent annually, slowing to 16 percent annual growth between 1835 and 1838, when 830,000 tons were consumed. By 1845, steamboats operating out of New York City and Philadelphia alone annually consumed nearly 150,000 tons of coal.[28]

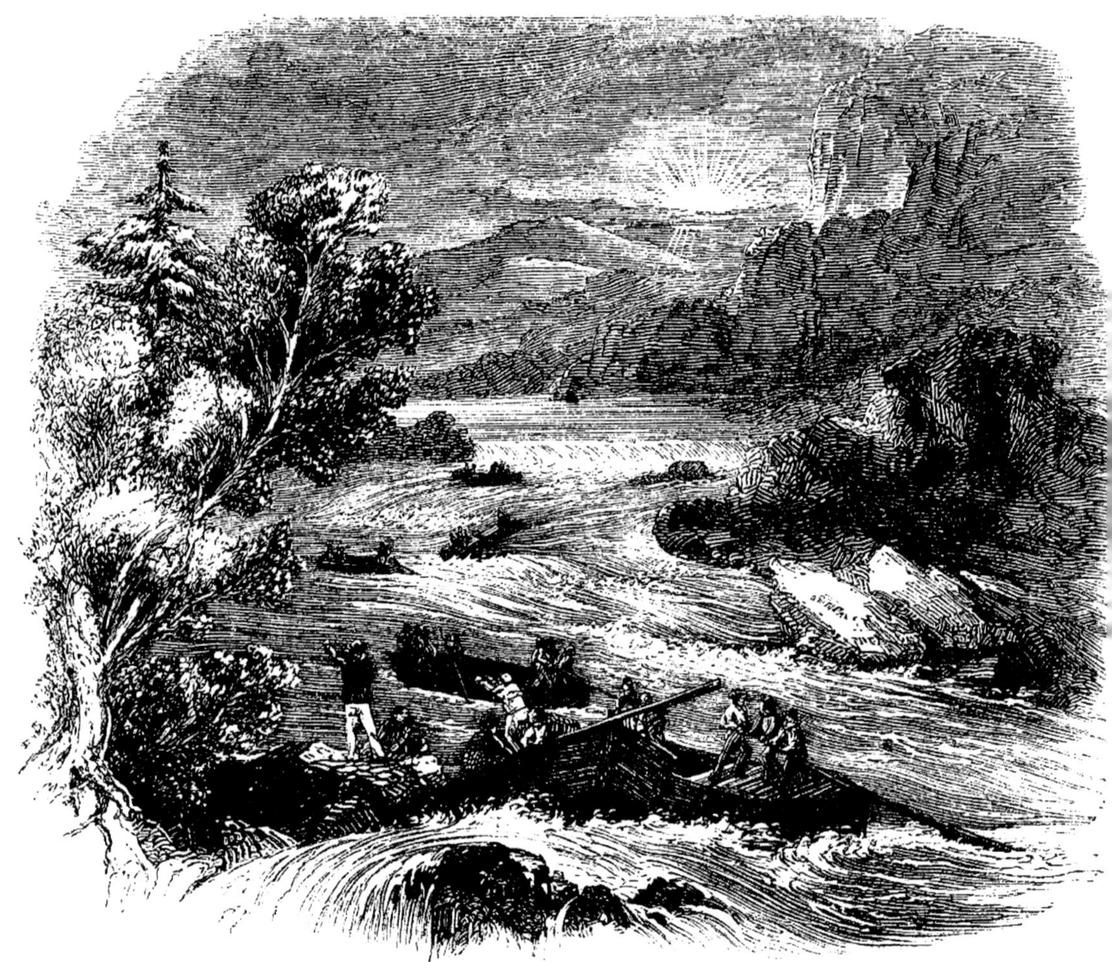

Boatmen with long oars steered coal arks downstream. At journey's end, the arks were sold for lumber, their crews walking home to Mauch Chunk. (*Harper's New Monthly Magazine*, 1857)

The coal rush was on. Charles Snowden presented specimens of Schuylkill anthracite to Cadwallader Evans Jr, president of the Schuylkill Navigation Company, in 1817, accompanied by a topographical survey that calculated the fall of the Schuylkill between the coal mines and tidewater in Philadelphia at 480 feet.[29] Manipulating a most reputable engineer to attract wealthy New York capitalists to his scheme, Snowden took Brigadier-General Joseph Gardner Swift, recently resigned superintendent of the United States Military Academy at West Point, to tour coal deposits near Orwigsburg, seat of Schuylkill County, in January 1820.[30] Stopping in Philadelphia on their return

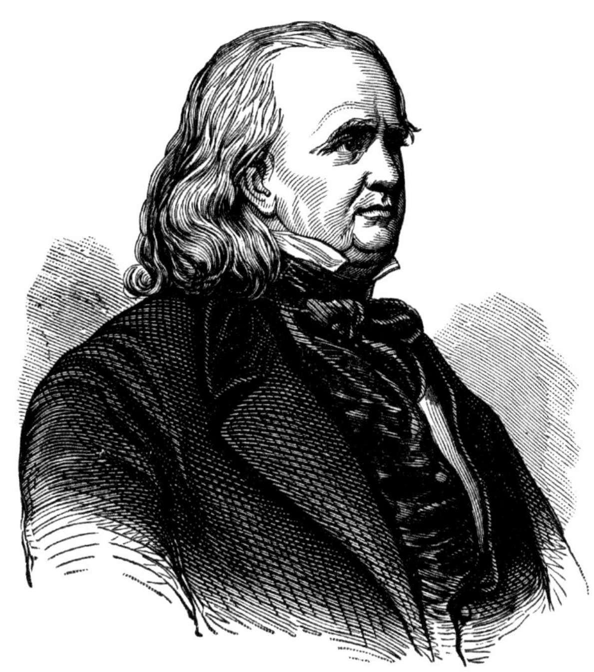

Brigadier-General Joseph Gardner Swift. (*Harper's Encyclopedia of United States History*, 1912)

to New York City, Snowden introduced Joseph G. Swift to Cadwallader Evans and to Samuel Mifflin, president of the Union Canal, then under construction between Reading and Middleton, Pennsylvania.[31] At Elizabeth, New Jersey, Swift dropped in on Governor Isaac Halstead Williamson to confer on a plan to open canal navigation between the Delaware River and New York Harbor. The legislature had incorporated the Delaware and Raritan Canal Company on 1 March 1820, naming representatives from Philadelphia, New York, Newark, New Brunswick and Trenton as commissioners.[32] The New Jersey legislature subsequently appointed Joseph G. Swift and Nathaniel Prime, a prominent Wall Street banker and stockbroker, to superintend the canal plan, but the project was deferred.[33]

Once home, Joseph G. Swift enthusiastically lit the first fire to burn Pennsylvania anthracite in New York City at his office, but the glow was short-lived.[34] The very next day, Snowden reneged on his agreement with General Swift, despite having borrowed $262 from his eminent companion to underwrite their promotional tour. Behind Swift's back, Snowden sold an interest in the Schuylkill coalfields to a new association of Wall Street capitalists at $2 per acre. Organized on 18 April 1823 to supply New York and other Atlantic cities with coal, the New York and Schuylkill Coal Company purchased the Peacock Tract, located between Pottsville and Minersville, for $9,000. In November 1824, they graciously allotted Joseph G. Swift some stock in compensation for his 'services in 1820 in bringing that coal into notice.'[35] Swift made $1,400 on the sale of this stock, 'which,' he lamented, 'is all the benefit I had from an enterprise, which, if Charles Snowden had been true to his bargain, had made my family opulent.'[36] From a mine opened in 1824, the New York and Schuylkill Coal Company began hauling anthracite to the Union Canal at Mount Carbon, transferring it from canal boats at the Upper Ferry on the Schuylkill, near Philadelphia, to 150-ton brigs for shipment to New York City. They sold the Peacock Tract in 1829 for $42,000.[37] By that time, its value reflected the immediate expectation of a water route opening across New Jersey to New York Harbor.

2

THE MORRIS CANAL AND BANKING COMPANY

Speculators in mineral deposits were not alone in chasing the spirit of internal improvements. The Morris County Agricultural Society elected George Perrott Macculloch, of Morristown, a Scottish trader with the East India Company born in Bombay, as its first president in December 1820.[1] Realizing the implications of reduced freight costs for farm products shipped along nearly 100 miles of the completed middle section of the Erie Canal, Macculloch compared the tedious progress of market wagons on rough roads and turnpikes across the Highlands. Gliding across Lake Hopatcong's waters, Macculloch listened to old fish tales intently, all the while trying to bring a farther horizon into focus. Gazing across hills denuded of wood, he heard the ringing anvil and hammerman's lament: *Come, penny, go, pound!* But was New Jersey's largest freshwater lake ample enough to fill an ambitious ditch across the Jersey Highlands?[2]

A plan began to form in his mind. In August 1822, Macculloch took Joseph G. Swift and Swift's former aide-de-camp, James Renwick, on an exploratory tour of the green, rolling hills.[3] They pondered whether a canal with Lake Hopatcong for a summit reservoir, following the valleys of the Rockaway and Musconetcong Rivers, would have sufficient water to connect Easton, Pennsylvania, to New York City. Macculloch 'prepared public opinion by a series of essays in the county newspaper.'[4] Writing under the *nom de plume* of 'Agrestis' in the *Palladium of Liberty*, Macculloch imagined canalizing the Musconetcong River from the Delaware River to Stanhope, cutting a canal from there to the Rockaway River, thence canalizing that river down to Paterson, circumventing the Great Falls by a flight of locks to reach tidewater.[5] Opening water communication between the Delaware and Hudson Rivers would bring Lehigh coal to tidewater, replacing wood and imported coal, and do much to revive the flagging iron industry of the Jersey Highlands.

Governor Williamson joined those who gathered at Drake's Tavern on 21 August 1822, to hear Macculloch advocate using Lake Hopatcong's waters

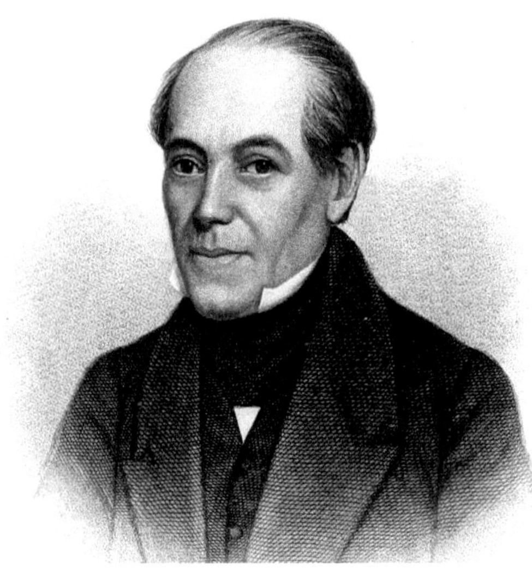

George P. Macculloch. (*The Biographical Encyclopedia of New Jersey of the Nineteenth Century*, 1877)

to open navigation between the Delaware and Passaic Rivers.[6] Westward, the canal might begin above Easton, Pennsylvania, and follow the Pequest Valley, or it might begin below Easton and follow the Musconetcong Valley. Since Lake Hopatcong and Green Pond offered two natural reservoirs at the summit level, the proposed canal would climb to Stanhope, crossing into the valley of the Rockaway River near Valley Forge (Wharton, NJ), and continue along that stream to Denville, whence at least two divergent routes might bring the canal to tidewater on the Passaic River.[7] East of Denville, possible routes included one by Boonton to Paterson or another by Morristown to either Paterson or Newark. Minimizing topographical impediments, advocates imagined a 90-mile canal traversing 'a rugged country, yet not such as to present any insuperable obstacles.'[8] As to advantages, the proposed canal would supply New York City and northern New Jersey with Lehigh coal at half the price then paid for Liverpool coal; it would conserve timber for lumber rather than charcoal and firewood; it would cheaply convey agricultural produce to city markets; and it would nourish new forges, furnaces and manufactories along the route.

Macculloch thought the legislature erred in incorporating a private company in 1820 to build a canal connecting the Delaware and Raritan Rivers.[9] Citing that failure, he insisted, 'In the hands of the people, a canal could be executed and managed as cheaply, and would produce more than if owned by a company.' Otherwise, he predicted conflicting interests 'in which the people will be arrayed against the canal, or the canal against the people.' In all such public works, he concluded, 'we ought to be subjected to no influence and bent under no control, save that of our representatives; nor should our greatest national effort become the sport of speculation or the avenue to a paltry spirit of jobbing.'

While naysayers disparaged Macculloch's proposal 'as the aberration of a dreamer [rather] than as the anticipation of a sane mind,' more reflective members of his audience were sufficiently aroused to recommend appointment of two citizens each from the counties of Essex, Bergen, Morris, Hunterdon and Sussex to a fact-finding commission.[10] On 22 November 1822, the legislature authorized George Macculloch, of Morris County, Charles Kinsey, of Essex County, and Thomas Capner, of Hunterdon County, to employ a scientific engineer and surveyor for $2,000. Recognizing that 'every neighborhood will very naturally desire to attract to itself the advantages resulting from the intersection of the Canal,' the new canal commissioners asked for public forbearance in local newspapers on 1 March 1823, as they began 'to explore, survey and form an estimate of the easiest and most practicable route from the vicinity of the mouth of the Musconetkonk to the tide waters of the Passaic.'[11] They were determined to recommend a single route only in their report to the legislature, while conceding several different routes were 'practicable in the wide extent of country between Paterson and Elizabeth Town at the eastern extremity, Morris Town and Boonton towards the centre, or between Musconetkonk and Easton at the western termination of the Canal.'

George Macculloch traveled to Albany in April 1823 to obtain assistance from New York's canal engineers.[12] Feeling this would not prove 'sufficient to counteract the apathy of friends or the prejudices and party spirit of opponents,' he wrote Secretary of War John C. Calhoun to procure professional opinions from General Simon Bernard and Brevet-Lieutenant Colonel Joseph G. Totten of the US Army Corps of Engineers.[13] Macculloch felt their involvement, combined with the volunteer services of Joseph G. Swift, would constitute 'a weight of authority sufficient to overpower cavil, ignorance and hostility.' He then journeyed with Benjamin Wright, chief engineer of the Erie Canal, to Little Falls, New York, to engage assistant engineer Ephraim Beach 'to take the levels and survey the routes, having previously conversed with him, and agreed with Professor [James] Renwick [of Columbia College] to entrust him with that task.'[14] He then spent the spring and summer of 1823

[...] collecting topographical and statistical information, as also in reconnoitering the various routes in company with the inhabitants of the vicinity. Here a singular fact should be stated, that the good sense and local information of our farmers, staked out the most difficult passes of the boldest canal in existence, and that in every important point the actual navigation merely pursues the trace thus indicated.

Ephraim Beach arrived in July 1823 to begin surveying under guidance of Professor Renwick, who acted in the capacity of scientific engineer.[15]

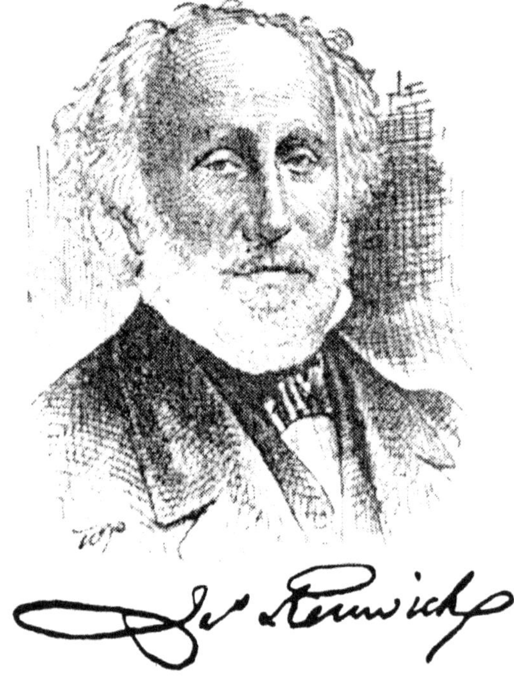

Professor James Renwick.
(*The National Cyclopædia of American* Biography, 1901)

A remarkable miscalculation lay at the heart of the initial optimism. Macculloch thought 'the summit level near the verge of Suckasunny plain, is 185 feet above the waters of the Hudson, and 115 above those of the Delaware, making a fall of about 300 feet to be overcome by locks.'[16] More careful measurements proved otherwise. The summit near Lake Hopatcong actually stood 914 feet above mean tide in the Passaic River, 53 miles distant, and 760 feet above the Delaware River at Phillipsburg, 38 miles distant, requiring boats to overcome changes in elevation amounting to 1,674 feet between Easton, Pennsylvania, and Newark. Astounded engineers thus

> [...] became aware, at an early period, that it could not be executed, within any reasonable limit of cost, by the ordinary method, and would not, if so executed, be of any great value, either to the state, or its stockholders, in consequence of the great length of time that would be consumed in passing through from 160 to 200 locks.[17]

As the Highlands posed appalling difficulties to lock navigation, James Renwick, professor of natural experimental philosophy and chemistry at Columbia College, advocated the use of mechanical inclined planes to overcome 1,400 feet of ascent and descent along the route.[18] To this end, he patented 'an economical form of inclined plane operated by a water counterpoise, the car at the upper end of the incline being filled with water until the weight was sufficient to lift the car carrying the boat at the lower level.'[19]

Renwick's idea was hardly revolutionary. William Reynolds, of Ketley, Shropshire, England, engineered the first successful inclined plane in 1787 on the Ketley Canal, built to convey iron ore and coal from Oaken Gates to his Coalbrookdale ironworks.[20] Rope winding around a large wooden barrel, mounted in a heavy wooden framework above a summit lock at the head of the inclined plane, simultaneously lowered a fully loaded boat, limited to about 5 tons, riding a framework plane car on one set of rails, while it dragged up a boat carrying no more than one third that weight in a similar plane car on a parallel railway. This counterpoise plane overcame a 74-foot change in elevation. In the summit lock, the boat settled upon a plane car that employed

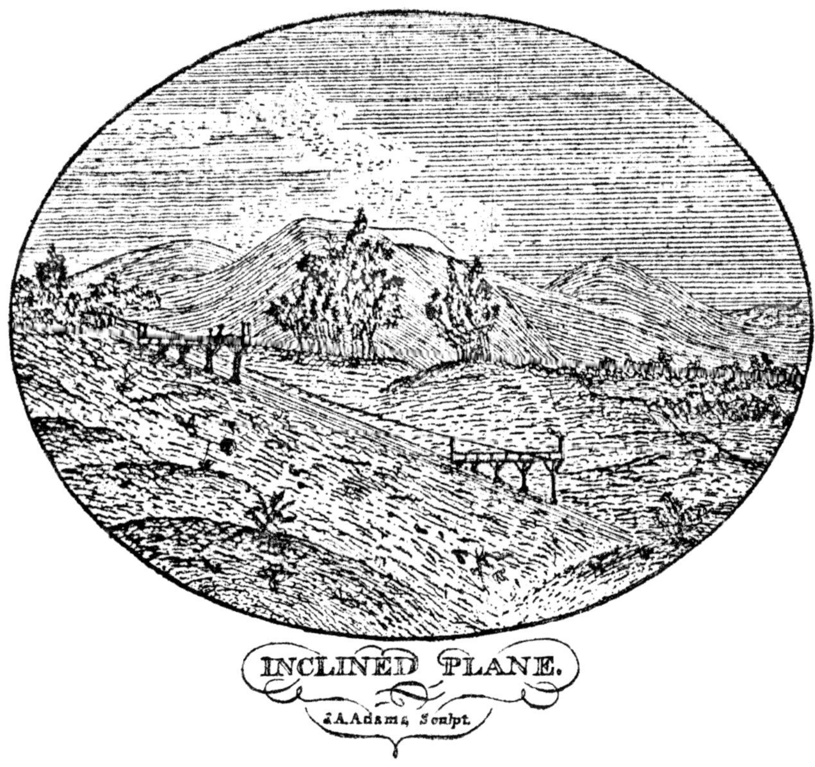

J. Alexander Adams, illustrator and engraver for the *Poughkeepsie Casket*, depicts moveable locks on an inclined plane as originally envisioned by James Renwick. (*Report of the Commissioners Appointed by the Legislature of the State of New Jersey, for the Purpose of Exploring the Route of a Canal to Unite River Delaware near Easton with the Passaic, near Newark, 1823*)

two pairs of wheels of different sizes to keep the boat nearly horizontal in transit. The apparatus, however, reduced the capacity of boats on the canal from 25 to 8 tons.

Resident engineer Henry Williams introduced three inclined planes on the Shropshire Canal, chartered in 1788, overcoming changes in elevation of 120, 126 and 207 feet. Attempting to remedy defects in Reynolds' design, these were built as summit planes, whereon boats cradled in plane cars crossed a slight elevation (instead of passing a lock) when entering or exiting the upper level. A small steam engine turned the rope barrel and pulley wheel, which assisted descending boats in raising empties on a double railway. Boats carrying 5 tons of freight were lowered down the planes for 3 pence each, and empties were raised at no charge.[21]

Francis Egerton, Duke of Bridgewater, constructed a double-lock plane in an inclined tunnel at Walkden Moor in 1797 to facilitate the subterranean navigation of his coal mines. Built on a slope 453 feet in length, the Duke's plane employed cast-iron rails fastened on wood sleepers. Boat cars on four wheels received or discharged boats in summit locks. Descending loaded boats dragged empty boats uphill by means of a heavy rope cable on a winding drum. Two men operated winches connected to the axle of a pinion wheel to set the apparatus in motion. Designed for 12-ton boats in 9-ton cradles, moving on four iron rollers, the lock plane on the Bridgewater Canal in the collieries at Worsley Delph, Salford, England, overcame an elevation of 106 feet. Boats had to be carefully supported in dry transit to preserve them from strain, thereby limiting their dimensions and the overall capacity of the canal.

American inventor Robert Fulton proposed a double inclined plane in his *Treatise on the Improvement of Canal Navigation*, published in London in 1796. In his model, a water-filled tub descending a vertical shaft hauled a small boat, riding uphill on a wheeled truck, as it lowered a descending

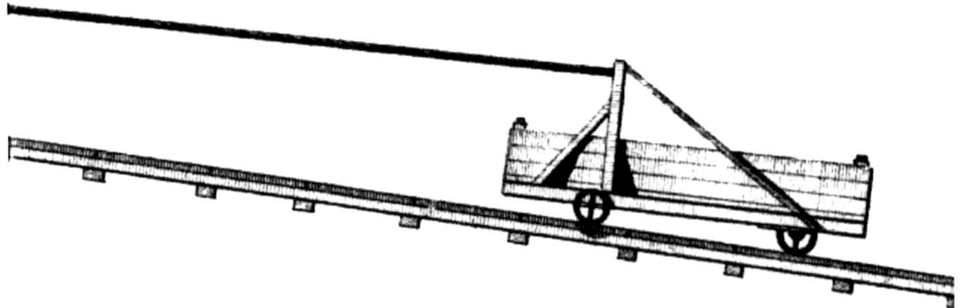

Plane car from the 'Plan and Elevation of the Inclined Planes upon the Shropshire Canal'. (Plymley, *General View of the Agriculture of Shropshire*, 1803)

boat by means of an endless chain, winding on a drum. To overcome greater heights, Fulton recommended an inclined plane with a single railway, using either a descending water-tub or an overshot waterwheel (depending on the elevation to be overcome) for motive power.

Dr James Anderson, of Edinburgh, introduced the concept of moveable 'locks' on an inclined plane in his *General View of the Agriculture, &c., of the County of Aberdeen*, published in 1794. Ironmaster James Fussell, of Mells, Somerset County, England, patented 'a balance-engine' in 1798, elevating and lowering boats in water-filled caissons, which counterpoised one another on a double-tracked inclined plane. Connected by chains, passing around revolving drums at top and bottom of the railways, the descent of one moveable lock 'necessarily occasions the ascent of the other.'[22] This was tried on the Dorset and Somerset Canal near Frome in 1800, but its efficacy was never fully tested due to delays in completing the canal.

English engineer William Chapman apparently imitated Fussell's counterbalance boatlift in his recommendations for the High Peak Junction Canal in 1813, proposing a short canal and tunnel, connecting Sheffield and Manchester, with six inclined railways powered by steam engines. Chapman dedicated his 1797 book, *Observations on the Various Systems of Canal Navigation*, to Francis Egerton, Duke of Bridgewater. In all such designs, the strength of the rope or chain proved a limiting factor.

There was also an American example: the Proprietors of Locks and Canals on the Connecticut River built a mechanical inclined plane in 1794 to raise and lower flatboats, replacing a portage around the South Hadley Falls, about 12 miles above Springfield, Massachusetts. Its engineer, Major Benjamin Prescott, of Northampton, Massachusetts, specialized in waterworks and canal projects. Reverend Dr Timothy Dwight, president of Yale College, described Prescott's canal plane—a tourist attraction popularly styled the 'Hampshire Machine'—in a travelogue published in 1821.[23] Fifty-three feet in height and 230 feet in length, the plane at South Hadley employed a stone ramp, covered with planks. Two waterwheels of 16 feet in diameter wound or unwound an iron chain on an axle, the opposite end being fastened to a boat carriage. Descending boats passed a summit lock through 'folding doors into a carriage, which admitted a sufficient quantity of water from the canal to float the boat.' A plane tender closed the lock and drained water from the boat carriage through sluices. Waterwheels set the contraption in motion, the slowly unwinding chain allowing the carriage to descend by its own weight. The process was reversed to draw a boat uphill. The carriage moved on three graduated sets of wheels, 'the second and third sets being so much larger than the first as to keep the [boat in the] carriage exactly level,' as it rode up or down the incline. According to Dwight's eyewitness testimony, 'The motion was perfectly regular, easy, and free from danger.'

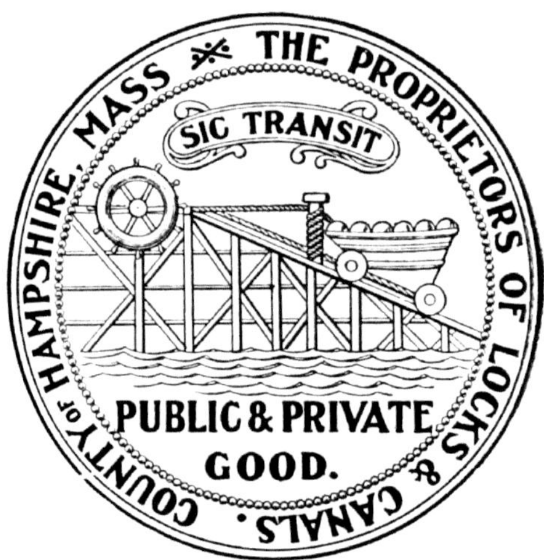

A loaded boat descends the inclined plane at South Hadley, Massachusetts, in a cradle car on a set of graduated wheels to keep it level, thereby reducing strain on its timbers. Two waterwheels wound or unwound either hemp rope or an iron chain around a vertical post to raise or lower boats along the track. The apparatus was depicted on the seal of the Proprietors of Locks and Canals on the Connecticut River, 1793. (Bacon, E. M., *The Connecticut River and the Valley of the Connecticut*, 1906)

The South Hadley plane accommodated boats 16 feet wide and 40 feet long, carrying 10 to 25 tons of cargo. Setting an unheeded precedent for the Morris Canal, construction costs exceeded estimates and a loan was floated in Holland to complete the work.[24] Cut to a shallow depth through 2½ miles of sandstone bedrock, the canal passed 7,000 tons of merchandise in a boating season, collecting a toll of 4 shillings and 6 pence per ton. The troublesome plane proved short-lived. Dwight reported,

> At first [hemp] cables were employed to raise and let down the boats, and were found insufficient, as well as expensive. The chains, which were substituted for them, were frequently broken; and thus embarrassed the regular course of the navigation.

A flight of five locks replaced the plane in 1805. Benjamin Prescott went on to serve as superintendent of the Springfield Armory from 1805 to 1815. He moved to Cohoes Falls, near Waterford, NY, in 1816 to work on the Champlain and Erie Canal.[25] Colonel Prescott died in 1826. His role (if any) in recommending the use of inclined planes on the Morris Canal is unknown.

Apparently undaunted by the unproven suitability of inclined planes to the project at hand, Ephraim Beach completed his preliminary survey in September 1823, avowing the practicality of either a northern route, 76 miles in length, passing through Paterson and reaching tidewater on the Passaic River at Acquackanonck (Passaic, NJ), or a southern route through Morristown, reaching tidewater at Elizabeth. Secretary of War John C. Calhoun ordered military engineers Simon Bernard and Joseph G. Totten to inspect the projected line of the Morris Canal. In anticipation of their arrival, General

Swift returned to Morristown on 16 September 1823 for consultations on Renwick's daring plan to incorporate two-dozen inclined planes, as well as fixed locks. As hoped, Bernard and Totten enthusiastically concluded,

> To us, [...] whether we consider the economy, the utility, or the durability of these inclined planes, *all is certain*; and we look confidently forward to the day when their introduction will be regarded as a most important era in the history of canal navigation, and especially in this country, to which they are so peculiarly adapted.[26]

George Macculloch and Ephraim Beach escorted New York Governor DeWitt Clinton, Judge Benjamin Wright, chief engineer on the Erie Canal, and General Bernard on a tour of the proposed route of the Morris Canal in October 1823.[27] Since Lake Hopatcong would supposedly furnish at least three times the required supply of water at the canal's summit, Governor Clinton foresaw no impediment to construction. Furthermore, the whole region being well watered, streams could partly be diverted into the canal along its whole route without interfering with existing waterpowers. While some might object to the high elevation of the summit level, he instead concluded,

> [...] altitude is like distance; it creates no insurmountable obstacle. It only augments the expense.

He heartily commended Renwick's proposal to substitute inclined planes wherever feasible along the route, 'from considerations of economy, and with a view to the rapid passage of boats....' At least on a theoretical level, Clinton seemed certain—'this measure cannot fail of success'—while acknowledging only preliminary experiments would ultimately relieve all doubts with respect to the efficacy of inclined planes.

Clinton estimated a canal 75 miles long, 32 feet wide at the waterline, 16 wide at the bottom and 4 feet deep could be built for $800,000 within three years.[28] Mouthing Macculloch's concerns, he recommended the state of New Jersey underwrite its construction, otherwise a private company might 'consult its own interests, not the prosperity of the state,' and make the public interest entirely 'subordinate to the cupidity of a private association.'[29] He further warned that foreign capital would quickly gain control and the canal would then primarily serve the interests of 'a non-resident company.'

Addressing potential advantages of such a canal, Governor Clinton emphasized the humiliating prevalence of 'foreign iron worked by foreign coal,' estimating local forge owners required between 1,000 and 5,000 acres of woodland to secure sufficient charcoal for their operations. A coal-carrying canal might therefore revive prostrated ironworks, which languished through

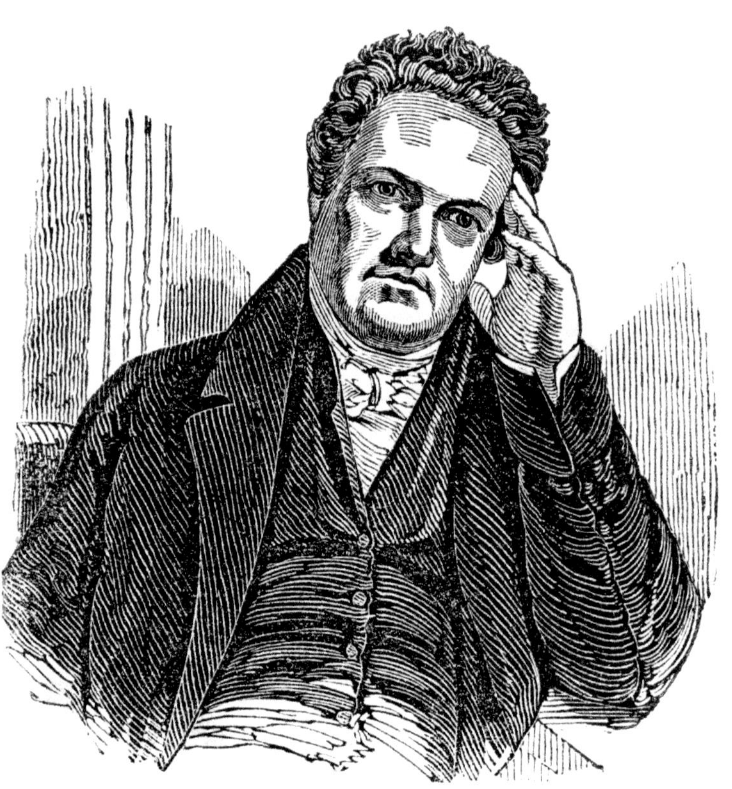

De Witt Clinton.

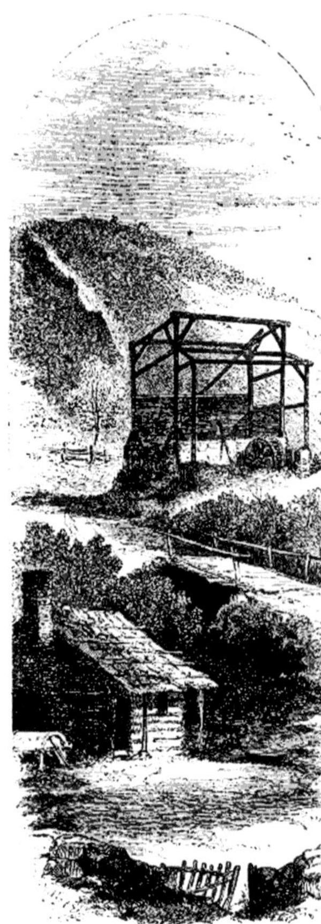

LORD STIRLING'S FORGE.

Above left: DeWitt Clinton. (*The American Magazine of Useful and Entertaining Knowledge,* Vol. 1, 1834)

Above right: John R. Chapin's 'Artist-Life In The Highlands of New Jersey', *Harper's New Monthly Magazine,* 1860. Log house and the ruins of an abandoned forge at a bridge across Hibernia Brook near (William Alexander) Lord Stirling's Hibernia mine (now the Wildcat Ridge Wildlife Management Area).

exclusive dependence upon the rapidly dwindling forests of northern New Jersey. Moreover, demand for coal in New York City would 'forever increase, and forever secure a great revenue from the canal.' Likewise, Paterson textile factories would thrive upon coal-powered steam engines. In short, Clinton enthusiastically predicted the canal would 'make New Jersey the greatest manufacturing country in America.' Reducing transportation costs, farmers would also enjoy a prosperous inland trade with city markets. With this endorsement in hand, George Macculloch submitted a favorable report to the legislature in November 1823.

Joseph G. Swift finely tuned the Morris Canal survey with fellow commissioner John Scott, ironmaker of Powerville, Morris County, and chief engineer Ephraim Beach in December 1823. Competition was sprouting under their heels—in April 1824, the New York legislature appropriated $1,000 to survey the route for a Sussex and Orange Canal, connecting the valleys of the Paulinskill and Wallkill, which, if built, promised to halve the price of Pennsylvania anthracite upon delivery in New York City. Macculloch again bent the public ear. Writing under the *nom de plume* of 'Publicola', he identified the iron industry as the region's primary engine of prosperity, seconded by water-powered manufactures. He warned the state's mineral treasures, though 'scattered in profusion near the surface,' would 'remain forever dormant until a water conveyance wafts coal in the vicinity of these ores.' He counted thirty-nine abandoned forges and furnaces in the Highlands, even as Americans imported European iron, valued at $3,330,000 in 1822 and $2,749,000 in 1823. He speculated the canal would allow iron to be manufactured 'almost 20 percent cheaper than at present, or in other words, the above enormous expenditures instead of being lavished upon England, Sweden, and Russia, will be concentrated in New Jersey.'[30] The wealth thus generated would trickle down to farmers, laborers, mechanics, merchants, physicians and lawyers.

Macculoch originally drafted a charter that provided for directors to be chosen from those counties intersected by the proposed Morris Canal, but advocates of the Delaware and Raritan Canal delayed its passage. Without Macculoch's knowledge and to his great chagrin, Wall Street lobbyists finagled inclusion of a provision granting banking privileges. Thus the Morris Canal and Banking Company was chartered on 31 December 1824, with a capital stock of $1 million.[31] George P. McCulloch and John Scott, of Morris County, Israel Crane, of Essex County, and Joseph G. Swift, Henry Eckford and David B. Ogden, of New York City, were appointed commissioners for receiving stock subscriptions. The legislature invested the new corporation with banking privileges for the term of thirty-one years (until 1855). The charter allowed the state to take the canal at an appraised value in 1924 and, if that should not happen, then the canal would become state property in 1974. Stock subscriptions opened in Morristown on 25 April 1825.

The Sussex Register reported chief engineer Ephraim Beach, 'with his attendants, commenced staking out the ground from the summit level eastward, for excavation,' on 17 May 1825, expecting work to commence by 4 June.[32] Since several possible routes covering the 20 miles approaching tidewater on the east each had 'their warm and highly interested advocates,' the engineers would not proceed farther 'than the point from which these several routes diverge, until the Directors, which are shortly to be chosen [on 4 June 1825], shall have finally settled the question....' Boosters of the southern route through Morristown and Elizabeth warily eyed their progress. *The Elizabeth-Town Gazette* complained 'that not a single share [of stock] has been granted to any of the applicants from this place.' And so, as the new directors ventured forth on a tour of inspection in July 1825, the same newspaper cautioned them to consult the greatest public interest in their determinations.

Proponents noted the southern route from Morristown to Elizabeth would be shorter, more practicable, cheaper to build, and more productive of freight and revenues. But nature conspired against them, raising concerns about a sufficiency of water. By August first, heat and drought seared the countryside about Elizabeth, forcing cattle to feed on hay for want of pasture. Farms flourishing in early July underwent a 'great and melancholy' change for the worse. Corn planted in May yielded a small crop and that planted late, produced nothing. Despairing farmers turned cattle loose to feed in cornfields. Drought also doomed prospects for gathering much fruit or potatoes.[33] *The New-Jersey Advocate* reported excavations for the canal would soon commence near Rockaway or Denville and the commissioners would decide at their next meeting which route leading eastward from that point would be most advantageous. *The Rahway Advocate* optimistically concluded, 'At present we believe it quite uncertain which will be eventually adopted.'

On 4 June 1825, stockholders of the Morris Canal and Banking Company elected fifteen directors at the house of Mayor William Lyon, innkeeper of Jersey City.[34] Contracts to excavate twenty sections of the canal were let on 9 July 1825. Actual construction began 'near Succasunny Plains' on 12 July 1825, as 700 laborers started digging their way towards Rockaway.[35] The canal company purchased Brooklyn Forge, situated on the Musconetcong River about a mile below Lake Hopatcong, and built a new dam to raise the lake waters another 5 feet (or 11 feet above its natural level), thereby flooding 460 acres of waterfront land acquired through condemnation.[36] While excavating the feeder lock at Lake Hopatcong, workmen unearthed

> [...] the skeleton of an Indian, the arm bone of which from the wrist to the elbow was eighteen inches, and from the elbow to the shoulder the same. The remaining parts of the skeleton were the same proportions. These bones would imply a height of nearly eight feet to this man of the forest.[37]

Joseph G. Swift traveled over the newly dug section to Lake Hopatcong, where he witnessed 'John Scott and Fay, men of six feet, and of great strength and dexterity, wielding the tongs and loupe with graceful ease' as they forged iron under a trip hammer at Brooklyn Forge.[38] He then went with Colonel Scott and Captain Beach to determine the location of one of the inclined planes and an aqueduct near Dover. After visiting the Great Falls at Paterson, Swift and his wife returned home to Brooklyn, New York.

By 1 October 1825, almost 8 miles of canal had been excavated between Succasunna and Rockaway and another 30 miles placed under contract. Chief engineer Ephraim Beach finally announced in December, 'that the Morris-Town route would cost about $130,000 more than the Boonton, besides incurring great danger for want of water.'[39] The directors accordingly set a course through Boonton, Pompton, Little Falls, Paterson and Bloomfield to Newark. The Morristown *Palladium of Liberty* grudgingly admitted,

If these points be correct, the determination of the Board is unquestionably correct; it is only matter of serious regret, that by much the largest portion of this County, in extent, population and trade, is thus excluded from all benefit in this public improvement.

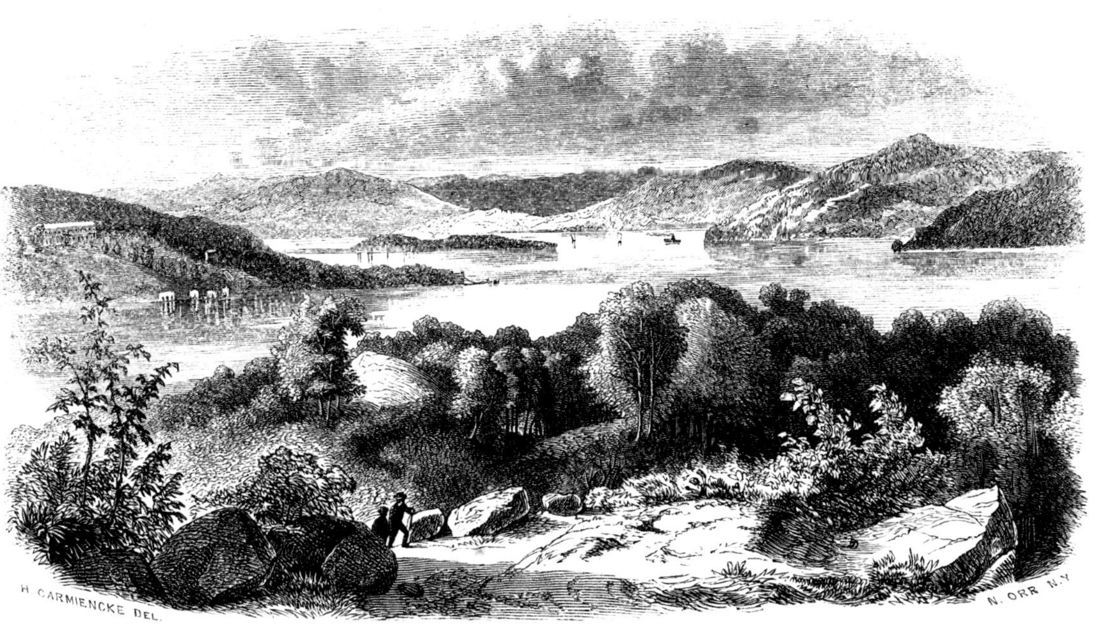

Hopatcong Lake, J. Hermann Carmiencke, delineator. (*Second Annual Report of the Geological Survey of the State of New Jersey for the Year 1855, 1856*)

Other Morristown residents ominously advocated erecting a railroad, which would be cheaper to build and have the advantage of providing year-round transportation.

Nearly 800 guests from New York, New Jersey and Pennsylvania watched president *pro tem* William Bayard turn a groundbreaking shovel of earth on the feeder at the outlet of Lake Hopatcong on 15 October 1825.[40] Innkeeper William Lyon, of Jersey City, catered 'an elegant collation.' George Macculloch warily saluted 'the Capitalists present and absent, of New-York—may the success of the present enterprise induce them to embark in future plans for the prosperity of New-Jersey.' In his remarks William Bayard reassured doubters that canal-building and not banking would be the company's 'first and greatest object.' He further promised, 'boats will pass from the Delaware River through this county to New York in less than three years.'[41]

Still complaining that legislators were foolish to grant banking privileges in the canal charter—thereby giving precedence to Wall Street speculation and stock manipulations over canal business—Macculloch soon parted company, his name disappearing from any further association with the canal. Hezekiah Niles, editor of *Niles' Weekly Register*, sourly concurred:

Canal-making and bank-making have no natural union between them. We shall, however, be glad to find by the result, that the two different projects have worked well together—and for the good of a new canal will be willing to bear with the evil of a new bank, if honestly managed; though the fact is that there are too many banks. But the pledge that the canal shall be made the primary object of the company, is very satisfactory.[42]

3

A Work in Progress

Professor James Renwick's audacious plan for inclined planes involved the use of moveable locks with their tops always horizontal and their bottoms parallel with the slope, measuring 60 feet in length, 3 feet in depth and 9 feet in width, each with the capacity to hold 45 tons of water. Fastened to an undercarriage with eight cast-iron truck wheels mounted on wrought-iron axles, each moveable lock would weigh 15 tons. The 60-ton weight of a water-filled lock would therefore be distributed over 60 feet of inclined plane during transit. According to Renwick's calculations, the moveable lock's pressure on the inclined plane would support 45 tons, requiring the chains to support only 15 tons. The slightly preponderant weight of a descending lock would draw an ascending lock up the plane on parallel railways. As hemp ropes would severely limit capacity, Professor Renwick substituted chain cables, manufactured at Dover, NJ, capable of sustaining 18 tons of weight.

In the estimation of an examining committee of the Franklin Institute, who reviewed his model, Renwick added '*one essentially novel, and highly important improvement*' to previous designs—namely, '*the substitution of two endless* chains, in place of *one single* chain; and a *new arrangement of the gearing of the drums, over which these chains revolve.*'[1] The additional chain not only provided redundancy (in case one chain broke), but it also ensured 'an equable motion in the locks….' According to Renwick's proposal, the ends of two strong chains were secured to a revolving drum at the summit of each railway, while the opposite ends were fastened on either side at the lower end of the moveable lock.

Wherever it was possible to excavate a 15-foot-deep cavity at the bottom of an inclined plane, drainable through lock gates, a single horizontal shaft and drum extending across both railways might be used to uncoil one pair of chains to lower the descending lock, while simultaneously coiling the other pair of chains in the opposite direction to raise the ascending lock.[2] Since this was not practical in most situations (as he soon discovered at Stanhope),

Renwick compensated by employing a separate shaft and drum for each railway to simultaneously wind and unwind chain cables, their opposite motions regulated through identical sets of spur wheels of two different sizes. Using a lever, the plane tender would engage the proper spur wheel on each shaft, so that in the time it took the heavier descending lock to reach water level at the bottom of its railway, the ascending lock would be drawn up the whole length and height of the inclined plane. At this point, employing chain stoppers (similar to those used on ships to regulate the descent of an anchor), the gears would be disengaged and the descending lock gently lowered into the water at the lower level. Anticipating the need for continual maintenance and repairs, spare lengths of chain would be kept on hand.

After due consideration, Benjamin Wright, chief engineer of the Erie Canal, was satisfied as to the practicability and utility of substituting inclined planes

> [...] at all eligible and favorable positions, to overcome 1,400 feet of ascent and descent, and the remainder to be conquered by locks of various lifts, to be constructed of hammered stone, and made upon the most economical plan, and durable construction.[3]

General Joseph G. Swift agreed, believing Renwick's 'new adaptation of the inclined plane' would henceforth obviate the difficulty of passing highlands with lock navigation.

Bolstering their case by citing European precedents, the Morris Canal commissioners optimistically claimed,

> [The Duke of] Bridgewater invented and adopted an inclined plane, which is found to economize three fourths of the cost of the apparatus which it superseded; the best French engineers have long used perpendicular lifts, or inclined planes, in preference to locks; in situations similar to those in which we are placed; and the canals of Ketley, Shrewsbury, Shopshire and Monmouthshire, are a standing proof of their practicability and utility. We trust we shall not be stigmatized as visionary theorists, in acceding to practices sanctioned by such high authority, and tested by the experiences of half a century.[4]

Directing a withering eye upon such suppositions, one detractor countered,

> On the abstract principal, that if planes were practicable for boats of five tons, they were equally so for boats of twenty-five tons burthen, a company was formed, a canal laid out, and sites for planes for boats of twenty-five tons duly located.[5]

This critic noted how various engineers and inventors had,

[…] at different periods, recommended various plans, improvements and modifications of planes for a canal navigation, but unattended by any practical results; indeed they possessed, generally speaking, little merit independent of the ingenuity displayed in their combinations. The Shropshire, Bridgewater, Ketley and Shrewsbury are the only canals on which they have been adopted with any advantage; and on these, even, the imperfections were so glaring, and the capacity of the canals reduced to so low a limit, in consequence of the restricted size of the boats, and the time expended in passing them from one level to another, that their further application, as a matter of expediency, was, to say the least, rendered somewhat problematical.

As Renwick's model involved the simultaneous ascent and descent of boats riding railways between levels in watertight wooden basins, his design not only limited the size of the boats and employed time-consuming locks, but it also required moving considerable water weight instead of cargo, which was likely to place an impossible strain on the chains.[6] As proponents were soon to learn, 'The practicability of inclined planes, in place of locks, will be tested on this canal.'[7]

Undaunted, Professor Renwick estimated the cost of building a plane of 100-foot ascent at $11,896, or, if the rails were supported on masonry walls, at $14,359, or about $150 per foot. Each plane was to be excavated to a depth of 18 inches and filled with gravel as a base to support stone blocks, set at 3-foot intervals, to carry the rails, with stone chips filling the intervals. Iron rails, cast in 3-foot lengths, were to be fastened into channels cut in the sleeper stones. Having laid the theoretical groundwork, Renwick shipped a model of his inclined plane to the legislature in Trenton. In 1826, the Franklin Institute awarded him the Franklin Silver Medal for his design. As originally conceived, the Morris Canal would have an estimated carrying capacity of 362,500 tons, transported in 14,500 boat trips of 25 tons each. If achievable, this seemed more than adequate for the time being, for 800 coal miners at Mauch Chunk sent 28,393 tons of coal down the Lehigh and Delaware Rivers to Philadelphia in 1825.

As the chief engineer advertised for contractors to excavate the section extending 5 miles west of the summit, the directors anxiously awaited completion of an experimental plane. Inexplicably, Renwick's plan for moveable locks was abandoned in all three prototypes. In his application to patent a 'Method of Raising and Lowering Boats', dated June 1828, William Knight, of Morristown, described:

[…] the plan now attempted by the Morris Canal Company, in this vicinity, *which is to draw the loaded boat over the plane dry*, in a sort of cradle, or frame, attached to four large wheels, moved by a vertical water wheel at the head of the plane; the whole apparatus resembling a large wagon moving up the plane, by a chain attached to the water wheel and the cradle frame with the loaded boat, moving under the wheels, and the whole weight resting on four points of the plane.[8]

He pinpointed the greatest difficulty with this design: 'the loaded boats, not resting on water, but supported only at certain points in the cradle frame, must incur much hazard of being made leaky, by overstraining the joints.'[9] Knight also clearly described a *summit* plane, where 'the boat, with its appendages, is to be carried *over* and *above* the water surface of the canal, and again descends by another plane into it….' No doubt observing the trials and tribulations of these modifications, Knight suggested reverting to a plan in which 'the boat is carried over the plane in a car filled with water, and is equally supported at all points, as when in the canal.'

The problem with using a timberwork plane car instead of a moveable lock to convey boats between levels (as English engineer David Stevenson noted) was that, in moving between the horizontal and the diagonal, one set of wheels supporting the boat car rested on the inclined plane, while the other remained on a level surface. With both axles no longer on the same plane, 'their change of position produces a tendency to rack the cradle, and the boat which it supports….'[10] Peter Freeman, a native of Morristown, is credited with patenting a simple solution in 1825 to overcome this twist.[11] Writing about the plane cars used on the Morris Canal, one later historian reported:

> They were constructed by a strong wooden crib or cradle on which the boat rested, supported on two iron wagons running on four wheels. When supported on the inclined plane, the four axles of the wagons are in the same plane. To guard against the tendency to rock the cradle, which occurred in other types of boat cars when the axles were not on the same level, the American engineers introduced two axles, which supported the entire weight of crib and boat, and on which the wagons turned as a center.[12]

Captain Ezekiel Kitchell and Captain Peter Freeman were hired to build a prototype, so 'the experiment may be fairly tested.'[13] Assisted by his son-in-law Calvin Howell, house-carpenter Ezekiel Kitchell accordingly embarked on building an experimental plane at Rockaway, NJ.[14] James Renwick noted Kitchell's experimental contraption was a 'double plane, but with power derived from a water wheel.'[15] Decades later, with benefit of hindsight, Kitchell's efforts merited the following description: 'This was a *Summit plane* with the machinery placed on a frame work over the track at the apex of the plane, and [eventually] proved an entire failure.'[16] To great relief, however, the Rockaway plane tested successfully on 6 July 1826, demonstrating its machinery could raise or lower a boat along 630 feet of track, overcoming a change in elevation of 52 feet.[17] According to the *New-York Evening Post*, 'the expectations of the friends of the plan were realized in the most satisfactory manner,' despite some initial reluctance on the waterwheel's part. Viewers beheld the plane car ascending and descending several times, with and without the boat, but carrying 'a large number of persons who had assembled to witness the interesting spectacle.' Ordinarily, six locks were required to overcome the same change of elevation with each taking at least eight minutes to raise or lower a boat. The trip over the inclined plane, however, took 'from 8 to 9 minutes, with less than half the head of water that could have been put on the wheel.'[18] Unfortunately, Kitchell's reluctant waterwheel required a continual stream of water, which exceeded that necessary to fill a flight of locks.[19]

Just as the experimental plane lifted investors' confidence, a July squall on Wall Street tipped the boat. Facing a growing mountain of bad debt, directors and finance officers of several New York insurance companies who had engaged in risky loan practices on the very fringes of the law brokered a series of fraudulent security exchanges to cover their losses, through the medium of banks they also controlled. To prop up the dangerously overextended

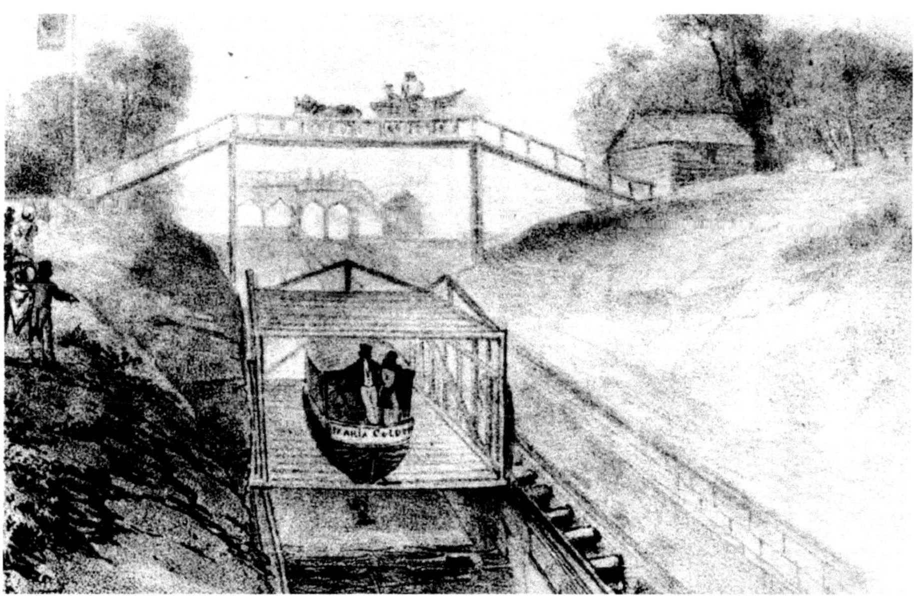

Auguste Hervieu's drawing of an 'Inclined Plane on the Morris Canal' was published in Frances Trollope's *Domestic Manners of the Americans* (1832). At Bloomfield, the plane car rode on four cast-iron wheels, eight feet in diameter, as depicted here. The packet boat *Maria Colden* also regularly traveled this section. The road bridge across the plane, however, suggests another location, possibly Major David Bates Douglass's prototype at Montville, NJ, built in 1830.

Life and Fire Insurance Company, its directors (at least nominally including assistant president Joseph G. Swift) procured 2,500 unpaid shares of Morris Canal stock with $250,000 in worthless securities on 10 May 1826. Since the same men formed the finance committee of the Morris Canal and Banking Company, this swindle was rather easily accomplished. William Bayard, president *pro tem* of the Morris Canal and Banking Company, conveniently signed blank certificates, which cashier James T. Talman then used without taking the trouble to enter them on his stock ledger to the credit of the Fulton Bank. The perpetrators immediately exchanged the Morris Canal stock for 2,000 shares of Fulton Bank stock, which they in turn transferred for $250,000 in dubious stock certificates of the Mercantile Insurance Company, another corporation under their control. As Thomas Vermilyea maneuvered to gain control of the Tradesmen's Bank, panic ensued when yet another interlocking lending institution, the Hudson Insurance Company, failed on 8 July 1826. This exposed the insolvency of the Life and Fire Insurance Company, which declared bankruptcy on 18 July 1826. This news in turn caused a run on the Fulton Bank, whose specie reserves quickly drained down to $3,000. Only the forced resignation of the Fulton Bank's directors restored public confidence. Discovery of the scheme, however, caused the 2,500 shares of Morris Canal stock to be thrown back on the company in August 1826 for a loss conservatively estimated at $7,000. According to the *Sussex Register*, accusations of securities fraud immediately threatened to suck the Morris Canal 'into the whirlpool in which several monied institutions have perished.'

A New York grand jury indicted four directors of the Morris Canal and Banking Company 'for a conspiracy to cheat, and for cheating.'[20] The charges related to their questionable handling as finance committeemen of 'certain certificates of stock in the Morris Canal & Banking Company, hypothecated to the Fulton Bank.' The indictment named: Henry Eckford, a wealthy shipbuilder, who was also president of the Life and Fire Insurance Company; General Joseph G. Swift, assistant president of the Life and Fire Insurance Company and director of the finance committee of the Morris Canal and Banking Company; New York City alderman William P. Rathbone, a director of the Life and Fire Insurance Company, of the Morris Canal and Banking Company and of the Fulton Bank; and, lastly, Thomas Vermilyea, a prominent merchant and broker who served as a director of the Life and Fire Insurance Company, of the Morris Canal and Banking Company, of the Mercantile Insurance Corporation and of the Fulton Bank.[21]

Attorneys Cadwallader D. Colden, Dudley Selden and William M. Price represented the accused men, who pleaded not guilty. The gang of four resigned from the board of the Morris Canal and Banking Company in August 1826. With faint praise, the surviving officers acted to replace them with 'gentlemen whose character will inspire confidence to the public, and give security to the Stockholders.' Within weeks, a committee of investigation tried to absolve cashier James T. Talman of blame, claiming his 'transfer of the 2,500 shares of Morris Canal Stock to the Fulton Bank for account of the Life and Fire Insurance Company, was made in virtue of a general authority from the Finance Committee.'[22] He resigned nevertheless and Robert Gilchrist, bookkeeper for Jersey City, was appointed in his place. The directors then asked a new finance committee, consisting of William Bayard Jr, Henry McFarlan Sr and Abraham Ogden, to submit a 'general view of the actual situation of the affairs of the company' at the stockholders' meeting on 21 September 1826. By their reckoning, the company collected $322,639 in cash or notes secured by stock. Of this sum, $233,239 had been expended on the canal to date. The company had outstanding debts of $70,575, including $50,000 owed to canal contractors. Stockholders subscribed $298,770 in cash or securities for 4,192 shares, but owed $36,590 to complete payments of 80 percent value. The company held 5,808 unsubscribed shares.

The new finance committee took several stockholders on a reassuring tour of the canal. They pointed out how the engineer's skill and good judgment overcame all difficulties in its location and there were accomplishments sufficient to demonstrate the practicability of completing the canal in the course of the next year at an expense not exceeding the capital stock of $1 million authorized in the charter. Stockholders were assured a full equivalent had been received in quality workmanship and materials for every dollar expended. If adequate funds were raised, then the directors promised to proceed with 'renewed vigor and increased confidence.' To repair losses accrued from the stock embezzlement scheme, the stockholders approved a new subscription so as not to be obligatory unless 3,000 shares were subscribed.

Cadwallader D. Colden, former mayor of New York City, tried to calm jittery investors, publicly minimizing financial losses suffered in the scandal. After examining the whole line of the canal, he went and purchased stock. The directors published his testimonial, dated 2 November 1826, to advertise steps taken to 'resuscitate the affairs of the Company, and place it upon a solid and durable foundation.'[23] Though the jaded New York lawyer had 'seen a great deal of canalling, both in our country and in Europe,' he everywhere admired the solid construction and ingenuity of the Morris Canal, so remarkably wrought 'with the limited means, which have been provided.' 'Indeed,' he opined, 'when at almost any point in the course of the canal, you see yourself surrounded by high hills it appears extraordinary that a path should have been found admitting of levels as extensive as those of the Morris Canal.'

Colden knew level-headed engineering was one thing, but hill-climbing quite another. His immediate objective was to see the Rockaway plane, where he watched as 'a large, clumsy, heavy scow loaded with stone, weighing eleven

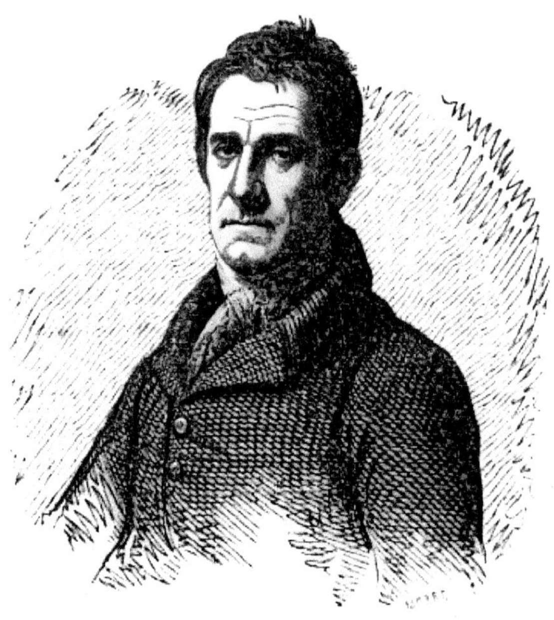

Cadwallader Colden.
(*The Family Magazine
or Monthly Abstract
of General Knowledge*,
Vol. 5, 1838)

tons, frequently passed from one level to the other.'[24] The apparatus seemed to do the job, even when operating at a disadvantage. Colden pointed out,

> Although there was but one vessel, and the operation would have been greatly facilitated if there had been another to act as a counterpoise; she was moved with perfect ease and security. The scow was repeatedly drawn up six hundred feet of the inclined plane, and conveyed into the water of the upper level in less than 12 minutes; whereas a boat would not pass the same height by locks in much less than an hour.

This persuaded Colden

> […] that the inclined plane, for passing any considerable elevation is preferable to locks, inasmuch as it is more economical as to the expense of water, time and money. I am quite sure it took less water to raise the boat on the inclined plane than it would have required to pass one boat up and another down by locks. The cost of the inclined plane is not over $140 for each foot of elevation, whereas the locks of the Erie Canal have cost $1,000 for each foot of lift; but as the locks of this canal are smaller, they will be proportionally less expensive.[25]

Although Colden found Kitchell's prototype

[...] perfectly satisfactory as to the evidence it affords of what may be done by this means, yet it is obvious, that it is not so perfect a machine of this kind, as might be made. It was built under the superintendence of the inventor, who is not a professed mechanic. The constructor is a house carpenter, and it may be easily imagined, that the machine is not finished in the style it might have been, if it had been made by a millwright or professional mechanic.

He decided the machinery could be 'improved and simplified.' Then there was the matter of safety: Even though boats were limited to a capacity of 25 tons, the chains used to draw them up were supposedly capable of sustaining 63 tons 'and, by a very simple contrivance, the boats may be instantly stopped in their ascent or descent, so that no very serious consequences could ensue; if the chain or any part of the machinery was to break.'

Forty miles, or nearly one half of the canal, was ready to receive water. Except for 9 miles of relatively easy work, the whole line was under contract and two thirds of all excavation was done. While only eight locks were fully operational, one half the lockage was nearly finished. Contractors also completed construction of two important guard locks and several dams. Although ground was prepared for several others, Kitchell's prototype at Rockaway (No. 6 East) remained the only one of the twenty-three projected planes to be completed. Smoothing investors' ruffled feathers, Colden promised the canal could be completed within the engineer's cost estimate. If an additional 2,000 shares were

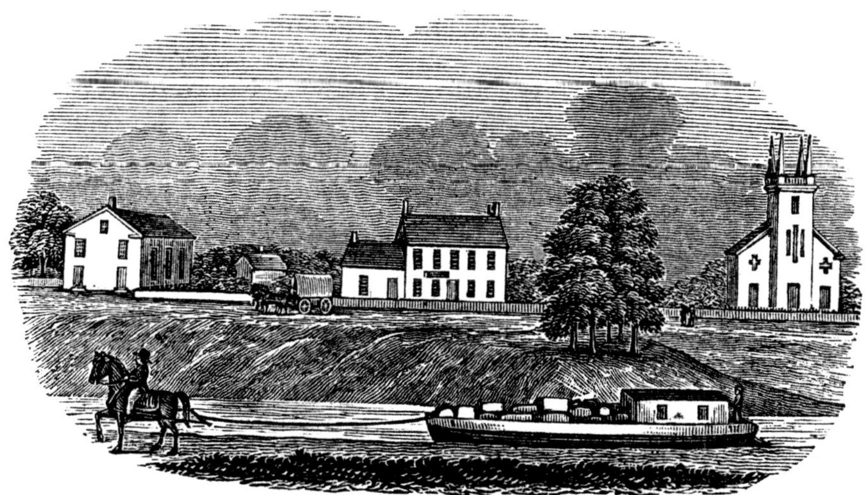

This 1844 woodcut shows a canal boat in the basin at the summit of Inclined Plane No. 6 East at Rockaway, NJ. *L to R*: the former Methodist Church (now a theater), the Kitchell House and the First Presbyterian Church still stand on Church Street. (Barber and Howe, *Historical Collections of the State of New Jersey*, 1844)

[...] immediately subscribed, so that materials for the locks and inclined planes may be provided and prepared this winter, the whole eastern section may be finished and navigated by the month of September next, and then the produce of the canal will be very considerable.

Falling five years short of the mark, Colden projected completion by the end of 1827, when the canal could begin producing 'a revenue equal to the most sanguine expectations that have ever been entertained.' He further noted 'contractors, and inhabitants of New Jersey, living near the canal line,' had bought 1,000 shares of stock since July, offering 'strong evidence that those who have the best opportunity of judging of the practicability of the Canal and of its advantages, and who are not prone to part with their money without due circumspection, have entire confidence that it may be accomplished, and that it will be profitable.' Before his letter appeared in print, Colden was elected president of the Morris Canal and Banking Company, replacing recently deceased president *pro tem* William Bayard.[26]

Since Kitchell's plane proved unreliable, President Colden offered $200 on 27 November 1826 for the best model of a mechanism to pass canal boats from one level to another. Nineteen competitors exhibited models, which were so similar in plan as to confound the judges.[27] Kitchell won the prize in February 1827 by simplifying the machinery employed in his own prototype at Rockaway, thereby reducing construction and operational costs.[28] To meet greater-than-expected costs, the Morris Canal and Banking Company sought a $300,000 loan, which was to be repaid from the proceeds of the sale of 3,000 shares of stock with subscribers receiving post-notes, payable in two years at 6 percent interest.[29] The Bank of New York loaned $25,000, which was to be made available when $200,000 had been subscribed.

Inspecting the line of the canal in August 1827, Colden found 1,500 laborers at work and more than five eighths of the excavation between Newark and Phillipsburg done. Except for finishing touches, lockage on the Eastern Division was completed and walls for three planes nearly so. While excavating on 20 July 1827, workers uncovered the remarkably preserved skeleton of a mastodon, about 3 feet below the surface, near Schooleys Mountain. According to Thomas P. Stewart, who examined the remains, the tusk, measuring 2 feet in circumference and 7 feet long, weighed 150 lb. Peter C. Bowne, who purchased the skeleton, said the grinders looked remarkably fresh, despite their great age, one weighing 4 lb.[30] One mishap, however, marred progress; the *Sussex Register* reported on 20 August that Christopher Flood, who had arrived in the United States from Ireland only a few days previously, 'was crushed to death a few days since, by a large stone, which loosened from the bank above where he was at work, and rolled upon him.' Meanwhile, masons worked on the foundations of a massive stone aqueduct

> # 100 Men Wanted.
>
> **T**HE subscribers, contractors on the *MORRIS CANAL*, are intending to imploy a large number of hands on said canal through the insuing summer and will give liberal incouragement to the young men of Sussex and Morris Counties, good efficient labourers will receive the highest wages going on the said line of canal, good accommodation and their pay monthly.
> DRAKE & SMITH.
> Brooklin, March 12, 1827–15–4ws.

'100 Men Wanted'. Contractors Drake and Smith, of Brooklyn Forge, near Lake Hopatcong, advertised in *The Sussex Register* on 12 March 1827.

with a single arch of 80-foot span at Little Falls on the Passaic River, built with freestone quarried a few rods distant.[31]

Riding the brow of Garret Mountain so as to preserve its level above the Great Falls, the canal skirted the manufacturing village of Paterson, which boasted fifteen cotton mills, two canvas factories, ironworks and machine shops, sustaining a population of 6,236 residing in more than 600 dwellings.[32] Near the falls, laborers cut a channel, averaging 16 feet in depth, through hard rock for nearly 265 feet. A wooden aqueduct, 236 feet long and supported on nine stone piers, carried the canal over the Pompton River near Mead's Basin.

To accommodate Newark merchants and artisans, the canal passed down one of the city's principal streets *en route* to the Passaic River. Making a direct approach to New York City, the canal builders planned to incorporate the old Newark road, abandoned for half a century, as its towing path across the Hackensack Marshes to Jersey City. At the summit level, a navigable feeder, ¾ mile long, connected with Lake Hopatcong, whose waters afforded navigation for another 9 miles to the north, accessing the mineral regions of Sussex County.

Two disasters struck in late September 1827. Fire destroyed Gamaliel Bartlett's forge at Stanhope on the 27th. The chain-cable proving shop at

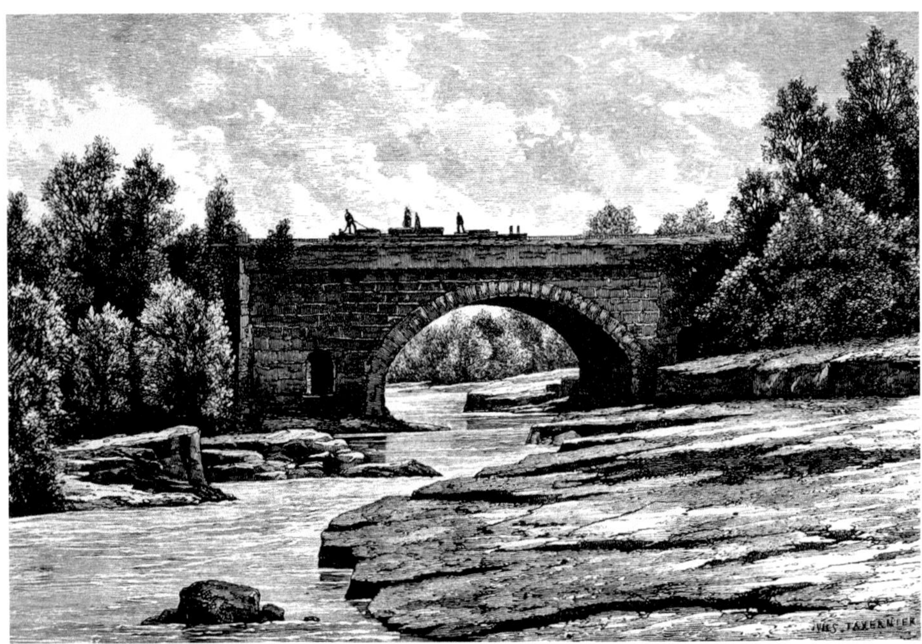

Jules Tavernier's rendering of the Little Falls Aqueduct on the Morris Canal. (*Picturesque America: Or, The Land We Live In*, 1872)

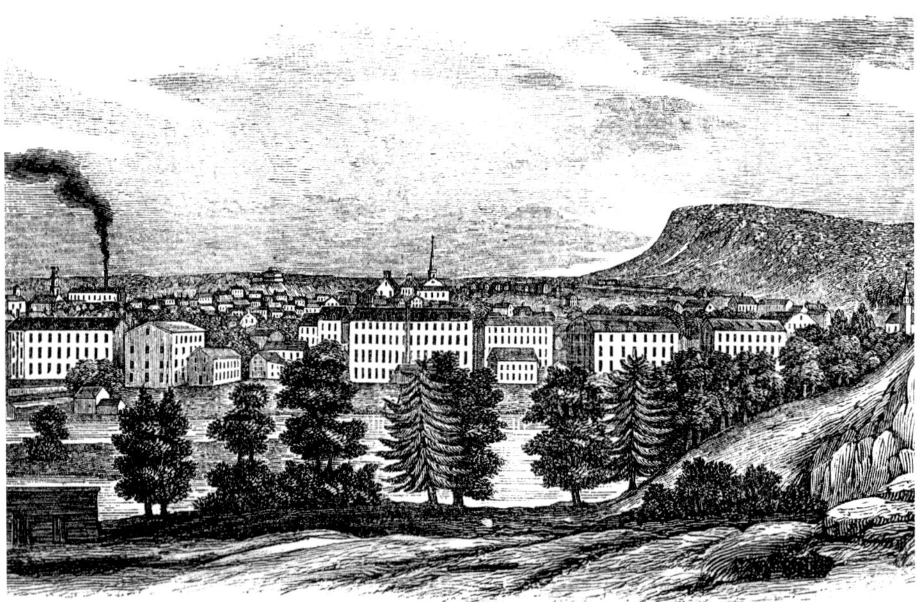

The Morris Canal runs along Garret Rock in this 'View of Paterson, NJ' from Barber and Howe's *Historical Collections of the State of New Jersey* (1844).

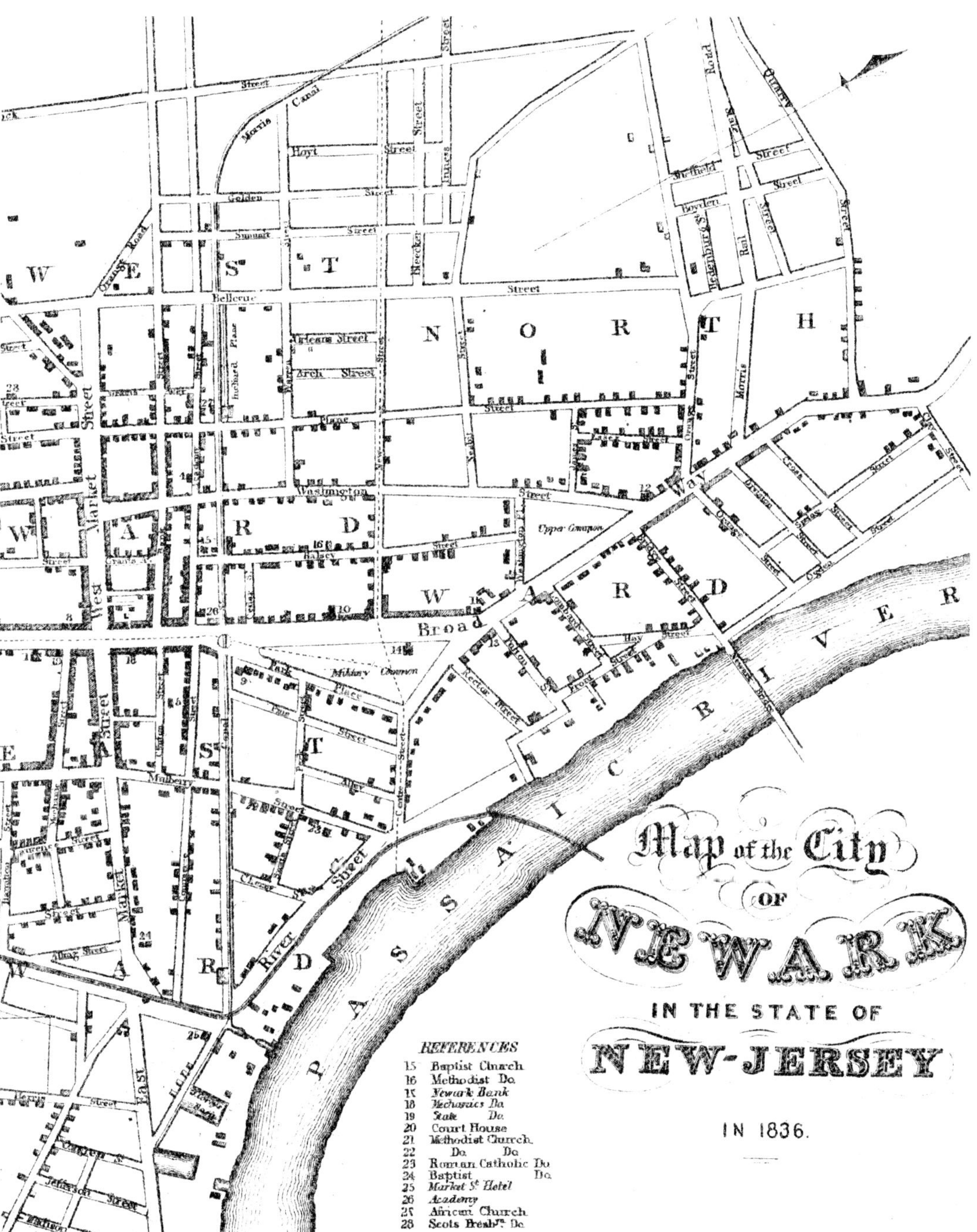

'Map of the City of Newark in the State of New Jersey in 1836' from Shaw, *History of Essex and Hudson Counties, New Jersey*, Vol. 1 (1884). Raymond Boulevard now follows the abandoned line of the Morris Canal. Jonathan Corey's basin was located about where NJ Transit stands today. Plane Street is now University Avenue. Bellevuc Street is now Martin Luther King Jr Boulevard.

Dover burned the following day, though the rolling mill was saved. Despite these mishaps, work continued into winter. On 16 January 1828, engineers, contractors and invited guests rode a large horse-drawn scow through the lock and feeder only a day after the waters of Lake Hopatcong first flowed into the summit level. They rode 'thence along the Canal West to [Plane] No. 3 [in Mount Olive], thence back and to No. 3 East [in Ledgewood], which work, being only completed the day before by Messrs Drake and Smith (the Contractors).'[33] On 28 January, a charter supplement authorized an 11-mile extension from Newark to the Hudson River. The company purchased 48 acres on the Delaware River in Phillipsburg, NJ, opposite the mouth of the Lehigh River, for its western terminus.

Success of the Morris Canal depended on a large intake of coal, and great progress was made to strengthen the rather precarious system of transport in the Lehigh Valley. The Lehigh Coal and Navigation Company partly canalized the Lehigh River, making it passable for 120-ton boats. Canvass White engineered the project to coincide with the start of construction on the Delaware Division Canal. To this purpose, Isaac A. Chapman, of Wilkes-Barre, spent the spring of 1826 surveying a series of levels from Mauch Chunk to the Delaware River, and several weeks more surveying locations for a sequence of dams at the head of the rapids in order to form pools in the channel of the Lehigh River at points where its bed was nearly level. Twenty-one dams and fifty-two locks were projected to overcome the change in elevation between Mauch Chunk and Easton.[34] To facilitate transport from the Beaver Meadows coal region, located 9 miles beyond Mauch Chunk, the upper section between Stoddartsville Falls and Mauch Chunk involved an even greater change in elevation, of 926 feet. This section would require construction of thirty-three dams along the river, which flowed the entire distance between high hills.[35] In September 1826, Chapman laid out a gravity railway for coal wagons, using a 'single-track edge-rail with turn-out places,' covering 9 miles from the Summit Hill mine down to Mauch Chunk.[36] The mine head stood 936 feet above the Lehigh River, but the mine railroad only descended to the top of the hill above the village at an elevation of 215 feet above the river. At this point, an inclined plane lowered loaded coal carts to the river's edge and hauled empties back to the head of the plane. A single mule could pull four empty carts back up the grade at 3 miles per hour.[37] Built in 1827, this gravity railroad reduced the cost of transporting coal from the mine to the head of navigation from $4.50 per ton by wagon to 25 cents per ton.[38] Soon, 100 coal wagons on the Mauch Chunk railway were delivering 180 tons of coal daily on the banks of the Lehigh Canal. Backers of the Morris Canal must have quietly fretted over these developments—while the Lehigh Canal would accommodate the passage of 120-ton boats, Morris Canal locks and planes limited boats to 25 tons.

As work on the Morris Canal continued, the most advantageous locations for trade swelled into hamlets and towns. Joseph Blackwell and Henry

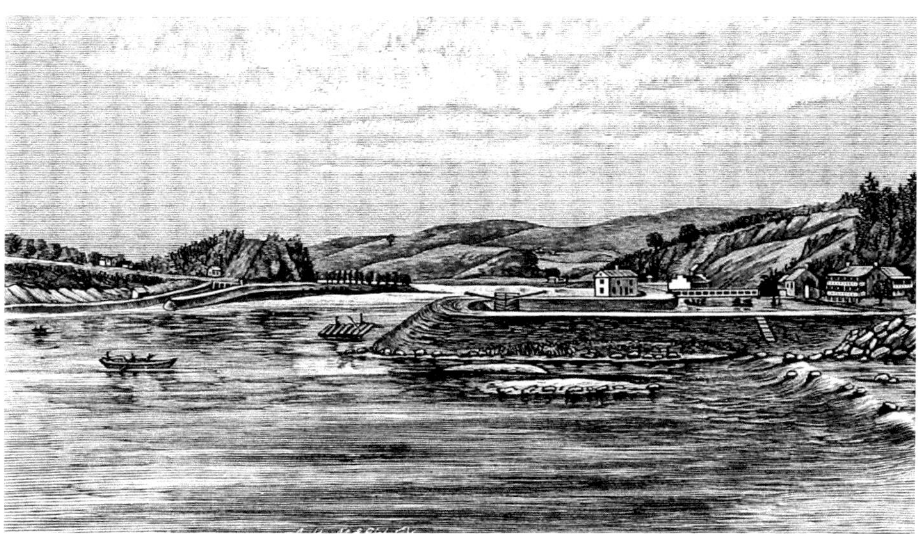

This woodcut depicts Easton, PA, (right) and Phillipsburg, NJ, (left) on opposite banks of the Delaware River. The guard and weigh lock on the Delaware Division Canal in Easton (at center) overlook the Forks of the Delaware River at the confluence of the Lehigh River. Mount Parnassus and the inlet to the Morris Canal and Inclined Plane No. 11 West are depicted to the left of center. (Condict, *The History of Easton, Penn'a*, 1885)

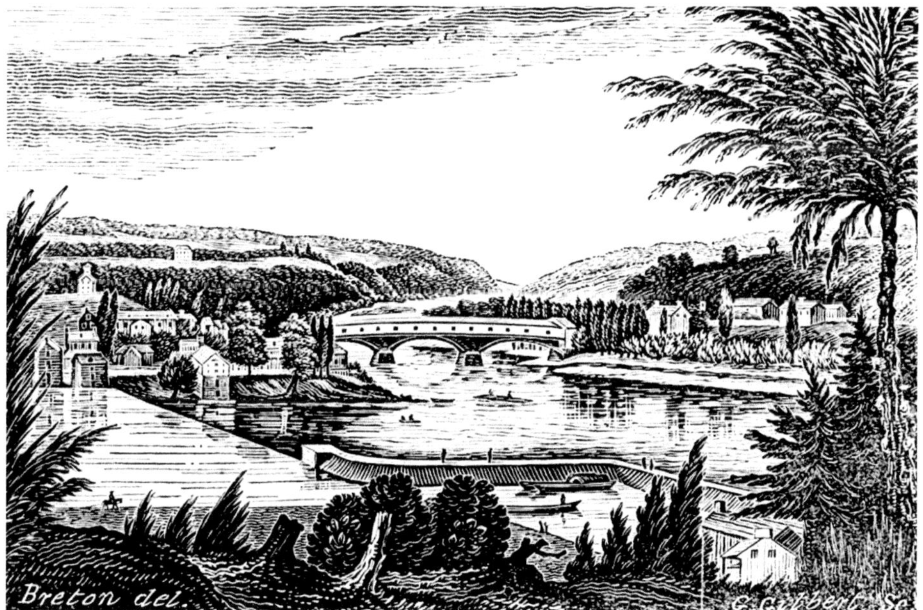

George Gilbert's woodcut of artist William L. Breton's 1835 view of Easton, PA, was taken from Mt Washington in Easton, looking north up the Delaware River. The Easton Dam formed a basin at the mouth of the Lehigh River, providing water for the intersecting Delaware Division Canal (lower right). Note the covered bridge on Northampton Street. (*Atkinson's Casket*, 1836)

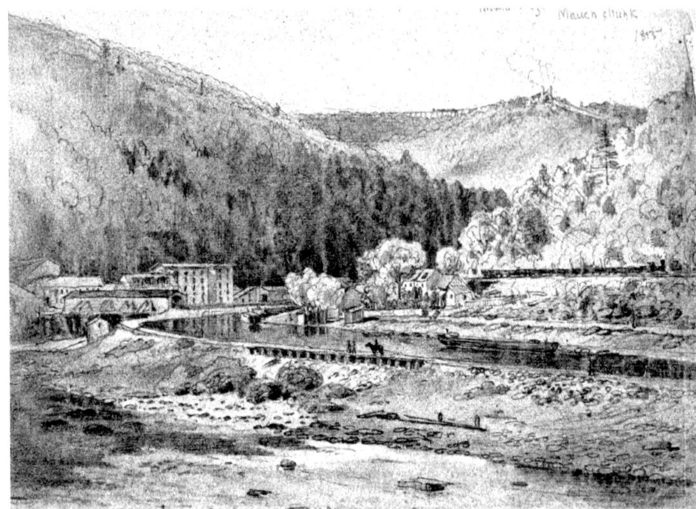

The covered bridge over the Lehigh River is visible at center left. The Mansion House stands behind it on Susquehanna Street (Route 209). The Lehigh Canal winds through the gorge, just below the Lehigh Valley Railroad. The switchback railroad descends from Summit Hill atop Mount Pisgah. Steam engines replaced mule power in 1844. *Mount Pisgah, Mauch Chunk*, graphite and charcoal drawing by James Fuller Queen, 1853. (*Marion S. Carson Collection, Library of Congress*)

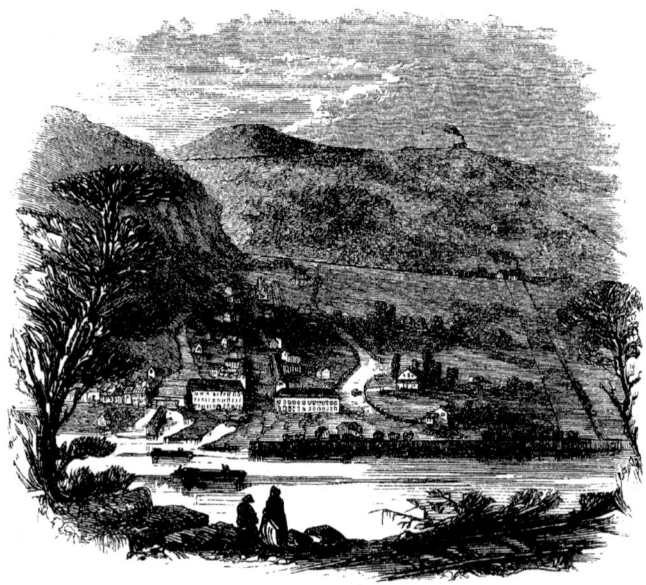

This 1857 view of Mauch Chunk was drawn from near the Lehigh Valley Railroad depot. The inclined planes on Mount Pisgah are visible. The wing dam in the Lehigh River is also shown. Broadway comes down to Market Square between the Carbon County Courthouse (right) and Asa Packer's store and post office (left). Behind the Courthouse, Alley Street winds around John Leisenring's mansion. Mauch Chunk Creeks empties into the river to the left. (*Harper's New Monthly Magazine*, September 1857)

McFarlan, proprietors of the newly incorporated Dover Manufacturing Company, laid out streets at right angles with a convenient canal basin, covering 2 acres, and then advertised an auction of fifty building lots in March 1827.[39] Their fledgling iron town included workingmen's houses, a large stone hotel, several stores, three rolling mills and two chain-cable shops, where nearly 1,000 tons of iron and chain cables were manufactured in 1826. Lehigh coal was delivered at less than $5 per ton. In their advertisement in *The Sussex Register*, Blackwell and McFarlan predicted: 'the lumber business from the Delaware River—the produce from the rich farming country of Sussex, and the inexhaustible iron mines of Morris County, must make this a place of very extensive business in a short time.'

The quest for a viable inclined plane was yielding mixed results. In the annual report for 1861, chief engineer William H. Talcott disclosed:

In 1827, another *Summit plane* was built at Boonton (No. 7 East), upon the plan and under the direction of Col. John Scott, with the machinery placed underneath the track at the apex of the plane, and worked with an endless chain. At the same time the 'Upper Montville' plane (No. 8 East) was built upon the plan and under the direction of Robt P. Bell—this also was a *Summit plane* with the machinery placed under the track like the Boonton plane, and worked by two water wheels on one shaft in place of a clutch to change the motion; both of these plans were successful experiments, and gave much satisfaction at the time.[40]

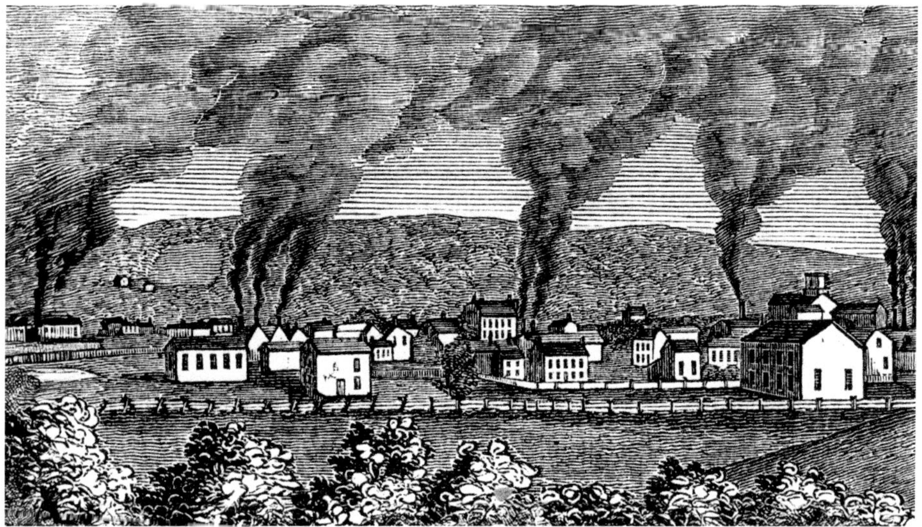

'Northern view of Dover'. (Barber and Howe, *Historical Collections of the State of New Jersey*, 1844)

According to the *Newark Sentinel* of 5 August 1828, a number of gentlemen from Newark and New York City viewed the operation of the plane at Boonton Falls with satisfaction on 2 August 1828, noting 'the machinery for the passage of boats from one level to another, has been improved and simplified from that used at Rockaway.' The Boonton plane overcame an elevational change of 80 feet, employing 1,000 feet of track. The boat passed over the plane in twenty minutes, whereas it would take eighty minutes to overcome the same elevation by ordinary lockage.[41] Whatever the advantage over a flight of locks, a twenty-minute crawl up the plane at Boonton was not a satisfactory outcome.

A joint-committee of the Governor's Council and General Assembly met with the directors of the Morris Canal Company at Jersey City on 1 December 1828, for a tour. They first viewed a 5-acre lot on Communipaw Bay, 400 feet wide on the Hudson River and 1,300 feet in length, adjoining the Jersey Ferry wharf, which the company purchased for a tidewater basin. Engineers anticipated the canal passing Bergen Ridge through a ravine, where an excavation only 18 feet deep and ½-mile long would allow it to cross the Palisades without either lock or plane. Engineers worked out a scheme to trap high tide on the Hackensack River with gates, thereby retaining 4 feet of water in the canal prism at low tide. From the Passaic River, the canal was to pass through Newark, employing two locks to ascend from the level of the Passaic River and a plane of 70-foot lift to climb the heights above the post office.[42] Starting at the head of the proposed Newark plane, the joint-committee walked 5 miles of towpath to Bloomfield, inspecting a finished lock (No. 16 East) on Lock Street, Newark, and two culverts *en route*. On this stretch, only a few yards of excavation awaited completion. Meanwhile, workmen fabricated a novel lock plane at Bloomfield, 683 feet in length, with a lift of 54 feet.

Like many others of his time, Ephraim Morris, son of a stage-driver, attended school at irregular intervals, obtaining 'merely the rudiments of a common education....'[43] Yet, he unexpectedly displayed great mechanical ingenuity in designing an inclined plane for the Morris Canal. According to his own account, Morris claimed he overheard canal commissioners, conferring upon the location of an inclined plane, regretting 'that a cheaper and more expeditious mode could not be devised for overcoming the irregularities in the surface of our country....' The amateur inventor ruminated overnight and then sought out the commissioners to reveal his plan. With no credentials to recommend confidence in Morris's abilities, they initially did not take him seriously. But he persisted, speaking 'with so much propriety' and exhibiting 'so clear a view of the feasibility of his plan, that many soon listened with astonishment, and were so much pleased with his genius that they immediately set him at work to make a model.' His design proved successful, 'and thus originated [...] one among the greatest mechanical inventions of the present century.' Morris patented his design on 13 October 1829.[44] But, as one reviewer more humbly concluded,

> Hitherto the inclined planes, which have been constructed, have disappointed the anticipations of their inventors; and, although we have often been told of perfect success in newly constructed works of this kind, the searching operator, time, has pointed out great defects, and has still left a good inclined plane, a *desideratum*. We are not aware that the plan now proposed offers any striking novelty, but should it remove the difficulties experienced in existing structures, its merits would be of high order.[45]

According to William Talcott's later description,

> In 1829, Ephraim Morris built a plane at Bloomfield (No. 11 East) on a new plan called a *Lock plane*, because the boat was received into a lock at the head of the plane, instead of descending into the upper level on the car as was done at the *Summit plane*.[46]

At Bloomfield, the plane car rode on four cast-iron wheels, 8 feet in diameter, with concave rims corresponding to the convex surface of the rails.[47] Mitered double gates operated at the end of the wooden summit lock adjoining the canal prism, but a single vertical drop gate, which lay flat in a

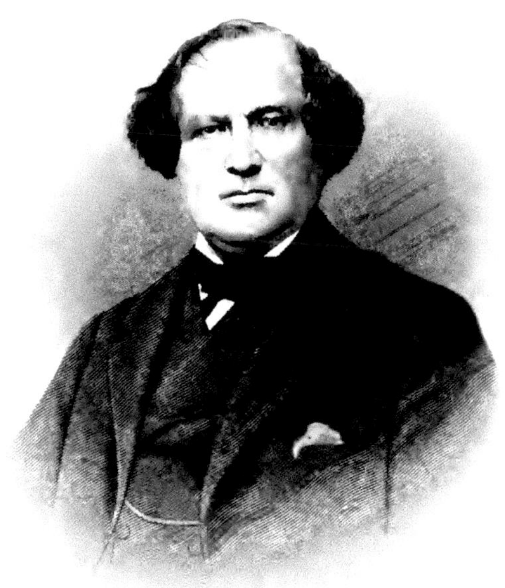

Portrait of Ephraim Morris
from Shaw's *History of
Essex and Hudson Counties,
New Jersey* (1884).

recess in the bottom of the lock chamber when open, allowed passage of the boat in its plane car. Boats in the lock either floated onto or from 'a cradle of the proper dimensions, suspended by vertical iron rods from the frame work of a large car.'[48] An iron chain, passing around an iron drum at the head of the plane, connected one plane car to its counterpoise on a parallel set of rails, so that as one descended, the other ascended. A water wheel of 20-foot diameter turned a horizontal shaft, extending out one side of the plane, which rotated a perpendicular drum through a 'double set of cog wheels, so proportioned as to enable [the shaft] to act upon the drum at a great mechanical advantage.' By shifting gears, cars could be raised or lowered in the desired direction on either set of tracks. Four-inch-wide cast-iron bars, 2½ feet long, were connected in series to form the railways. Two parallel sets of cast-iron rails were fastened atop heavy oak cross ties, carried on four masonry walls, 3½ feet high and 2½ feet wide. Boats on the lower level entered or floated free of the plane car without assistance. According to *Niles' Weekly Register* for 17 October 1829,

> [...] a boat and load weighing 25 tons, was not long since, passed up the plane in the space of 27 minutes, in the presence of the commissioners of the canal, and others, who had assembled to witness the experiment. Of its perfect action to all purposes of navigation, there is as yet some considerable doubt, even in the minds of those who have had experience in the business.[49]

While Mr Morris was building his plane at Bloomfield, Mr Eliphalet Miller built a *Lock plane* at Beavertown [Lincoln Park] differing materially from Mr Morris' plan. When a correspondent for the *New York Commercial Advertiser* visited 'Miller's Plane, [from the name of the builder], at Pompton,' he noted, 'The principle of this plane is different from that at Bloomfield,' even though both were lock planes.[50] At Montville, the correspondent's party ascended 'another plane, constructed upon still a different principle....' Finally, they proceeded 'to the great plane at Booneton Falls,' concluding:

> This was the fourth plane, which we had ascended, each of which was constructed upon principles somewhat different, but all of which were successful. The first plane, however, at Bloomfield, struck us on the whole as the most perfect model.

Newark millwright and patternmaker Eliphalet Miller ultimately left his work unfinished, apparently due to frustration and insolvency.

Mechanical experimentation could not proceed indefinitely, with capital drying up and estimates for construction of the extension to Jersey City exceeding the company's means and expectations. Consequently, on 23

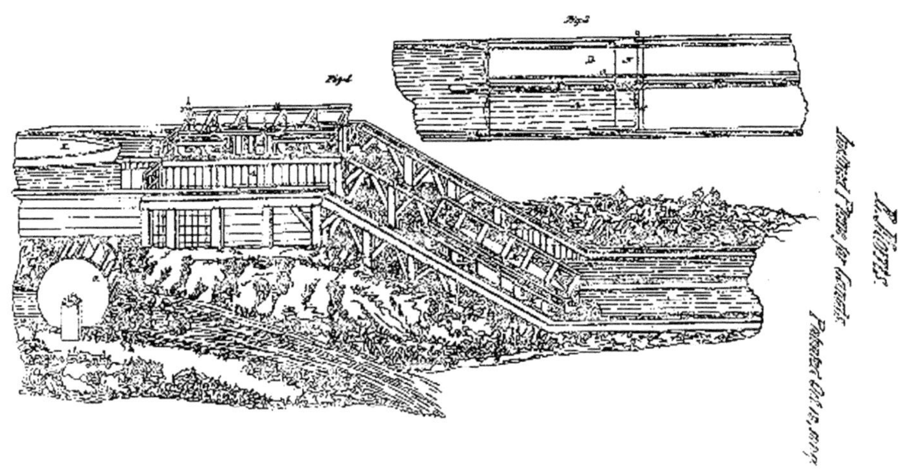

'Inclined Plane for Canals, Ephraim Morris, patented October 13, 1829.' Ephraim Morris built an inclined plane on this design at Bloomfield, NJ.

February 1829, the legislature authorized the Morris Canal and Banking Company to borrow $500,000 by issuing post-notes and to pledge the canal, its appurtenances and chartered rights, as collateral. The company sought a new loan from the Bank of New York in March 1829, agreeing to take $25,000 in post-notes already held by the bank, which were nearing maturity, as payment. The bank agreed on condition the whole amount of $500,000 should be subscribed.[51] To pay off their post-notes, the Morris Canal and Banking Company negotiated a mortgage loan at 5 percent interest in Amsterdam, accepting a draft on William Willink Jr, its agent and negotiator in London, for $750,000 on 29 March 1830.[52] This financial burden soon became known as the 'Dutch Loan'.

Unhappy with the Bloomfield and Pompton planes—which cost between $180 and $200 per lift foot—President Colden invited Major David Bates Douglass, of Brooklyn, retired engineering professor at West Point, to view the operation of the planes at Upper Montville and Boonton on 1 December 1828. Behind a public display of confidence, the company harbored great doubt as to what course to adopt with regard to the planes. The five in operation were each different, built according to the design of their respective contractors, but none worked efficiently enough to make the canal economically viable. According to Major Douglass's testimony,

[...] the one at Rockaway had to be entirely rebuilt; the walls of that at Boonton failed in the first experiment; and the cars and machinery required essential alterations to make them operative, after I took charge of the work. The same was equally true of the Upper Montville plane; and as to the plane at Pompton, I found it incapable of operation—abandoned, in despair, by the projector, and consigned in utter perdition by the President of the company, with whom it had formerly been a favorite. [53]

Douglass discovered 'several thousand perches of masonry, of a very inferior quality, built; so that nearly six thousand perches in all had to be condemned, as unfit for the purpose, after it had been duly estimated, and paid for.' According to an anonymous critic, 'Major Douglass submitted a plan, which he considered preferable, the maximum average cost of which would not exceed $160 per foot; thus offering a saving to the company of $40 per foot from the estimate of their engineer....'[54]

One contemporary observer opined,

In 1825, the excavations were prosecuted with alacrity, while the planes were deferred; an arrangement which experience proves should have been reversed, since the latter could be perfected only by many and tedious experiments. The erection of the planes, too, was entrusted to ordinary mechanics, who, deficient in scientific knowledge and manual skill, caused much disappointment, which was aggravated by great and useless expenditure; but, finally, proper engineers were employed, and the planes have become effectual to establish a regular intercourse along the line of the canal with the Delaware and Lehigh Rivers, and with the Hudson.[55]

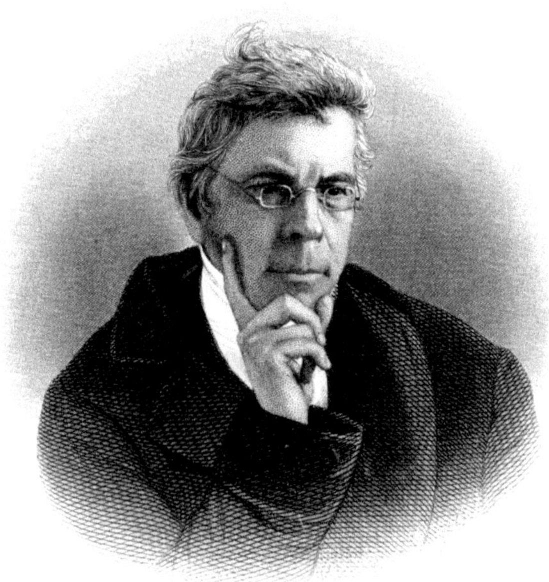

Portrait of Major David Bates Douglass. (Stuart, *Lives and Works of Civil and Military Engineers of America*, 1871)

Another anonymous critic in 1833 laid blame on Ephraim Beach:

> [...] the engineer engaged, enjoying no higher claim to the title than was embraced in the profound knowledge of the practical art of surveying, and a laudable contempt of all physical science, having progressed that far in his work, abandoned all further responsibility in favor of his employers. As might have been anticipated under the circumstances, the company, thus thrown on their own resources, after having selected from the multifarious models that were daily offered for trial, and sunk in futile experiments on them thousands and thousands of dollars, were on the point of abandoning the work in hopeless despair, when a ray of light beamed on them from West Point, and served to re-animate their drooping spirits.[56]

Hoping to silence infighting among competing inventors, designers and mechanics, President Colden employed Major Douglass as chief engineer of the planes on 15 September 1829 at a $4,000 annual salary.[57]

Competition was building and further indecision and delay was not an option. On 17 October 1829, *Niles' Weekly Register* commented ominously on the Bloomfield plane 'that a railway might as well have been constructed through the whole route.'[58] Only three months later, on 11 January 1830, Joseph C. Hornblower presented the General Assembly with the Morris Canal Company's remonstrance against a contemplated railroad from Paterson to the Hudson River at Jersey City. Proving a competent administrator and problem solver, Douglass engaged the West Point foundry in February 1830 to make castings and other ironwork for planes at Old Andover (Waterloo) and Montville on the same terms the company had previously engaged Messrs Blackwell and McFarlan. He imported English iron plates and rails. Ironically, as the canal's engineers sought iron castings and chain from foreign suppliers, distressed bar iron manufacturers from northern New Jersey founded the East Jersey Iron Manufacturers in January 1830. [59] In that year, New Jersey ironworks manufactured $657,000 worth of products, processing 1,671 tons of pig iron, valued at $30 per ton; 5,615 tons of castings, valued at $60 per ton; and 3,000 tons of bar iron, valued at $90 per ton. The United States produced 180,000 tons of pig iron in 1830.[60]

In April 1830, Douglass advertised in the *Sussex Register* for contractors and millwrights to build machinery for the planes, based on his prototype at Montville. His specifications included laying way-timbers and attaching iron rails; building and hanging waterwheels 20 feet in diameter with 9-foot buckets; flooring the wheel pit; building a flume; building plane cars; hanging and gearing the millwork, including one horizontal and one upright shaft; brake and rack work with all necessary fixtures; installing pulley platforms and pulleys; bolting down standards for the friction pulleys on stone blocks; and building a stage for the plane attendant.

Major Douglass 'made *Summit planes* of all but the one at the Delaware River (No. 11 West). That was made a *Lock plane*, but different from either of the other *Lock planes*.'[61] His plan resembled other prototypes in having the motions of ascending and descending plane cars reciprocate on double railways.[62] In place of summit locks, plane cars passed over a summit curve, rising about a foot above the upper water level. By design, the plane car crossed the summit with equal bearing on its eight wheels. Plane cars descended the summit hump into the upper level by gravity, advancing independently of the machinery. At both head and foot of each inclined plane, boats floated free of the plane cars with sufficient velocity to speed them on their way without assistance. Although chains were manufactured to withstand a strain of 15 tons without breaking, the weight they had to sustain was calculated never to exceed 6 tons. In abandoning water-filled moveable locks, the greatest difficulty to resolve was 'that the boats, which as a rule are very light in construction, suffer much damage while out of the water on the cars because of the weight of their loads, especially when they are heavily loaded.'[63] As slimly built canal boats could not be grounded on the smooth surface of a plane car without straining their timbers, Douglass designed smaller and more substantially made boats to withstand amphibious transit.[64] These boats, called 'flickers', could carry 25 tons of cargo.[65]

William Pragnell began building boats at Dover in May 1830, 'after a model recommended by Professor Douglass, of West Point—engineer of inclined planes, Major Beach, canal engineer, & Col. Scott, canal commissioner.'[66] In 1837, English engineer David Stevenson described Morris Canal boats as '8½ feet in breadth of beam, from 60 to 80 feet in length, and from twenty-five to thirty tons burden.'[67] On 9 June 1830, canal contractors Drake and Bartlett offered liberal wages for 100 men to work at Stanhope. At Phillipsburg, engineers decided to terminate the canal on the Delaware River with a plane and guard lock. Major Douglass personally supervised construction of one of the Montville Planes, where his improvements 'allowed the passage of loaded boats at the average rate of six minutes and a half.'[68]

Douglass demonstrated his accomplishment before a committee of directors on 23 October 1830. Two days later the committee, 'being satisfied with the operation of the machinery, and the solidity as well as the durability of the whole work, and feeling confident that it will realize in practice the most sanguine expectations,' congratulated everyone involved 'upon the happy result of this experiment.'[69] Finally satisfied, they employed plane tenders at $30 per month and lock tenders at $12 per month.

Five canal boats laden with iron ore made a trial run between Dover and Newark on 11 November 1830. On Friday 10 December 1830, the first boat passed through Newark on the recently completed inclined plane.[70] At about ten o'clock in the morning, a correspondent for the *New York American*

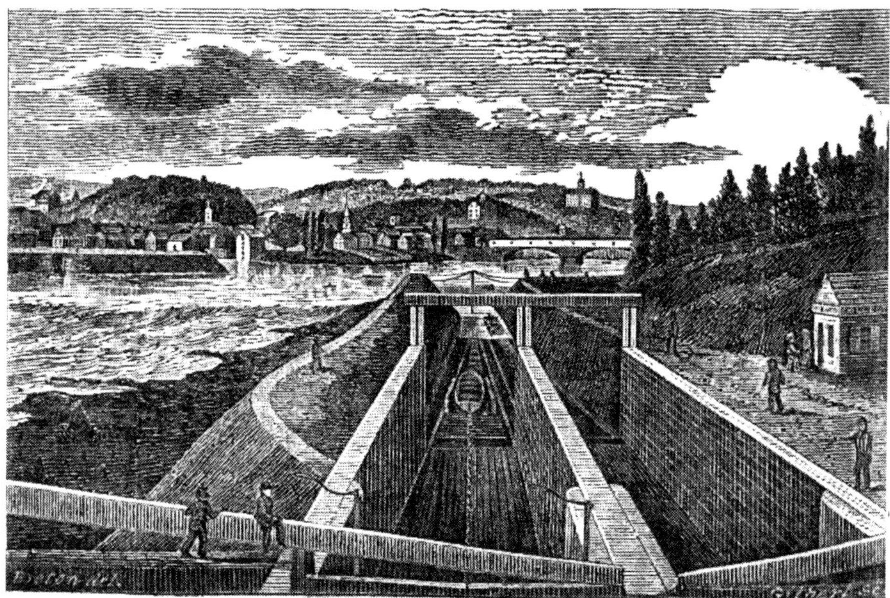

Inclined Plane of Morris Canal, opposite Easton.

George Gilbert's woodcut of artist William L. Breton's 1835 view of Inclined Plane
No. 11 West. David B. Douglass submitted a plan favoring summit planes, except for
a lock plane at the Delaware River, which differed from other lock planes along the
route. Note the covered bridge across the Delaware River between Phillipsburg and
Easton. (*Atkinson's Casket, Gems of Literature, Wit and Sentiment*, 1836)

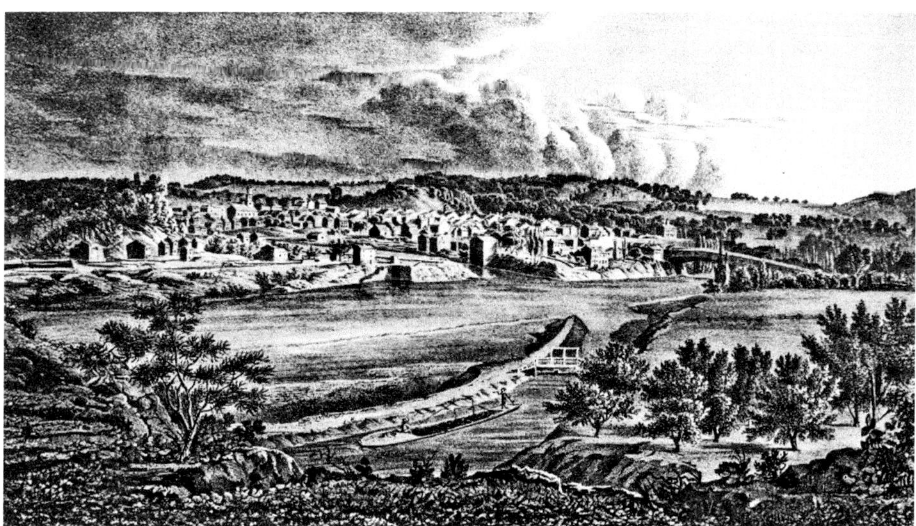

This view of Easton, PA, was drawn in 1832 from near Mt Parnassus in Phillipsburg,
NJ. As a coal laden 'flicker' enters the inlet of the Morris Canal, its captain sounds his
horn to alert the plane tender to his approach. (Weaver, *The Forks of the Delaware
Illustrated*, 1900)

watched horses tow Jonathan Cory's boat (named *Dover*, after its place of origin) into the immersed plane car on the upper level. At Major Douglass's command, water was fed to a waterwheel (24 feet in diameter), situated a short distance downslope. The cable-chain pulled the boat, securely housed within its frame, with about 200 persons aboard, up the summit hump in one minute. Onlookers, watching from the bridge at the foot of the hill, marveled as its bow, crested for the first time, admiring 'a boat sixty feet long sailing over a mountain seventy feet high, without any visible agent being employed to propel her forward, the large wheel and all the other machinery being underground and concealed from view.' The *New-Jersey Eagle* reported the boat crossed the summit,

> [...] with all the ease that a ship would cross a wave of the sea. As the forward wheels of the car commenced their descent, the boat seemed gently to bow to the spectators and the town below, then glided quickly down the wooden way.[71]

In six-and-a-half minutes the boat descended 1,040 feet of railway into the lower level. Once it floated free from the carriage, 'two horses and as many boys as could get hold of the towline' drew the boat through Newark to the lock at the Passaic River, where she took on a load of iron before returning to the plane. This time, as she ascended, the *Dover* passed the packet boat *Maria Colden* about midway.[72] The *Newark Sentinel of Freedom* gleefully commented,

> The whole operation is performed with a celerity, even beyond the calculation of the engineer. It was performed about sixty times in the course of Friday and Saturday last, carrying boats variously loaded in twelve cases; and once with a boat ascending and another descending at the same time; the load of the ascending boat being about twenty-one tons. The time of the operation has generally been about eight minutes—some times less than seven—never more than nine. Five operations can with the greatest ease be performed in an hour, allowing large intervals for the entrance and exit of boats, and for other purposes; and as two boats may pass at each operation, the plan will accommodate the arrival and departure of ten boats per hour, with a tonnage of 250 tons; or 6,000 tons per *diem*, which is nearly four times the whole commerce of the New York canal to Albany. The detention of boats will not, according to the experiments, exceed seven minutes (the remaining time on the plane being compensated by the motion *forward*), which is only a detention of *one minute* for every ten feet of lift. This is a saving of at least nine-tenths in comparison with locks, and reduces the detention on the voyage from Easton to this place, from twenty-four hours, which it would be if locks were used, to less than two hours and a half. [73]

The *Sentinel* concluded with the observation,

> There are now three inclined planes on Professor Douglass' principle, finished, and in operation; the others are in a state of forwardness that warrants the expectation of their being done by the opening of the navigation in the spring. All the masonry, and a large part of the carpenters' work, are already completed, and very little remains to be done except to place the machinery, which can be done without inconvenience in the course of the winter. The experiments upon the plane excited much interest, and called forth repeatedly the warmest plaudits of the spectators.

On 31 December 1830, the acting manager of the Lehigh Coal and Navigation Company informed concerned stockholders:

> I am credibly informed that the Morris canal is ready for use excepting some of the mechanical work at a few of the inclined planes; and an intelligent friend has informed me, that a visit to the inclined planes on that canal completely dissipated all his former doubts and convinced him of their efficacy. He stated that the planes caused little or no detention, as the boats had completed the passage on them in nearly the same time that the horse walked the same distance.[74]

As work on the planes hurried to a conclusion, John Prior placed notice in the *Sussex Register* in March 1831, offering to build canal boats 65 feet in length and 8 feet in breadth for $200 each. *The Morristown Jerseyman* reported in July 1831 that several boats would 'pass from one extremity of the Morris Canal to the other, unless the embankments have been injured by the powerful rains of last week.'[75] The eastern section of the canal was already 'covered with boats laden with ore, iron, &c.'

Major Douglass declared all planes operational on 9 August 1831, signaling commencement of navigation along the whole extent of the Morris Canal. There was, however, some dissatisfaction with inadequate water in some levels. Without funds to complete construction to Jersey City, the canal terminated on the Passaic River in Newark, where Jonathan Cory operated two large basins and a dock outfitted with storehouses, wharf room and stables. Cory's sloops traveled between his Commercial Dock and Whitehall in New York City. Farther inland, Samuel Sayre advertised in the *Sussex Register* on 12 August 1831 to 'Country Merchants and others giving me freight,' that his boat would make regular trips to Newark, leaving Sayre Place, 1 mile west of Stanhope, each Monday to arrive at Newark on either Tuesday evening or Wednesday morning. He planned to leave Newark the same day or the following morning and arrive at his basin on Saturday. Sayre delivered freight to Cory's Basin or the Newark Dock, where it could either be stored or forwarded to New York as directed. Freight wagons destined for Sayre Place departed 'the Sussex Turnpike at Lockwood, passing [New] Andover Forge— distance one mile and a half, good road.' On 30 October 1831, the *Sussex Register* noted the first shipments of mackerel, coal and flour passing to and from Easton upon the canal.

Twenty feet wide at bottom and 32 feet wide at the waterline, the Morris Canal was dug 4 feet deep.[76] It took five days for an 18-ton boat, drawing 3 feet of water, to cross 90 miles between Easton and Newark. While Phillipsburg and Newark were only 70 miles apart, long levels were surveyed not only to avoid expensive banks and cuts, but also to reduce the number of planes and locks required to adjust boats in elevation, which 'added many miles of unnecessary sinuosities to the length of the canal.'[77] On the Eastern Division, twelve planes overcame 758 feet in elevation and sixteen locks overcame 156 feet. The Western Division required eleven planes to overcome 691 feet in elevation and seven locks to overcome 69 feet. Locks were built 9 feet wide and 75 feet long between miter-sills. Their lifts varied from 8 to 12 feet. In the end, the planes cost an estimated $400 per lift foot, amounting to $560,000 on 1,400 feet of lift.[78] When all was said and done, it cost nearly $2,439,534, or $27,105 per mile, to construct the canal between the Delaware and Passaic Rivers—almost treble the original estimate of $817,000. President Colden justified the overrun, insisting, 'that inclined planes for boats of heavy burthen, is entirely a new project, and that large sums were expended on experiments on these costly machines, before those were constructed which so well answer the purpose.'[79] Their haphazard development, however, resulted in variations of type: three lock planes and twenty summit planes. From the outset, numerous breaches and accidents interrupted navigation. English-made chains soon replaced eight iron chains of American manufacture, which broke repeatedly. English chains were soon substituted on all the planes.[80] Even that did not solve the problem— in July 1831, an English chain 1½ inches in diameter broke six times on the Boonton plane. Disgruntled American ironmakers were quick to point out that an American chain only ¾ inch in diameter, used to lengthen the English chain, stood the trial of passing the boat.

In February 1832, Major Douglass wisely ordered brakes for stopping the plane cars in case of accident, but problems persisted. In May 1832, a boat belonging to Colonel Joseph Jackson, named *Electa* for his wife, was carrying iron to Newark with the captain, his wife and two children on board. Just as the boat passed the summit of the Boonton plane, the chain broke. The plane car sped down

> [...] with great velocity, striking the water with such force as to throw an immense wave over the towing path, which carried the boat with it down an

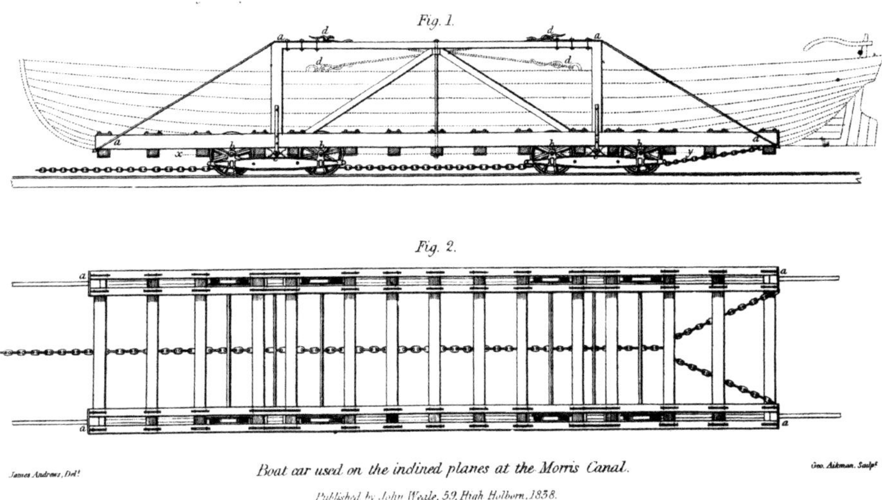

George Aikman's engraving of James Andrews' drawing of a 'Boat car used on the inclined planes at the Morris Canal', Plate 6, 1837. (David Stevenson, *Sketch of the Civil Engineering of North America*, 1859, Library of Congress)

embankment from fifteen to twenty feet in height and landed it on the rocks below, amid some trees standing there, but fortunately without striking any. People hastened to the boat to ascertain the fate of those on board. On opening the cabin door the wife, with her two children, was found sitting there rather composedly, and uninjured. When told what had happened she seemed surprised, and said she 'thought the boat went down very swift, but supposed that was the way the thing worked.'[81]

A contemporary report in the *New-Jersey Eagle* indicated the boat broke in two pieces near its center and lay in 'a heap of ruins not worth picking up....' It mentioned a woman and three children aboard the boat at the time of the accident, but also suggested, 'The captain and hands probably went on shore to walk down the plane, which is frequently done.'[82]

Despite mishaps, Major Douglass was generally admired for his ability to reduce 'his principles to practice.' One anonymous New Yorker invited his fellow citizens to see the results for themselves:

The proximity of one of these planes to the city enables any person, within an hour's ride, to be on the scene of action, where curiosity may be amply gratified by the exhibition of boats, heavily loaded with the rich mineral and agricultural productions of the country, passing and re-passing each other on the plane in rapid succession. It is, indeed, an interesting sight to observe the facility with which the boats pass from one level to another; when within about twenty feet of the foot of the plane, the towline is detached, and the boat, under the guidance of the steersman, passes gracefully into the car there ready for its reception. So soon as secured, which is the delay of a moment, a sign is made by the waving of a small flag to the tender at the summit, and directly the pattering of water on the wheel, and the clinking of the chain over the sheaves, tells you that the car is in motion. Presently emerging, boat and all from the water, you find yourself ascending slowly and majestically for the distance of eight or nine hundred feet towards the summit; and there pausing for a moment, as the car is relieved from the restraint of chain and machinery, she plunges headlong, as it were, under the influence of her gravitating force, for a hundred and fifty feet, towards the termination of the plane in the upper canal—whence the boat, from the impetus received, glides freely from the car; and the horses, which in the interim have passed round, resume their duties in propelling the boat to the next plane, where a similar operation elevates her as before to a higher level.[83]

At the outset, an insufficiency of boats limited carrying capacity. President Colden admitted,

As to the number of boats on the canal, there have been very great disappointments. The company made contracts, which had they been fulfilled, the company would have 100 boats of their own employed early in the season; but several of the contractors failed altogether to comply with their contracts; and one, who was to have supplied twenty boats, although he did build some of them, yet he constructed them so badly that they were worth nothing and could not be accepted. The interruptions on the canal have discouraged individuals from providing boats, but yet there are more, and probably considerable more than one hundred and fifty boats on the canal; and now that it is seen that the navigation will be made permanent, boats are building with great spirit, and before the season closes, or certainly in the spring, the number of boats will far exceed two hundred.[84]

Anticipating the first full boating season, secretary Robert Gilchrist published rates of toll per mile in February 1832 for various commodities from ashes, bricks, coal and charcoal to wheat, whiskey and window glass.[85] Whether carrying cargo or not, boats paid 2 cents per mile, if over 45 feet in length, and 5 cents per mile, if under that length. The passenger rate was 1 cent per mile. Water was let into the canal in April 1832, but a break near Phillipsburg delayed its opening for another month. While several coal-laden boats reached Newark from Mauch Chunk in November 1831, a boat named the *Walk in the Water*, carrying a consignment for Stephens and Condit, became the first vessel to navigate the entire length of the Morris Canal to Newark after its official opening, arriving in Newark on 19 May 1832.[86] City merchants and consumers hailed the arrival of two canal boats loaded with coal from Mauch Chunk, which immediately reduced the price of this indispensable fuel. Soon, fifteen to twenty boats were delivering coal, wood, bark, iron ore and farm produce daily to Newark. Three horses gently tugged the packet boat *Maria Colden*, conveying passengers daily between Newark and Acquackanonck (Passaic), except on Sundays. On 24 May 1832, President Colden wrote to Daniel K. Minor, editor of the *American Railroad Journal*. He boasted, 'The Canal is now, so far as I know, in perfect order, from one end to the other, and I think is, at last, about to realize our expectations.'[87] Major Douglass having accepted a professorship at New York University, Ephraim Morris took his place, changing Planes Nos. 7 East (Boonton) and 8 East (Upper Montville) to lock planes during the winter of 1832–33.[88] On 20 April 1833, the *Newark Sentinel* reported the recent arrival of a canal boat named the *Lady Clinton*, which left Easton with 108 barrels of flour, delivering 27 barrels after selling the other 81 *en route*. The only interruption in its transit was a delay at the Montville inclined plane, where alterations were not quite completed. The *Lady Clinton* was

> [...] one of 4 or 5 boats, that are on their way with similar cargoes. There are, as we are told, 223 boats on the canal, all of which will be in activity in a few days.—There are besides a number of new boats building; and there is every appearance that great business will be done upon the canal this year.[89]

At least one scrutinizer, however, had doubts.

> [The Morris Canal is] deeply in debt, and pays no dividend to the stockholders; but its use has been most beneficial upon the business of the country through which it passes, and its portage will increase with population and business; and should anthracite coal be successfully applied to the extraction of iron from ore, the consumption of that article alone will add greatly to the tolls.[90]

At that time,

> [...] a ton of iron might have been brought to New York from Archangel [Russia, on the White Sea], at nearly the same price it could have been transported from Berkshire Valley; and thus, this great branch of manufacture, alike interesting to the State and the Union, was in imminent danger of perishing.[91]

In March 1832, New Jersey legislators authorized the United Railroad and Canal Company to build the Delaware and Raritan Canal and the Camden

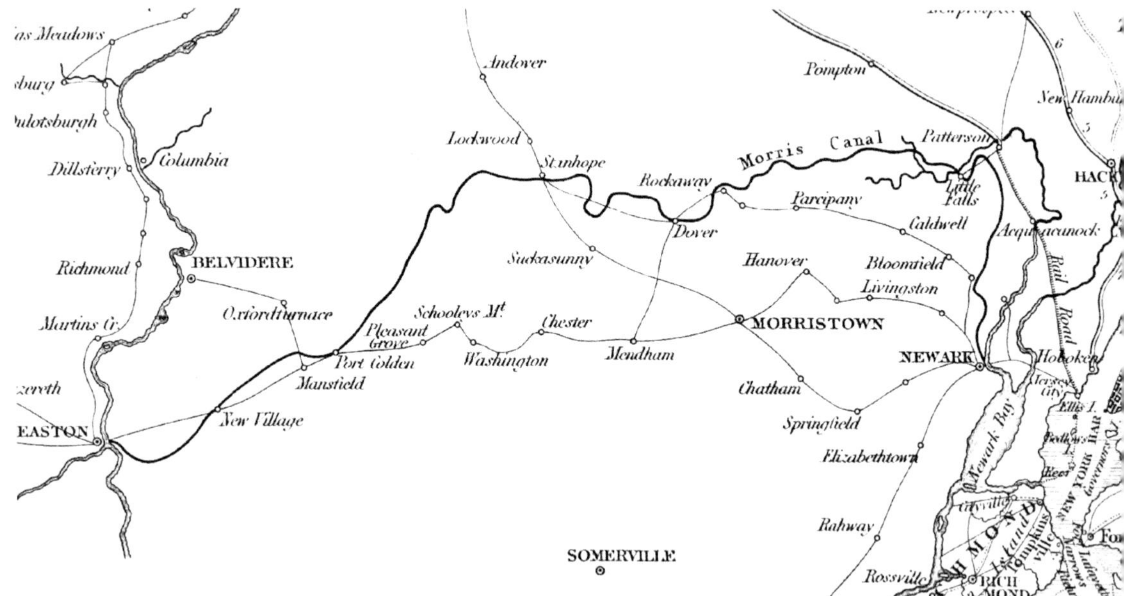

Route of the Morris Canal between Easton, PA, and Newark, NJ, in 1839. (Burr, *Map of New York, Exhibiting the Post Offices, Post Roads, Canals, Rail Roads, &c.*, 1839, Library of Congress)

and Amboy Railroad across the relatively level inner coastal plain, conceding the enormous privilege 'that no other railroad should be constructed, which might compete with that road.'[92] To protect this monopoly, the United Companies conveyed 1,000 shares of its joint stock to the state, guaranteeing an annual income of $30,000 to the public coffers. This canal instantly became a favorite project,

> [...] with speculators desirous to deal in a marketable commodity; with capitalists seeking for safe and profitable investments; and with many statesmen of New Jersey, who believed they saw in it the means of creating a permanent and large revenue for the State, which would forever relieve her citizens from taxation, for the ordinary support of government.[93]

Morris Canal stockholders, however, immediately understood, 'the transportation of the Lehigh coal to the New York market, originally counted on by the projectors of this canal, will be effected by the Delaware and Raritan Canal.'[94] To what degree, no one could say. And no one seemed prepared to calculate the transportation potential of the Camden and Amboy Railroad.

Water was admitted into the feeder of the Delaware and Raritan Canal in April 1834, gradually filling the main channel, 43 miles long between Bordentown and New Brunswick, fully 7 feet deep and 75 feet wide at its

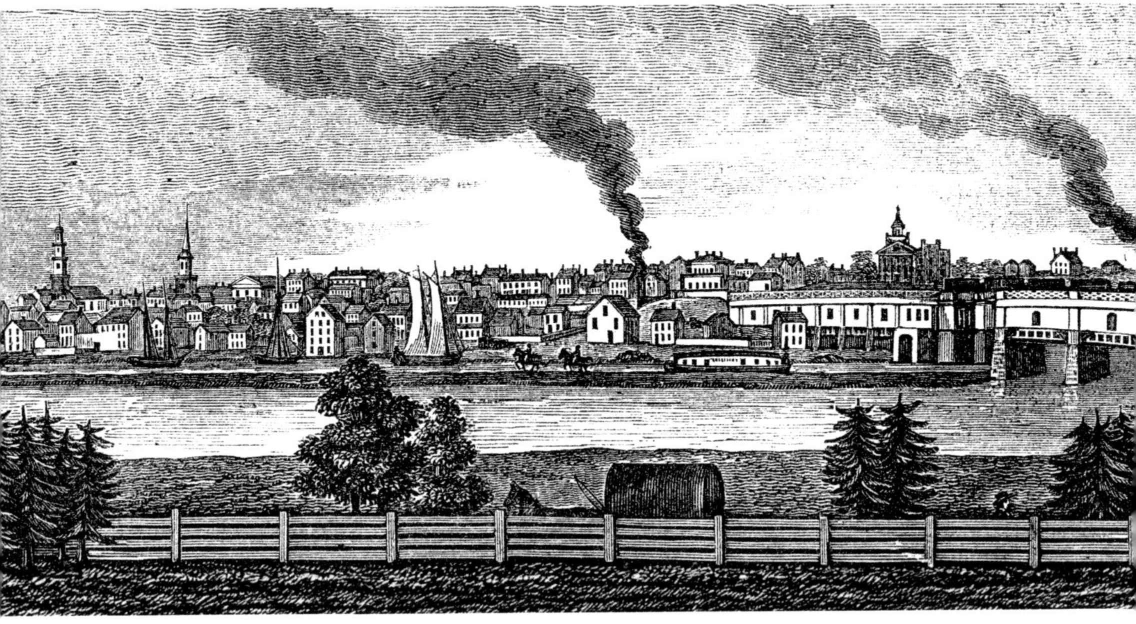

This 1844 woodcut view of New Brunswick, taken from Highland Park, shows two horses drawing a boat on the Delaware and Raritan Canal on the far bank of the Raritan River. The spires of the First Reformed Church and Christ Church on Neilson Street are visible to the left. The central column of smoke most likely rises from a paper factory on Water Street. The cupola of Old Queen's College (Rutgers) dominates the skyline to the right, flanked by Van Nest Hall and the President's House. The Buccleuch Mansion on Easton Avenue can be seen to the far right. A train on the New Jersey Railroad, which opened in 1838, is shown crossing the river. (Barber and Howe, *Historical Collections of the State of New Jersey*, 1844)

surface. Fourteen locks, measuring at least 24 by 118 feet, were capable of passing sloops of 50 to 100 tons' burden.[95] On 28 April, two boats with coal from Mauch Chunk arrived in Trenton, having descended the Delaware Division Canal to Bristol, where they crossed the river to Bordentown.[96] Boats carrying lumber were already traveling between Trenton and Kingston. Signaling the opening of navigation between the Raritan and Delaware Rivers, the directors rode a barge from Bordentown to Trenton and then up the 24-mile feeder to Lambertville on 25 June 1834. The party proceeded to New Brunswick the following day. Through the exertions of president and chief engineer Robert L. Stevens, of Hoboken, the Camden and Amboy Railroad opened between Camden and South Amboy on 19 December 1834, completed at a cost of $30,000 per mile.

After Cadwallader Colden died in Jersey City on 7 February 1834, New York merchant and investment banker James B. Murray was elected president of the Morris Canal and Banking Company.[97] Between March and September 1834, 1,085 boats carried 20,000 tons of merchandise over the Morris Canal, indicating an average cargo weight of 18 tons.[98] *The Newark Daily Advertiser* reported in August 1834 that 247 boats passed through the city over the course of ten days: 95 boats carrying Lehigh coal and 152 boats carrying products of the forest, mines, mills and manufactures along its route. Shippers of firewood paid $17,134 in tolls the previous year and transportation of this precious commodity was increasing.[99] Tolls for pig iron amounted to $4,812 and for stone amounted to $4,855.

But all was not smooth sailing. Easy credit, inflation and incautious optimism sucked foreign and domestic venture capital into labor-saving inventions and new technologies, but also into wildcat schemes and risky speculations. Without a national currency or any meaningful federal regulation, state-chartered banks circulated notes whose values fluctuated according to distance from their points of issue and varying rates of exchange governing their redemption for specie. After the War of 1812 drained federal coffers, President Madison chartered the Second Bank of the United States in May 1816, not only to mediate the exchange of state bank notes in expanding regional economies, but also to generate investment capital. Through mismanagement and speculation, however, the bank soon floundered, deepening a post-war depression and feeding public suspicions. Many blamed the selfish manipulations of a privileged elite for the Panic of 1819.

The economy recovered in 1823, just as Nicholas Biddle began to build the Second Bank of the United States into a central bank, developing its role as fiscal agent for the United States Treasury into a stabilizing influence upon money markets. President Andrew Jackson and his rising Democratic Party heralded a new breed of 'self-made men,' however, who demanded a level playing field. Leading the charge, Jackson attacked Biddle's Second Bank of the United States, whose twenty-year federal charter was set to expire in 1836. After Whig supporters failed to pass a re-charter bill, the President moved to starve the 'Monster Bank', ordering Acting Treasury Secretary Roger Taney in 1833 to disperse federal deposits among selected 'pet banks'. Biddle retaliated by curtailing loans to the amount of $5.5 million in only two months, causing a sharp contraction in credit. Financial panic gripped the nation during the winter of 1833–34. Although Biddle rescinded his policy in July 1834, he unwittingly demonstrated the danger of a 'monied aristocracy'. Responding to hard times, the Morris Canal reduced tolls from 3 cents to 2 cents per mile in August 1834, offering 15 percent discounts on freight traveling over 70 miles.

As one financial correspondent observed in August 1833,

In the secret history of Wall Street, during the last six or eight years, Morris Canal stock has frequently cut a very conspicuous figure. This curious stock has floated more money out of pockets than ever it did corn or grain to market.[100]

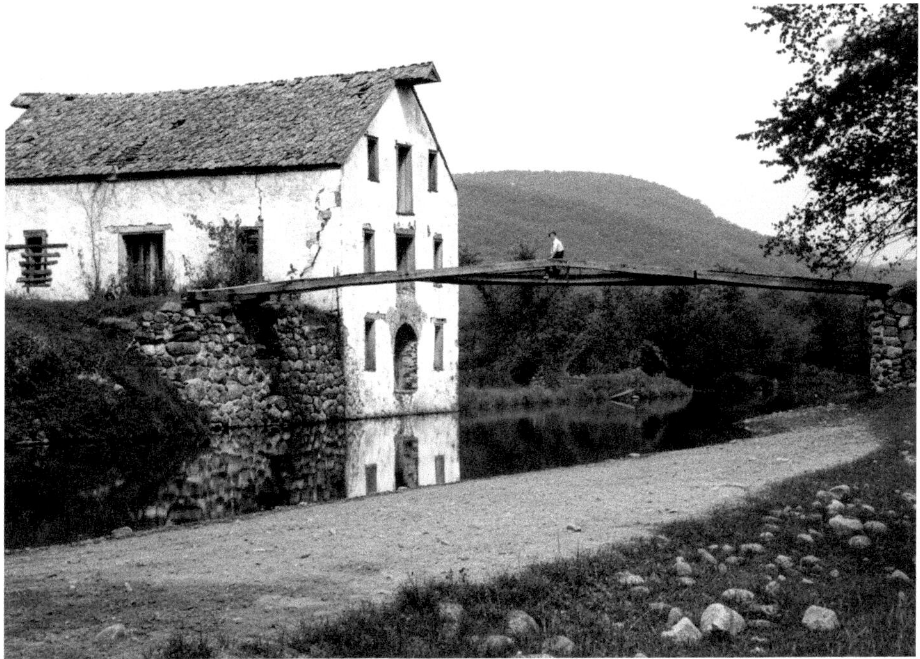

Royal Hopkins built this storehouse in 1834, half a mile west of Waterloo, and a blacksmith shop on the opposite bank of the canal in 1837. Carpet manufacturer John Humphries, born in Kidderminster, England, purchased the property in 1838 to erect a mill to manufacture linen-warp twine. He named the locale *Stourport* after the site of his first carpet factory on the River Stour. New York shoe-thread manufacturer James French acquired the property in 1851–53, renaming it *Byram Village*. He built the footbridge across the canal when the township refused to open a road connecting his new chemical works and twine-and-cordage factory to the Waterloo Depot in 1860. *(Photograph by Olin F. Vought (?), courtesy of James Lee Sr to the author in 1979)*

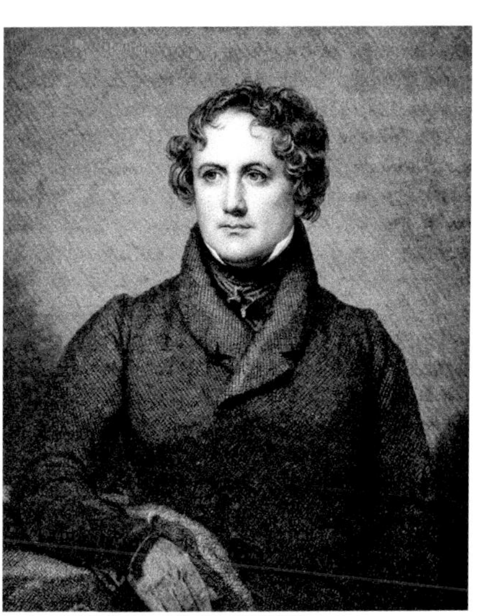

Portrait of Nicholas Biddle.
(Wilson, *A History of the American People*, Vol. 4, 1931)

The Morris Canal and Banking Company won legislative approval to increase its capital stock by $600,000 in $100 shares on 19 January 1835, on condition that no part of that sum could be diverted to banking purposes. A month later, the company opened subscription books to its additional capital stock, requiring investors to pay $10 on each share subscribed. An immediate infusion of cash was needed not only to pay off debts and claims incurred in the canal's original construction and to fund its extension to Jersey City, but also to enlarge it so it could become competitive with other carriers. A considerable hubbub, however, was soon raised 'about many large contracts made in New York between the bull and the bear gamblers in Morris Canal stock' in consequence of a carefully laid plot to corner the market. Innovative stockbroker Jacob Little led a pool of Newark and New York City speculators in quietly buying up Morris Canal stock far below par and lending it freely to short sellers, who expected to profit by repurchase at a cheaper price in a weakening market.[101] Once Little set his 'bear trap', he manipulated a rise in the price of Morris Canal stock from $10 per share in December 1834 to $185 per share in January 1835, and then called in the loans, forcing short sellers to cover their position.[102] The *Journal of Commerce* neatly surmised:

> [...] some gentlemen have contrived to buy up all the [Morris Canal] stock, and to buy a great deal more, deliverable ahead. Under these circumstances the bears have burned their claws, for they have promised to deliver what is not to be had but of the bulls themselves. Poor fellows! It is not the first time they have been caught in that trap.[103]

The New York Stock Exchange Board decided, twenty-eight to twenty-four, to take no cognizance of existing contracts in the Morris Canal and Banking Company, but later restored its stock to the brokers' list.

Former Treasury Secretary Louis McLane, who declined President Jackson's order to remove federal deposits from the Second Bank of the United States, was elected company president in May 1835 with an annual salary of $6,000, succeeding James B. Murray.[104] A new board of directors, comprising 'some of the first men in [New York] city for character and wealth', was also chosen. *The Evening Post*, however, claimed speculators in Morris Canal stock had paid James B. Murray a large sum to resign as president of the Morris Canal and Banking Company.[105] *The Evening Post* further implied some on the new board of directors received company stock, 'amounting, virtually, to a bonus of some $10,000 or $15,000, to induce them to be directors,' so as to 'bolster up a tottering company with their reputation....' The editor also noted a general suspicion 'that the present market value of the stock of that company far exceeds its real value.' Colonel Murray responded by suing for $10,000 in damages to his reputation.

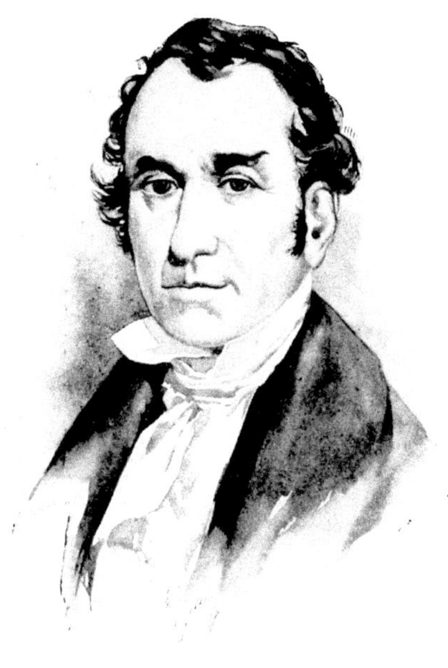

Louis McLane. (Wilson, *A History of the American People*, Vol. 4, 1931)

With loads averaging 20 tons apiece, toll collectors counted 2,096 boats clearing Phillipsburg for Newark and intermediate points between March and July 1835, moving 41,211 tons of freight.[106] On 27 July 1835, toll collector Thomas McGauran counted 185 boats arriving at Newark from Mauch Chunk, Easton, Washington (NJ), Port Colden, Stanhope, Dover and other places, over the previous twelve days. Of this number, 126 boats carried 2,531 tons of coal.[107]

Chief engineer Roswell Mason closed the canal on 12 November 1835, to make 'contemplated improvements to facilitate the navigation of boats with an increased tonnage.'[108] To allow longer boats to crest the planes, Ephraim Morris supervised conversion of the remaining summit planes over the winter of 1835–36 to lock planes, which were widened by 2 feet and their machinery strengthened at a cost of $230,000.[109] According to a detailed description of Plane No. 9 West, two lock chambers were constructed of stone at the summit. A small water wheel, turning two beveled cogwheels, 12 inches in diameter, was engaged to raise or lower the upper gates. The lower gate opened on a horizontal hinge joint, allowing it to lie flat upon the floor of the lock chamber. As the upper gate was lowered to fill the lock with water, the lower gate was lifted to seal the chamber. A wooden overshot waterwheel, 26 feet in diameter and 8 feet wide, moved the boat upon the inclined plane.[110] Its shaft turned a cast-iron pinion wheel, 5 feet in diameter, which worked a cogwheel, 4 feet in diameter. The push of a lever selected one of two beveled cogwheels, each

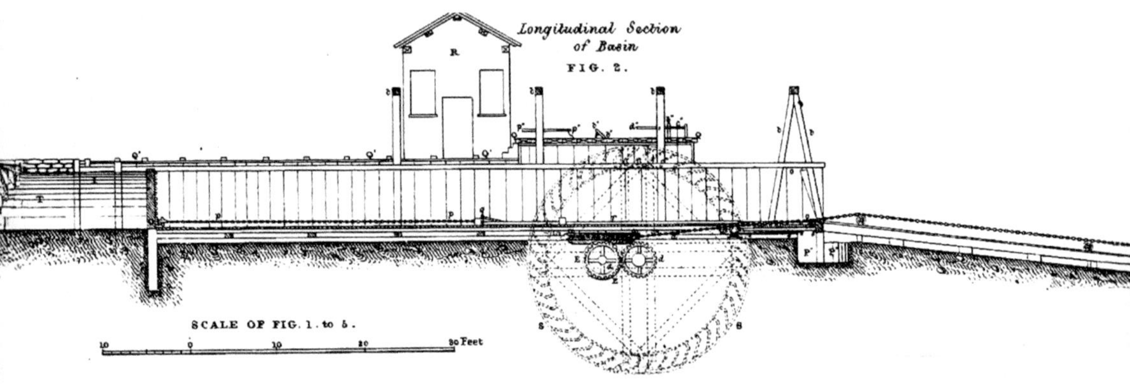

Longitudinal section of lock plane. (*Civil Engineer and Architect's Journal, Scientific and Railway Gazette*, Vol. 5, 1842)

5 feet in diameter, to either wind or release chain around a pulley, 9 feet in diameter, thereby raising the plane car on one pair of rails, while lowering another on a parallel track. Each plane car moved on four pairs of wheels, each set of two pairs being fixed on a moveable axle or primitive swivel-truck. Ideally, a boat floated onto a plane car in the summit lock, while another floated into a plane car at the foot of the plane, the boats being secured by chain to a sidebar of the plane car. A strong chain, one end fastened at the top of the plane and the other end at the bottom, traveled over guide pulleys set along the centerline of each pair of rails, running around a horizontal pulley mounted underneath the lock chamber and around pulleys attached to the ends of the plane cars.

[…] thus when the truck is descending the chain is lengthening, and at the same time it is shortening with the ascending truck; by this arrangement, the trucks nearly balance each other, and the only work of the water-wheel is to overcome the friction and the small difference in the weight of the up and down truck.[111]

A help-chain, fastened to the side of each plane car, passed down the center of the railway and around a pulley at the foot of the inclined plane, to be used for 'drawing the ascending trucks up to the end of the [lock] chamber; as by the winding-apparatus the ascending truck is only just brought to the top of the incline.' A lever and a brake regulated the speed of the waterwheel. As boatmen fastened their boats onto the plane car unassisted, a single plane tender was able to manage the machinery. Lock planes supposedly accommodated boats weighing from 7 to 8 tons, each carrying between 20 and 30 tons of freight. It required about fifteen minutes to pass boats up the longest plane of 1,100 feet,

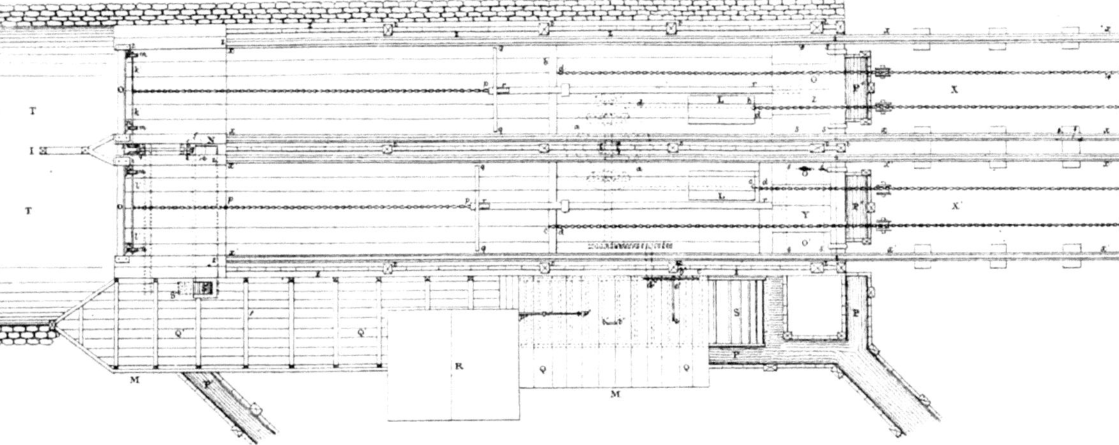

Plan of lock chambers at summit of inclined plane. (*Civil Engineer and Architect's Journal, Scientific and Railway Gazette*, Vol. 5, 1842)

overcoming a rise of 100 feet. It was 'generally reckoned' that about six boats could pass each way per hour.[112]

The enlarged canal demanded more water. On 5 March 1836, supplemental legislation authorized construction of a feeder from Greenwood Lake (then known as Long Pond) and creation of additional reservoirs.[113] In a water-powered age, this was a touchy subject. To prevent destruction of valuable manufactures, the company was prohibited from diverting

[so] much of the waters of the Musconetcong Creek [...] as to deprive the owners of mills or manufactories on said creek, below the dam at Saxton's Falls, of sufficient water to turn one wheel at present used to drive two run of millstones, with the necessary fixtures for the same, during eight weeks in the year, and at least two wheels, each of the same power, during the residue of the year, without the consent of the owners.

Roswell B. Mason advertised in July 1836 for contractors to build the Long Pond feeder, 5½ miles in length, and a stone dam to tap Greenwood Lake, raising the water level 8 feet.[114] Engineers searched the headwaters of the Musconetcong and Rockaway Rivers for other potential reservoirs.

On 13 June 1836, superintendent Thomas Wright advertised to 'let or hire' all available canal boats to transport coal between Mauch Chunk and Newark and intermediate places along the canal. The rate for each boat was set at $5 per trip for loads of 20 tons with an additional 50 cents for every ton over and above 20 tons for crossing the whole line of the canal and in proportion for shorter distances. The freight rate for coal carried from Mauch Chunk was fixed for the season at 1¼ cents per ton per mile. Unfortunately, greater tonnage strained even the improved machinery of the planes. On 11 July 1836, the waterwheel shaft broke at Old Andover (Waterloo), while one boat was descending and another boat ascending. According to one report,

> [...] the machinery being thus freed from all restriction whirled impetuously, in a ratio corresponding to the speed of the descending boat—which plunged into the basin, with prodigious force, and instantly sunk; while the ascending boat rushed with equal velocity against the lock at the top of the plane and carried it away.

Fortunately, no one was injured, but it took 'some time and much money to repair the damage.'[115]

Enlarging the canal was a matter of utmost urgency, as the Lehigh Coal and Navigation Company announced in December 1836 the completion at White Haven of one of its 'high dams and high lift Locks, which, on practical trial, meets the most sanguine hopes of its friends.'[116] This new lock, designed by engineer Edwin A. Douglass, was 20 feet wide, 100 feet long, with a 23-foot lift. It filled or emptied in two minutes. It was especially suited to the Lehigh River between Mauch Chunk and Wright's Creek, where 75 locks of 8-foot lift would have been required instead of 29 locks of the new design. The Lehigh Company employed 200 boats in transporting coal and their business was increasing by 50 percent annually.

Through the Philadelphia brokerage firm of Thomas A. Biddle and Company, headed by Nicholas Biddle's cousin, the newly state-chartered Bank of the United States in Pennsylvania acquired a (25 percent) controlling interest in the Morris Canal and Banking Company in 1836. In combination, these financial institutions built a large commission business, selling bonds issued by developing Midwestern and Southern states to finance internal improvements. As middlemen, they 'purchased' bonds on extended credit.[117] Except for a few American buyers in New York and Philadelphia, brokers largely resold these bonds for cash in London before full payment came due. In the meantime, state improvement authorities depended entirely on monthly installments on their bond issues to pay contractors—the only security they held being the broker's untarnished reputation for punctual payment.[118] However prestigious their roster appeared on paper, the officers and directors of the Morris Canal and Banking Company probably looked better at a distance than up close; in point of fact, the company's principal asset was the canal and its furnishings, which were heavily encumbered by debt, especially the Dutch mortgage, and its stock was a 'football' for Wall Street speculators.[119] Once credit dried up, excessive borrowing for large-scale, speculative public improvements provoked a 'sovereign debt crisis' that shook the financial world to its very sandy foundations.[120]

On 27 January 1836, Indiana legislators passed an act to fund a general system of internal improvements, embracing canals, turnpikes and railroads. State officials negotiated $2.4 million in loans for this purpose, essentially selling bonds on credit in the New York market. In November 1836, Indiana fund commissioners sold $1,029,000 in bonds to Thomas Biddle and Company and the Morris Canal and Banking Company on extended credit, expecting these brokers to pay the state interest in monthly installments until the principal was paid through re-sale of the bonds for cash.[121] The State Bank of Indiana issued another $1 million in state bonds to the Morris Canal and Banking Company on credit in 1837. Also using the Morris Canal and Banking Company as its designated agent, the State of Michigan sold $4,194,249 in twenty-year bonds at 6 percent interest to fund public works projects in 1837.[122] It deposited $2,700,000 in bonds with the company in exchange for their obligation to repay in regular installments. Michigan commissioners of internal improvements entered into $800,000 worth of contracts, but soon realized the quarterly installment payments would be insufficient to meet expenses. To make matters worse, there was growing concern about whether the funded transportation improvements would, upon completion, ever generate sufficient revenue to pay interest on the bonds, much less the capital when it came due.[123] The near impossibility of raising additional funds in depressed foreign and domestic money markets suddenly raised the possibility of default.[124]

To many, internal improvements were irresistible as a vehicle for economic expansion and as a bright badge of civic pride. Nicholas Biddle and his cousin, Edward R. Biddle (now a Morris Canal director), promoted the interconnection of canals and railroads to join New York City and Philadelphia to points as far distant as Pittsburgh and Lake Erie. Two hundred and four delegates from sixteen Pennsylvania counties convened the Northumberland and Erie Railroad Convention in the German Church at Erie, Pennsylvania, on 16 November 1836. After electing Nicholas Biddle as chairman, they agreed on 'the importance of an immediate connection by railway between the waters of [Lake] Erie and the city of Philadelphia.'[125] Delegates likewise urged the legislature to support

> [...] the intersection of the main line of railway from the [Great] Lakes to the Susquehanna, by a railroad from Catawissa, at some point between Williamsport and Sunbury, to be determined by the company incorporated and now engaged in making a railway from the Susquehanna to the Little Schuylkill....

Once the Lehigh Coal and Navigation Company completed their canalization of the Lehigh River from Mauch Chunk to White Haven in 1837, coming within 15 miles of Wilkes-Barre and the Susquehanna River, this link was vitally important.[126] To close the gap, they amended their charter to allow for a railroad across the Pocono Mountains, reaching the anthracite coalfields of the Wyoming Valley.

Determined to complete and control a through route to the Great Lakes, Nicholas Biddle financed a consolidation of the Morris and Lehigh Canals, the Beaver Meadow Railroad and the newly chartered Little Schuylkill and Susquehanna (LS&S) Railroad to open a direct line of 'communication to the verge of the bituminous coal field' across 250 miles. To realize this vision, the LS&S Railroad leased the Morris Canal for five years, starting 1 December 1836, for an annual payment of 4½ percent on its total capital stock of $4,100,000.[127] At the same time, the Morris Canal and Banking Company invested $230,000 in LS&S Railroad stock and $100,000 in the Beaver Meadow Railroad.[128] The Bank of the United States subscribed $250,000 in the LS&S Railroad, allowing the company to commence grading 48 miles of double track.[129] John C. Montgomery, president of the LS&S Railroad, announced he would operate locks and planes on the Morris Canal around the clock, offering premiums to industrious boatmen ranging from $10 to $100. He also arranged for 'a constant supply of Coal at Mauch Chunk and Parryville, for the Morris Canal Boats, and for obviating the detentions which have previously existed there.' The canal was to be

> […] placed in the most thorough repair, and all possible exertions will be made to keep it in the best order, and to prevent accidents or detentions at the Inclined Planes or elsewhere during the ensuing season.

Boats would be

> […] rented to respectable persons at 50 cents per day for the purpose of the Coal trade; and 1½ cents per mile freight will be paid for transporting Coal on the Morris and Lehigh Canals.

Although the lessees had not yet laid a single mile of track, they spent $2 million, largely provided by the Bank of the United States, to buy up thousands of acres of coal deposits.

The Morris Canal and Banking Company advertised for general contractors to extend the canal from 'Newark to the Hudson's River, at or near Jersey City' on 17 April 1834.[130] The delay proved costly—having lost passage through the only natural gap through the Palisades to the New Jersey Railroad, the canal was forced to take a circuitous detour around Bergen Ridge.

PREMIUMS.

FOR the purpose of developing the capabilities of the Morris Canal, and with a desire to reward active industry and enterprise, the following PREMIUMS will be paid to the owners or renters of Boats navigating the Morris Canal during the year 1837.

To the owner or renter of the boat which pays to the Company in the year 1837, the greatest amount of toll, $100

To him whose boat pays the next greatest amount, 80

To   do   3d greatest am't, 60
To   do   4th   do 50
To   do   5th   do 40
To   do   6th   do 30
To   do   7th   do 20
To   do   8th   do 10

To the owner or renter of the boat trading to Mauch Chunk which traverses the greatest number of miles on the Moris Canal, $100

To him whose boat traverses the next greatest distance, 80
To the 3d, 60
To " 4th, 50
To " 5th, 40
To " 6th, 30
To " 7th, 20
To " 8th, 10

The above Premiums will be paid after the navigation closes, by the Canal Cashier; so soon as it can be ascertained from the documents of the officers of the Company, which boats have earned them.

Arrangements have been made by the Company for securing a constant supply of Coal at Mauch Chunk and Perryville, for the Morris Canal Boats, and for obviating the detentions which have previously existed there.

The Morris Canal with all its appendages, will be placed in the *most thorough repair*, and all possible exertions will be made to keep it in the best order, and to prevent accidents or detentions at the Inclined Planes or elsewhere during the ensuing season.

The Planes and Locks will be worked NIGHT and DAY.

The Company's Boats will be rented to respectable persons at 50 cents per day for the purpose of the Coal trade; and $1\frac{1}{2}$ cts. per mile, freight will be paid for transporting Coal on the Moris and Lehigh Canals.

JOHN C. MONTGOMERY, *Pres't.*

L. S. & Susquehanna Railroad-Co.

Philadelphia, Feb 27, 1837.   6w.

John C. Montgomery, president of the LS&S Railroad, advertised 'Premiums, for the purpose of developing the capabilities of the Morris Canal' in *The Sussex Register* on 27 February 1837.

Moreover, the extension from Newark to tidewater, opposite Manhattan, proved 'a difficult one to construct, most of it being marsh, and another portion of it requiring a heavy sea wall.'[131] About $600,000 was expended before water was let into the new section. On 30 November 1836, a deputation of Jersey City residents welcomed the packet boat *Maria Colden*, carrying the canal company directors, the Mayor of Newark, and other officials. Two canal boats laden with Lehigh coal, two laden with Beaver Meadows coal and two laden with cordwood from the interior of New Jersey closely followed in their wake.[132] In March 1837, the president and directors of the Morris Canal and Banking Company not only informed stockholders of their lease arrangement with the LS&S Railroad, but also proudly reported, 'The canal has been completed to Jersey City.'[133]

Shovels also shaped the new feeder connecting Greenwood Lake to Mead's Basin (Mountain View). Construction of reservoirs at Mount Pleasant, Cranberry Lake and Bear Swamp Pond added to expenses, but promised

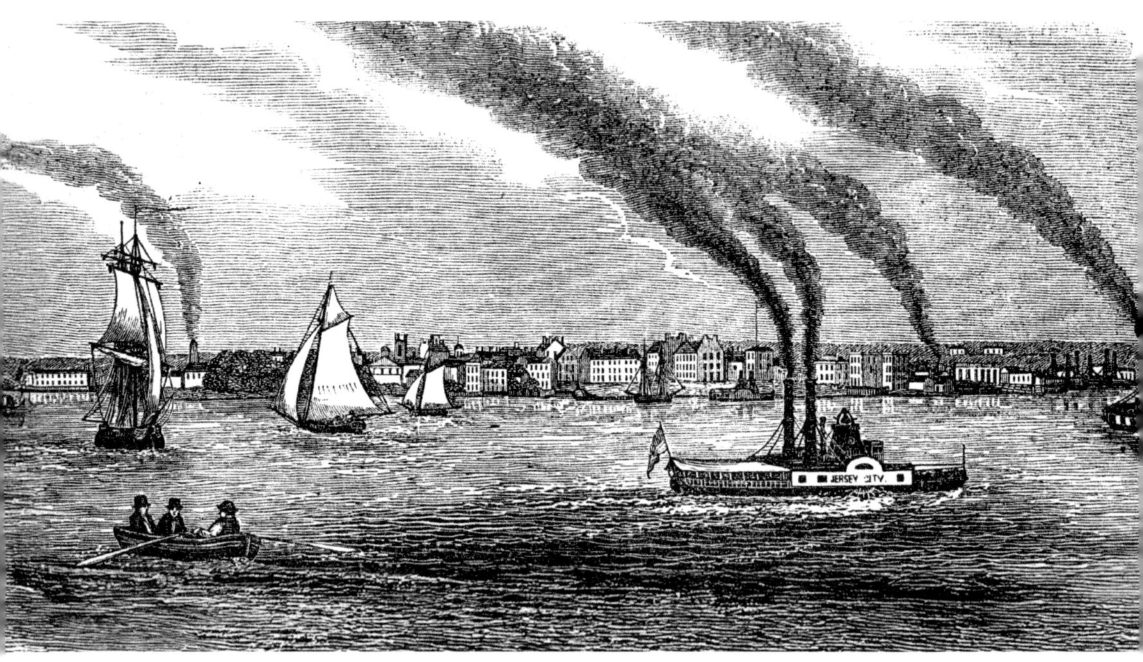

'S. E. View of Jersey City, From New York'. (Barber and Howe, *Historical Collections of the State of New Jersey*, 1844)

an abundant water supply, even in times of drought, as well as additional opportunities to develop waterpowers along the canal's banks. From start to finish, the Morris Canal required twenty-three lift locks, twenty-three planes, eleven guard locks, five dams, thirty culverts, twelve aqueducts, and two hundred bridges to cross 102 miles of country.[134]

That spring, Thomas Vail Johnson purchased the late Jonathan Cory's Morris Canal Line of Packets, employing three ships to convey cargo between his Newark Dock and White Hall, New York.[135] In May 1837, Pierson and Williams, of Stanhope, advertised use of 'Three Superior Boats, with covers, navigated by experienced captains and other hands' on their freighting line, 'from Stanhope to Newark, or to the city of New York, after the canal is finished.' They proposed making three trips weekly. An attempt was also made to charter the Bottle Hill and Montville Canal, which was to run from Bottle Hill (Madison) in Morris County, through Hanover and Pequannock Townships, to the Morris Canal within a mile of the lowest inclined plane at Montville, and also to construct a raceway from the main canal to the Rockaway River, near the old Boonton Ironworks.[136] Expanding capacity did not proceed without mishap, for, on 22 December 1837, Joseph Buchanan was buried while undermining a bank of earth during construction of a new canal basin and boat yard at Washington, NJ, covering 2 acres. He survived only three hours after being extricated.

4

Troubled Waters

While workmen made tangible progress enlarging the canal, financial markets continued to expand on a shimmering, thin-skinned bubble. To rein in speculation, President Jackson required payment in specie for public lands in July 1836. As farmers continued to gather inflated prices for grain, the *Newark Daily Advertiser* asked, 'Who can want a better gold mine than a good Sussex county farm?' On the other side of the coin, thousands of workingmen without recourse to their own gardens joined a bread riot in New York City on 10 February 1837, protesting high rents and exorbitant prices for bread, meat and fuel. On 15 May 1837, banks refused to redeem their notes in specie at par value, triggering a panic. While the ranks of unemployed Americans grew, $10 million in foreign imports flooded New York, undermining domestic producers. The effects were particularly devastating wherever communities concentrated upon a single industry. To worsen matters, machinery steadily supplanted handicraft, displacing outmoded workers. As desperation mounted, the New Jersey legislature convened to consider relief measures on 22 May 1837.

Looking for a figurehead of national prominence to replace Louis McLane when he left to head the Baltimore and Ohio Railroad in January 1837, directors of the Morris Canal and Banking Company persuaded Senator Samuel L. Southard to accept the company's presidency that June.[1] Ever the opportunist, this genial but ambitious Flemington attorney served as judge of the State Supreme Court upon his first election to the General Assembly in 1812.[2] Chosen to represent New Jersey in the Senate in 1821, he worked with Henry Clay to achieve compromise over Missouri's admission as a state. Never one to refuse offers of gainful employment, he served as Secretary of the Navy under Presidents James Monroe and John Quincy Adams. Returning to Trenton upon Andrew Jackson's election, he filled the office of State Attorney General in 1829. His party having obtained a majority in the legislature in 1832,

[…] he allowed himself to be elected Governor; and then with great difficulty prevailed on his friends to elect him Senator, thus producing the necessity of resigning as Governor, and helping so to distract his party that they lost their majority in the State, and did not regain it for several years.[3]

He was re-elected to a full term in 1838. When Vice-President Tyler succeeded to the Presidency in 1841, Southard rose to the powerful office of Senate President.

On 8 January 1838, the Morris Canal and Banking Company published notice of its intention to seize several ponds and streams along the line of the canal and its Pompton feeder, namely, at Saxton Falls in Warren County; at Cranberry Lake, the Punk Horn Creek, and Bear Swamp in Sussex County; and at Mount Pleasant and Lake Hopatcong in Morris County. Joseph C. Hornblower, Esq., Chief Justice of the New Jersey Supreme Court, appointed three disinterested Freeholders from counties not intersected by the canal to equitably appraise the value of lands seized from owners and to compensate any interested parties for their losses. Feeling aggrieved, mill owners in the Musconetcong Valley demanded compensation for damages to their water privileges. In November 1838, Robert P. Bell, of Stanhope, brought suit for $8,000 in compensation for damages sustained between 1833 and 1837 when the Morris Canal Company dammed the source of the Musconetcong River, overflowing his lands and

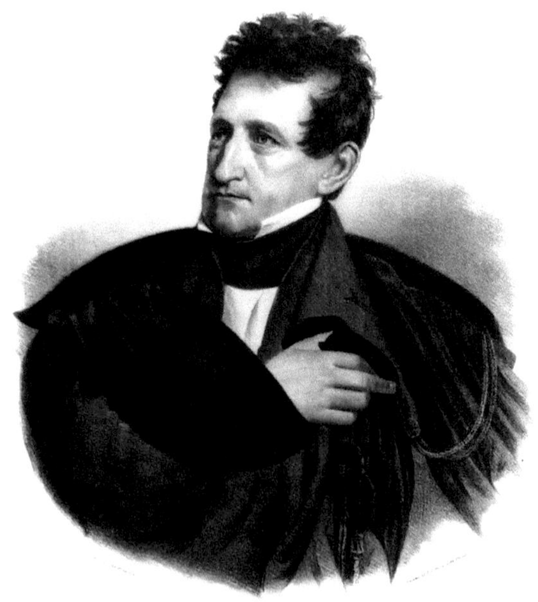

'Sam L. Southard, Senator from New Jersey'. (*Library of Congress*)

diverting water to the injury of his forges. Sixty witnesses were examined and counsel took two days for their summaries. After remaining out overnight, the jury reported their inability to agree on a verdict.[4]

Despite protest from its Democratic minority, the New Jersey legislature allowed banks to issue bills under the denomination of $5 on 31 January 1838, but required them to publish monthly financial statements in three state newspapers. Governor William Pennington ordered banks to resume specie payments on 15 August 1838, but times did not so readily mend. After serving little more than a year, Southard resigned as president of the Morris Canal and Banking Company, ostensibly to devote full attention to his national leadership post. As a prominent Whig in a presidential election year, he sought to distance himself from an ongoing battle—led by disenchanted visionary George Macculloch—to prevent any legislative enlargement of the canal company's banking privileges, while its officers desperately sought to stave off bankruptcy.[5] Regarding Southard's nominal leadership of the Morris Canal, a friend and contemporary later kindly confided:

> It is not probable that he possessed any special financial ability, or that the directors of this institution expected him to perform any onerous duties connected with the station. But he had a high character for integrity and ability, and was now universally known and respected throughout the country; characteristics for which it was thought worth while to give him a good salary, and thus obtain the benefit of his name in aid of an institution that needed the support of a strong pillar.[6]

In his place, Edward R. Biddle was elected president and Edwin Lord, nephew of Eleazer Lord, president of the Erie Railroad, was elected vice-president.[7] In keeping with his new station, Biddle rented a house at 20 Washington Square, on fashionable Waverly Place, for $1,200 and furnished it for $8,000.

On 26 January 1839, a terrific storm swept across a vast swath of countryside. Raging streams washed out bridges and milldams, submerged meadows and flooded highways. At Hackettstown, Nathan Stiger's milldam and half of the stone bridge below it were lost. Scarcely a bridge over the Musconetcong survived. Floodwaters burst the banks of the Morris Canal at Stanhope and undermined an aqueduct over a small stream about a mile below the village. Another break near Phillipsburg destroyed Enoch and Richard Green's store. Across the Delaware River in Easton, ice floes carried away 75 feet of the embankment of the canal basin. The canal between Newark and Jersey City vanished under the floodtide, which carried away a wharf with its large burden of coal before abandoning canal boats on the marshes. A loud and angry gale toppled the chimney and tore off part of the roof of the Morris Canal Banking House in Jersey City. Some took this as a sign of divine disfavor upon an unpopular corporation, widely regarded as the corrupt play-thing of Nicholas Biddle and his cronies.

Ignoring signs of an approaching storm in financial markets, Indiana fund commissioners sold $400,000 in bonds of the Wabash and Erie Canal on credit to the Morris Canal and Banking Company in January 1839, a portion of which were re-sold in March 1839 to the Bank for Savings in New York City.[8] This was done even though the Morris Canal

> [...] was largely in debt to the State of Michigan, much embarrassed in its affairs, and its stock selling at 56 percent. The proceeds were payable in ten installments, of which $20,000 only was realized....[9]

With the benefit of hindsight, Indiana fund commissioner James Farrington defended selling state bonds on credit. According to him, the Morris Canal and Banking Company

> [...] had some of the most distinguished men of this country to preside over its operations, and the board of directors for the last four years, and up to the time of these sales, collectively and individually, have generally been among the most respectable and intelligent business men of New York. Whilst the stock of the company has ranged low in value from the first it has of late years negotiated some millions annually, and from the State of Indiana within the last two years and up to the date of these sales she had purchased and paid for $3,200,000 of her bonds, and up to the month of January, 1839, the date of the last sale made whilst I was in office, it had in no instance, within my knowledge, failed in its payments, but had frequently made advances to the State beyond the amount due by contract. These considerations, with the known fact that the Bank of the United States at Philadelphia (then in public estimation, perhaps the highest in credit of any moneyed institution in the country) had a large interest in this company amounting, if I recollect rightly, by the exhibit made by it, to over $900,000, led me to place confidence in the Morris Canal & Banking Company, and when, *after trying in vain, to obtain from other institutions and companies terms equally advantageous as offered by this company*, I did not hesitate in sanctioning it. But for the revulsion that has taken place in the financial world, impairing, and in many instances prostrating the credit of all State stocks, as well as the moneyed institutions of the country, I still think, the Morris Canal & Banking Company would, as she had hitherto done, have continued to fulfill, in good faith, her engagements to the State.[10]

The Morris Canal and Banking Company sold $1,362,000 in Michigan bonds for cash and, on 29 January 1839, persuaded Michigan officials to accept promissory notes of the Bank of the United States of Pennsylvania for three quarters (about $2,360,000) of the remainder, and the guarantee of the Morris Canal and Banking Company for the remaining quarter (about $786,000), bearing 6 percent interest, due in quarterly installments over a period of four years.[11] This bought little time. With skies darkening, Nicholas Biddle resigned as president of the Bank of the United States on 29 March 1839. Directors of the Morris Canal and Banking Company met with officers of the Bank of the United States on 1 August 1839, before officially informing the State of Indiana the company would default upon a $100,000 installment due on 1 September, which it owed on half of the $2.1 million in state bonds it reportedly re-sold in London. On this news, the whole financial system shuddered. The Bank of the United States of Pennsylvania suspended specie payments on 9 October 1839, fueling a run on banks in Southern and Western states. On 16 November 1839, Michigan Governor Stevens T. Mason sent Kintzing Pritchette to negotiate cancellation of the contract with the Morris Canal and Banking Company and the Bank of the United States for as much of their $4-million loan as remained unpaid.[12] It was quickly ascertained that the Morris Canal and Banking Company and the Bank of the United States 'had hypothecated some three or four millions of the [Michigan] State bonds to European bankers, at about fifty cents on the dollar, as a security for the payment of their own debts to those banks.'[13] Overall, English fund-holders owned at least $200 million in American stocks and bonds, which could not be sold for more than 80 cents on the dollar. London bankers and fund-holders consequently demanded the re-charter of a national bank and federal assumption of state debts—a politically untenable step, given growing disunion among Whigs over the issue of slavery.[14] Times were hard. Grain prices sank 50 percent lower than two years earlier and farmers were soon unable to sell produce on any terms. By February 1840, an estimated quarter of the population of the United States was unemployed.

Amid prevailing gloom, a promising glow did steadily brighten. While Josiah White experimented unsuccessfully with a heated air blast to smelt iron with anthracite coal in a small furnace near Mauch Chunk in 1826, Welsh ironmaster George Crane, of the Ynyscedwyn Ironworks near Swansea (Wales, UK), finally perfected the hot-blast method in a small cupola furnace in 1837.[15] Reproducing his success, Joseph Baughman, Julius Guiteau, Henry High and Francis C. Lowthrop produced iron with anthracite in their experimental furnace, below Mauch Chunk, in October 1838, consuming 2 tons of coal to make 1 ton of iron.[16] Josiah White and Erskine Hazard secured George Crane's assistant, David Thomas, to superintend an anthracite blast furnace alongside the Lehigh Canal at Catasauqua, Pennsylvania, in 1840. Here, in 1841, they manufactured a malleable iron 'T'-rail for use on a 4-mile, horse-powered section of their 20-mile railroad connecting White Haven on the Lehigh River with Wilkes-Barre on the Susquehanna. Within nine months, three furnaces were built to produce anthracite iron, each turning out 40 to 50 tons of pig iron weekly.[17] Eighteen blast furnaces and six large rolling mills with puddling furnaces, using stone coal for fuel, were in various stages of operation or construction by November 1840. Thirteen of these furnaces and five of the mills were located along the Lehigh and Morris Canals, creating a demand for ore, coal, limestone and pig iron amounting to 227,500 tons.[18] With the successful application of anthracite to smelting iron, one Pennsylvanian editor gleefully predicted:

> [...] *America must soon become the great iron market of the world*, as she will be able to furnish the article much cheaper than it can be obtained anywhere else [...] Thus then, the tide of trade will be completely turned, and instead of paying to Europe interest for money to make our railroads and canals, we shall not only be able to cancel our State debt, but receive millions of Europe in return for the iron and coal of our mountains.[19]

Banker Nicholas Biddle had been 'among the first to contribute his money and influence to the successful prosecution of the business' of making iron with anthracite.[20] Edward R. Biddle and Edwin Lord, respectively president and vice-president of the Morris Canal and Banking Company, borrowed $180,000 in company funds to finance construction of three anthracite iron furnaces at Danville, Pennsylvania and a large rolling mill and nail factory in South Wilkes-Barre. The security bonds were payable in iron delivered in New York by Biddle, Chamber and Company. They also invested $100,000 in the Morris and Sussex Manufacturing Company at Stanhope, headed by Edwin Post, of New York City, another director of the Morris Canal and Banking Company.[21] On 23 March 1840, the *Sussex Register* announced that William Nelson Wood and Andrew A. Smalley, of Stanhope, were putting New Jersey's first anthracite furnace in blast, modeled after those at Pottsville and Mauch Chunk.[22] It was generally agreed that the 'employment of anthracite in the process of smelting opens a new era in this important branch of productive industry.' On 1 October 1840, the Sussex Iron Company, owners of Stanhope Anthracite Steam and Water Furnace No. 1, advertised for 5,000 bushels of charcoal. Ore came from the Irondale mine, 3 miles distant.

To avoid clamorous creditors, the Morris Canal and Banking Company closed its offices at 45 William Street in the heart of Manhattan's financial district on 4 February 1840. Due to rising anxiety among investors, shares in the Bank of the United States and the Morris Canal and Banking Company sold at gradually declining prices throughout July 1840.

Recriminations over the flailing economy embittered the political contest between Van Burenites and Whigs as Election Day approached. Despite

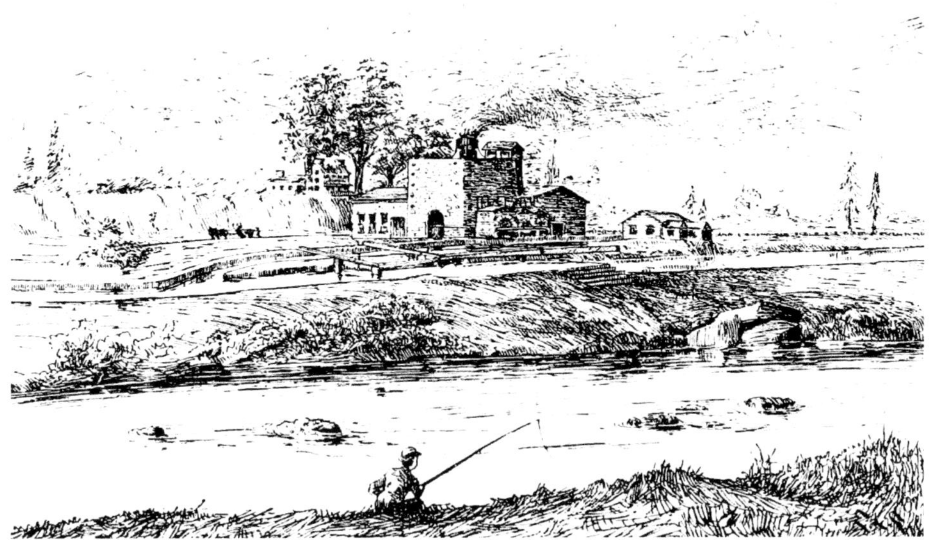

Engineer William F. Durfee's pen-and-ink drawing of the early anthracite-iron furnace at Catasauqua, PA. (Youmans, *The Popular Science Monthly, November 1890 to April 1891*)

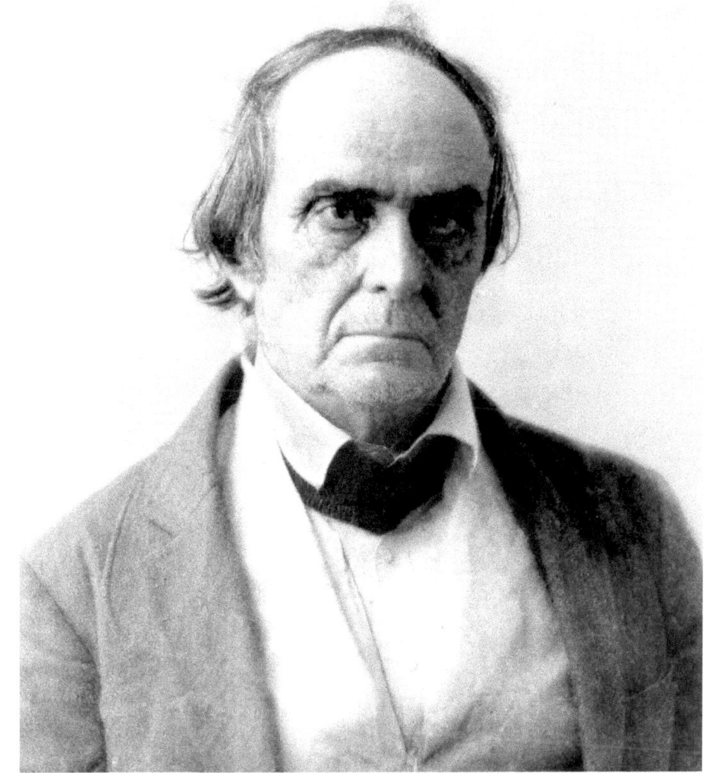

Matthew B. Brady's daguerreotype of Daniel Webster, made between 1845 and 1849. (*Library of Congress*)

drenching rains on 13 August 1840, the honorable Daniel Webster, of Massachusetts, addressed 5,000 people at a three-county Whig meeting held on the Stanhope Green (where the Hanowitz and Almer buildings were built in 1901). Symbolic log cabins preceded processions from Newton, Stillwater and Branchville. The Tippecanoe Club of Warren County 'arrived in canal boats and formed their procession on the tow-path as they left the boats.'[23] Besides thousands from north-western New Jersey, large numbers attended from Essex, Somerset and Hunterdon, some in the audience traveling upwards of 40 miles. Judge William P. Robeson, of Warren County, and David B. Ogden, Esq., of New York City, spoke first, then Mr Webster was introduced. After speaking for about half an hour, a downpour of rain 'drove him and such of the audience as could gain admittance into the storage-house, where he finished his address.' This was the old Parker House, where trap doors were opened so that people on the floors above and below could hear the great orator. Numerous banners and flags displayed partisan slogans, such as 'No Direct Tax upon the people, No Standing Army to consume it.' Ladies of the Newton Tippecanoe Club waved a blue silk flag, inscribed, 'Who would be free, themselves must strike the blow.' On 3 November 1840, the Whigs' national candidates William Henry Harrison and John Tyler were swept into office. With a bare working majority in Congress, the new President hoped to calm the economic storm, encouraging measures to establish a new national bank and revise tariff duties. President Harrison, however, died on 4 April 1841, only one month after his inauguration. John Tyler, an independent Southern Democrat, became President, effectively scuttling the Whig agenda.

On 6 October 1840, the Morris Canal and Banking Company mortgaged the canal extension between Newark and Jersey City to the State of Indiana to secure payment of $190,000. On the following day, they gave a second mortgage on the entire canal to the same party to secure payment of $960,000. The Indiana commissioner agreed to advance $100,000 to enable the Morris Canal and Banking Company to enlarge their locks.[24] With few good alternatives, Robert Stuart, treasurer of the State of Michigan, also negotiated a settlement with the Morris Canal and Banking Company on 9 December 1840, obtaining $621,000 in assignment of assets against an outstanding debt of $823,000.[25] He recognized revenues would eventually improve through the Morris Canal's connection with other transportation lines, as well as with coal companies and iron foundries operating on the borders of the canal. He also knew there was great promise of many more blast furnaces being established,

> [...] as it is ascertained that iron can be made with anthracite coal, at fifteen dollars per ton, which must drive foreign competition out of our markets, the price being thirty to thirty-two dollars in the city of New York.[26]

By treating Michigan and Indiana as preferred creditors, however, the Morris Canal and Banking Company provoked the ire of unpaid investors and contractors in New Jersey, who worked to build and enlarge the canal, as well as foreign mortgage holders. In November 1840, the company failed to pay $5,000 in taxes, owed on their banking capital, to the State of New Jersey.

On 1 January 1841, the Morris Canal and Banking Company defaulted on its interest payment on the 'Dutch Loan'. The Bank of the United States resumed specie payments on 15 January 1841, only to suspend them again on 4 February after paying out $6 million. On 10 February 1841, the bonds of the Morris Canal and Banking Company were formally protested, as it owed at least $1,672,000 in various financial obligations. The Stanhope anthracite furnace was put in blast on 5 April 1841, its daily output averaging 6½ tons; but after producing 800 tons of iron in four months, it was blown out on 30 July 1841, in order to repair the hearth.

Hindered by the inadequacy of its planes, the Morris Canal could not compete with other canals in carrying Lehigh coal to New York. The work of widening the inclined planes by 2 feet and of enlarging lift locks to 95 feet in length and 11 feet in width commenced in January 1841, employing several hundred men. Work on all but widening the planes was quickly suspended until April, due not only to deep frost, but also to word that the Lehigh Canal would not be navigable until June.[27] Facing financial collapse, the company issued post-notes in March 1841, payable in twelve months, to fund the enlargement, but a want of confidence in its financial condition discouraged takers. After repairs occupying nearly the entire boating season, the canal partially opened on 2 September 1841, with facilities to accommodate boats 86 feet long and 10½ feet wide.[28] When fully loaded, they had a draft of 3 foot 10 inches, and required two hands and a single horse to operate. Boys ranging from twelve to seventeen years of age drove the horses, receiving $10 per month in wages.

After meeting only three installments, the company defaulted on a payment of $67,187 to the State of Michigan on 1 April 1841. According to an investigatory report in the *New York Herald*, 'the bonds of [Nicholas] Biddle were given to the State of Michigan as part security for the balance of the $5,000,000 taken by the Morris Canal and made over to the US Bank.'[29] On 22 May 1841, Michigan treasurer Robert Stuart visited Jersey City, where he learned the Morris Canal and Banking Company not only could not pay $823,000 in overdue installments owed to the State of Michigan, but also $100,000 it owed the State of Indiana, as well as interest on its foreign debt. Confronted on 1 July 1841, vice-president Edwin Lord bluntly informed Stuart, 'I cannot pay it.'[30]

The inevitable could no longer be postponed. Despite several years of heavy business losses, Edward R. Biddle and his cronies maintained expensive offices and residences, collecting handsome executive salaries. The directors fired president Edward R. Biddle and vice-president Edwin Lord on 15 October 1841, without naming their successors. The board justified its action thus:

> [...] these officers had loaned their friends or themselves $180,000 of the funds of the bank, to establish or improve certain iron works in Danville and Wilkesbarre, besides various other financial operations.[31]

That same afternoon, furniture from Biddle's residence on Washington Square was partly sold at auction.[32] The *Newark Daily Adviser* immediately winced, crying, 'This indicates an urgency pregnant with more financial disaster. What's the amount this time?'[33] Five days later, on 20 October 1841, Wilhelm Willink Jr, banker for the United States at Amsterdam and trustee for the holders of the original Dutch Loan, sued in the Court of Chancery to foreclose on the first mortgage, seeking authorization for lenders to take possession of the canal and to apply any income and profits therefrom to the discharge of the debt. On 10 December 1841, a Philadelphia grand jury indicted officers of the Bank of the United States for colluding to defraud stockholders by using bank funds for friends' and their own benefit.

The New Jersey Court of Chancery appointed Elias B. D. Ogden, of Paterson, Stephen P. Britton, of Elizabeth, and Dudley S. Gregory, of Jersey City, as receivers for the Morris Canal and Banking Company on 29 January 1842, with authority to dispose of its property and effects.[34] On 3 February 1842, the newly appointed receivers informed the public:

> All persons along the line of the Canal and elsewhere are forbid taking, selling, or converting to their uses, any of the property or effects of the Company, and from purchasing the same from any of the former agents or managers of the Company, and also from making payments to any persons but the Receivers, or their lawfully constituted agents, under such penalty as may fall upon them.

The receivers even offered to rent dwelling apartments in the Morris Canal Company's banking house in Jersey City.

New Hope civil engineer and contractor Lewis S. Coryell leased the canal in April 1842, expecting to complete repairs so as to make the canal navigable by 1 August.[35] The State of Indiana filed suit on 12 July 1842 to recover over $2 million, claiming the Dutch mortgage did not cover the canal extension between Newark and Jersey City. On that same day, the Sussex Iron Company declared bankruptcy and suspended operations at Stanhope, delaying completion of Furnaces No. 2 and No. 3 for another three years. The Corporation of Newark threatened in August 1842 to fill in the canal

'Notice, Receivers
for the Creditors and
Stockholders of the
Morris Canal and
Banking Co.', *The Sussex
Register*, 3 February 1842.

NOTICE.

PUBLIC notice is hereby given, that the subscribers have been appointed by the Court of Chancery of this State Receivers for the Creditors and Stockholders of The Morris Canal and Banking Company.

All persons along the line of the Canal and elsewhere are forbid taking, selling, or converting to their uses, any of the property or effects of the Company, and from purchasing the same from any of the former agents or managers of the Company, and also from making payments to any persons but the Receivers, or their lawfully constituted agents, under such penalty as may fall upon them.

ELIAS B. D. OGDEN.
S. P. BRITTON.

Receivers for the Creditors and Stockholders of the Morris Canal and Banking Co.
Jersey City, Feb. 3, 1842.   2w

unless dilapidated bridges were rendered safe for public use. A public notice posted in local newspapers on 19 December 1842 invited 'Creditors of the Morris Canal & Banking Company, including the Bill and Post Note holders, Contractors, Laborers, and particularly those Creditors who became so on account of the late Enlargement of the Canal' to meet at Nathan B. Luse's hotel in Morristown on 5 January 1843. Creditors representing claims for $40,000 attended and appointed a committee to devise a legal strategy.

Newark coal-and-lumber dealer George S. Mills and Lorenzo Augustus Sykes, chief engineer of the New Jersey Railroad and former resident engineer of the Morris Canal, leased the canal in February 1843 for $3,000.[36] They not only looked forward to the 'good promise of a brisk and profitable season' in the transport of Lehigh coal, but also noted,

[…] the iron business at the various establishments on the route has been resumed and is to be extended during the season. The Stanhope Works are to be put in full operation, and, in addition to the old works at Boonton, a large nail factory is now in progress by a New England Company, which will be completed in the course of 60 days, and which is then expected to turn out some tons of nails daily. Preparations have also been made for the transmission of large supplies of ore from the rich iron mines of Morris County.[37]

Decidedly in a slump, manufacturers looked to the strongly protective Whig tariff of September 1842, passed over President Tyler's opposition, for a return

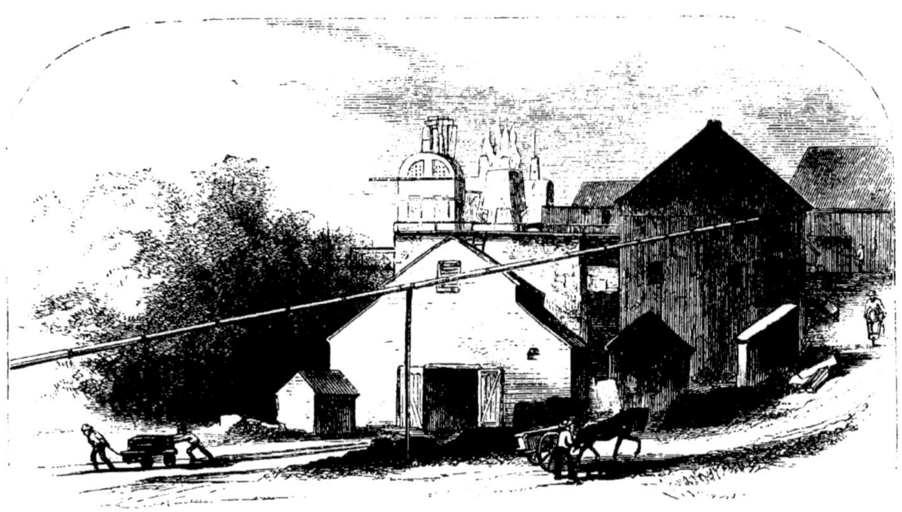

The blast furnace at Boonton measured 40 square feet at its base and stood 40 feet tall, surmounted by two ovens to heat the air blast, which was powered by water from the Morris Canal. Iron ores came from the Hibernia and Andover mines. (*Harper's New Monthly Magazine*, 1860)

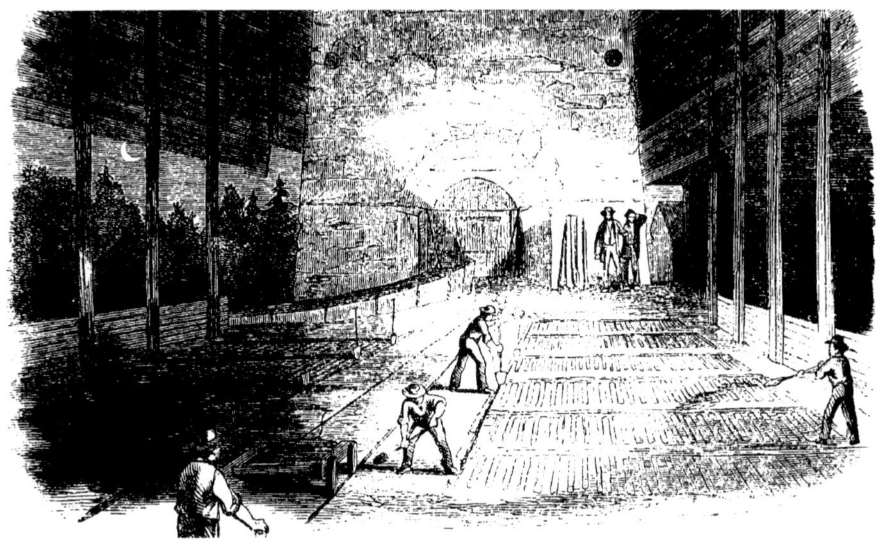

A track ran down the center of the sand floor of the casting room, dividing sixteen beds of gutters for running out molten iron into two matching sets of eight beds. Eight lateral gutters called 'sows' each fed twenty-six perpendicular gutters called 'pigs'. A man with a spade prevented molten metal from flowing down his sow until the bed below was filled. Another man shoveled earth onto filled beds to keep the heat down. Sows were broken into four pigs, thus a single casting produced 480 pigs, amounting to 11 tons of pig iron. (*Harper's New Monthly Magazine*, 1860)

to prosperity. New tariff duties allowed such American-made articles as pins, wire and screws to compete with English imports. The Whig tariff stimulated an expansion of capacity as companies built new furnaces, enlarged old ones and engaged in new lines of business. It also sparked a rise in wages as a rapidly reviving domestic market promised better prices for farmers and manufacturers. At the same time, mechanization reduced production costs—for example, invention of a steam hammer in 1842 made welding heavy iron masses a comparatively easy and reliable process. Stagnation, however, again followed prosperity in the iron and woolen business. Panic seized Morris County ironmakers in September 1843, when a new British tariff compelled a reduction in wages or suspension of work. Continued dissatisfaction brought a Whig avalanche at the polls in 1843.

On 12 August 1843, a severe summer storm caused nine breaks in the beleaguered Morris Canal between Newark and Little Falls, resulting in $2,000 in damages and a ten-day suspension of navigation. Four hundred striking Lehigh boatmen forcibly prevented passage of any Pennsylvania canal boats, though they allowed Morris Canal boats to go to the mines and supply the market. Civil and military authorities at Easton refused to interfere, allowing belligerent boatmen to keep a constant guard over all boats under blockade and to drive off any men the coal companies sent to release them. The Lehigh Canal Company responded in August 1843 by draining their canal and discharging employees, not only in the hope of dispersing the strikers, but of ending all operational expenses (despite the fact the business of the Morris Canal boats would nearly cover them). Suspension of this important source of supply drove up the price of coal and caused shortages.

Sparking back to life, the Stanhope Iron Company began manufacturing a new type of rail for the New York and Erie Railroad Company in December 1843, carting its finished product to Morristown for shipment on the Morris and Essex Railroad.[38] Competition proved good for business. Canal enlargement and the spread of railroads reduced freight charges, resulting in a decline in the price of coal and other commodities. But overall, a destructive summer storm, the British tariff on iron and the Lehigh boatmen's strike ruined any prospect of the Morris Canal meeting its heavy financial obligations. Saddled with a second mortgage to the State of Indiana since October 1840, the company could not collect sufficient tolls or float $290,000 in bonds to meet $459,000 in debt payments. The boating season ended on 6 December 1843, and resumed on 15 April 1844. Ira C. Whitehead, master in chancery, sold the Morris Canal on 21 October 1844, under a court order of foreclosure at the suit of Wilhelm Willink, to recover $855,625. One critic observed,

> This miserable little ditch [...] has been very famous in its day as the tender and decoy for the late National bank [...] As a work of public improvement,

it is, in a financial point of view, nearly, if not quite, valueless. By means of the banking powers attached to it, however, it has been the means of more dishonor to the Union, and loss to individuals, than any other of the many bubble companies that floated on the ocean of paper credits with which the country for the last ten or fifteen years has been deluged.[39]

On 23 October 1844, Asa Whitehead, John J. Bryant and Benjamin Williamson purchased the canal for $1 million (about one quarter of what it cost to build) on behalf of the trustees of the Holland Loan, issuing stock to the full amount of $1 million as authorized by the charter. The company, formed from the old stockholders, reorganized on 30 November 1844, with the election of twenty-three directors.[40] Daniel Tyler, a military engineer who studied at the French Artillery School, was chosen as president in place of Benjamin Williamson, who resigned. Tyler, a Connecticut Yankee who had rescued the Norwich and Worcester Railroad from bankruptcy, was credited with building the first American blast furnace to make iron using bituminous coal. With a competent engineer at its helm, the reorganized company now struggled to make the canal a paying proposition. Shortly after announcing Tyler's appointment, the company published its intention of completing the enlargement of the canal to double its capacity. Though Wall Street speculators hammered down Morris Canal stock in October 1844, a great demand for coal all along the line made operations profitable. The Stanhope iron furnaces alone consumed 7,000 tons of coal annually. Dover iron manufacturers flourished and Dudley B. Fuller and Company completed their large new nail foundry at Boonton.[41]

Daniel Tyler had 2,000 men at work on 1 April 1845, enlarging the waterway to 25 feet at bottom, 40 feet wide at the water line and 5 feet 3 inches in depth.[42] Hinged section boats capable of carrying 65 tons were introduced to transport Hazleton coal from Penn Haven and Lehigh coal from Mauch Chunk directly to Jersey City, a distance of 155 miles. Extensively used in the original construction of the planes, wood became 'so much decayed and weakened, that frequent failures of some of their parts occurred when passing sections of boats loaded with 25 tons,' that some permanent solution had to be found.[43] Building 100 section boats, Tyler strongly recommended a return to the use of summit planes, but only two old lock planes were actually converted—one at Montville and the other at Port Colden.[44] During the winter of 1845–46, the Newark plane was converted to a summit plane, but even this improvement only allowed one section of a boat at a time to pass, at the rate of two boats per hour. Since the new boats could not be passed over the old planes when loaded with more than 50 tons, private owners continued to run nearly 100 old 'flickers' each with a carrying capacity of 25 tons. The capacity of a Morris Canal plane was thus limited 'to one quarter of what could be passed through a lift lock.' Complicating matters, two sprocket wheels for

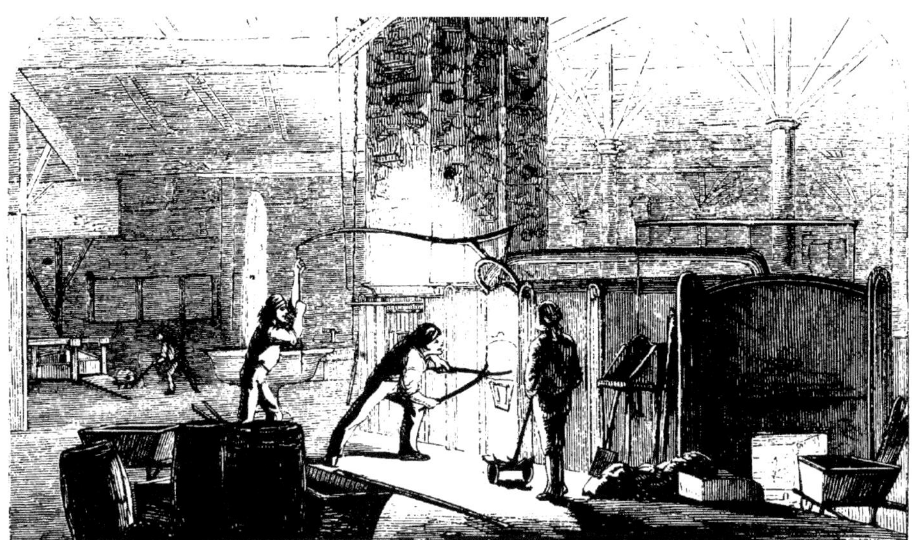

At a puddling furnace in the Boonton nail works, a puddler would churn a semi-molten iron ball with a long iron rod for about two hours to rid it of impurities, such as sand and cinder, and to mix the various melted ores. Another worker stands by with a 'ball-trolley' to convey the puddled iron ball to a squeezer, where any remaining cinder was forced out and the metal compressed into a sold mass. This was then rolled into flattened bars. (*Harper's New Monthly Magazine*, 1860)

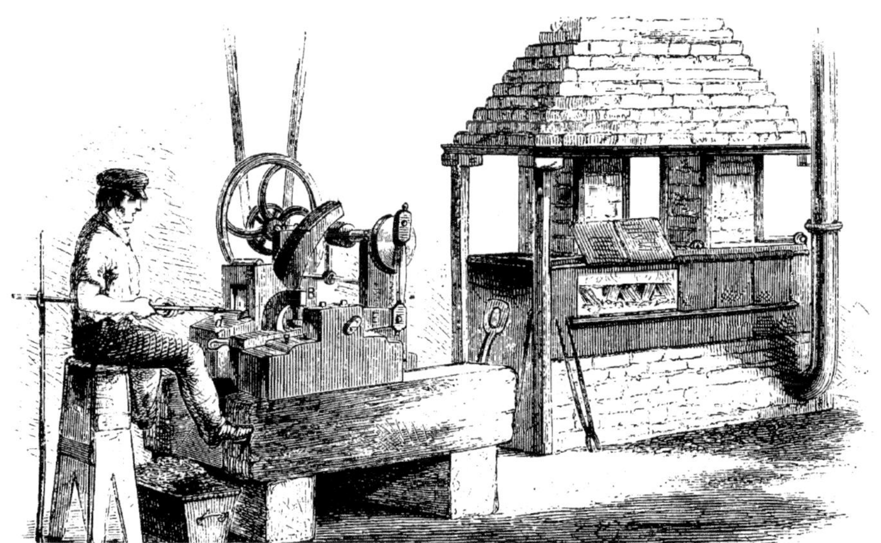

Water-driven shears cut flattened bars into nail-plates, which were reheated and passed between rollers. Cooled nail-plates were sawn into foot-long lengths of different widths for cutting into various sizes of nails and spikes. An adjacent cooper shop manufactured casks for shipping cut nails. (*Harper's New Monthly Magazine*, 1860)

winding the chains failed due to manufacturing defects.[45] Drought so lowered the water level in Lake Hopatcong as to prevent navigation until late in the boating season. Adding further delay, the work force employed in enlarging the canal struck for pay in May 1845. In the most serious incident, several hundred laborers rioted near Dover on 9 May 1845, when a subcontractor, who bid the job too cheaply, ran out of money to pay them.[46] The workmen broke into the lock tender's house as company president Daniel Tyler was dispensing back wages, forcing him to remove the money and call for the sheriff, who arrested the ringleaders.

William Hubbard Talcott was employed as resident engineer and superintendent of the Western Division in 1845. A year later, he became chief engineer and superintendent. He was another 'self-made man', who attended only the winter session at his local school and taught himself higher mathematics 'while tending a grist mill.'[47] He moved to Albany in 1830 to study engineering under John B. Jervis. Shortly thereafter, the Mohawk and Hudson Railroad employed him as superintendent and engineer. He was also engaged to survey the Albany and West Stockbridge Railroad. Talcott was appointed constructing engineer of the Genesee Valley Canal in 1837, which was planned to open navigation between Rochester and Olean, NY, over a distance of 107 miles. Upon its completion in 1841, he became a resident engineer upon the Erie Canal enlargement and relocated to Fort Plain, NY

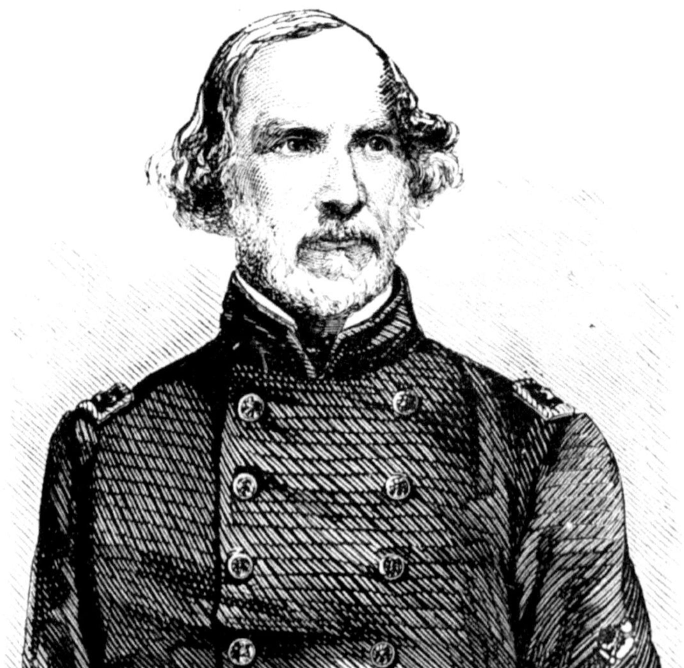

General Daniel Tyler, *c.* 1865. (Moat, *Frank Leslie's Illustrated History of the Civil War*, 1895)

On 17 April 1845, the Morris Canal Company issued $500,000 in 6-percent bonds to enable the work of enlargement to continue, despite sweltering heat and some of the lowest water levels in Lake Hopatcong ever reported. Due to drought, the Stanhope furnaces used the lake waters without restriction in the winter and spring, leaving insufficient water to supply the canal until late summer. As fissures in the baked bed of the enlarged canal absorbed water faster than it could be replenished, it was August before the prism was filled.

Drought heightened contention over water rights. Roswell L. Colt, of Paterson, controlling stockholder of the Society for Establishing Useful Manufacturers, disputed the canal's right to use water from Greenwood Lake. Acting on his behalf, Edward Dickerson, clerk of the United States District Court and son of judge Philemon Dickerson, led ten men at high noon on 8 August 1845, to destroy the canal's waste gate at Garret Rock, above Paterson.[48] This act drained 7 miles of the 17-mile level, suspending navigation. Division engineer James Moore soon appeared on the scene to fill the gap left by the demolished gate, with a cemented stone wall about 10 feet thick planked in front.

Finally, on 1 September 1845, the *Sussex Register* reported,

> The Morris Canal has been for some ten or fifteen days in good navigable order, and doing an unprecedented business. The close of the season is near at hand, yet the enlargement of the Canal has so materially increased its capacity, that in the short time intervening an immense amount of transportation will be done.

But much remained unfinished, including the crucial enlargement of the section between Jersey City and Newark, estimated to cost $18,500. Moreover, the canal's banks had not yet been raised high enough to hold more than 4 feet of water on considerable stretches west of Newark. Work proceeded on the aqueduct at Mountain View, whereby the canal passed over the Pompton River, and on construction of an additional reservoir near Stanhope, inundating 90 acres to form Lake Musconetcong. When the Sussex Iron Company at Stanhope converted to steam power, the Morris Canal gained exclusive use of water issuing from Lake Hopatcong. A new bulkhead also had to be built across the Delaware River to deepen the channel to at least 5 feet at low water, allowing boats to pass between the Lehigh and Morris Canals. Moreover, considerable repairs to locks were not completed, and new bridges had to be built over the widened canal.[49] One hundred new section boats with a capacity to carry up to 65 tons were purchased. All this had to be accomplished with limited means, due to heavy indebtedness and the greater capacity of competitors. Inevitably, coal traffic went to the Delaware Division Canal and the Morris Canal increasingly depended on local trade to meet expenses.

As the canal struggled to its feet, the price of railroad iron made a spectacular rise in April 1845 from $60 to $85 per ton. New furnaces with steam-driven blowing engines produced 300 tons weekly and nearly 15,000 tons annually to satisfy demand. In May 1845, the Speedwell Ironworks at Morristown employed 150 men in the annual production of 5,000 tons of iron, manufacturing parts for locomotives, railcars and steamboats. The newly re-organized Sussex Iron Company opened books at Morristown on 19 February 1846 for subscriptions to $350,000 in capital stock.

Benjamin Williamson was elected president in March 1846. The Morris Canal lost an eleven-year battle to unfairly capture a large share of the Lehigh coal trade when, on 20 April 1846, the governor of Pennsylvania signed a bill authorizing the Delaware Division Canal to construct an outlet lock at the head of Wells Falls. This was about ½ mile below New Hope, and thus opened a direct connection to the feeder of the Delaware and Raritan Canal.[50] This saved the time and expense of running canal boats an additional 52 miles round trip, to and from Bristol, and of towing boats across the Delaware River to Bordentown, thus reducing the average trip via the southern route by a full day to 21¼ days. With the cost of enlargement exceeding expectations, the reorganized Morris Canal and Banking Company needed shortly to raise at least $245,948 to pay contractors, to purchase boats, and to meet operating expenses and debt service. To prevent impending foreclosure, unidentified financiers offered in October 1846 to advance $290,000 in return for being allowed to purchase 20,000 shares at $7 per share. Asa Whitney Sr, of Philadelphia, one of the company's largest shareholders, became president in March 1847. On 1 April 1847, the company made its semi-annual payment on $28,000 in interest due annually on $400,000 in bonds, newly issued at a 7-percent rate. Once again open for boating, the enlarged canal began earning $1,500 weekly in tolls.

The railroad age was fast dawning. Peter Cooper fabricated the first American steam locomotive in 1830 for the Baltimore and Ohio Railroad. Moving operations to New York City, his rolling mill was the first to burn anthracite coal to puddle iron.[51] In 1845, he built a rolling-and-wire mill in South Trenton, NJ, conveniently situated on the Delaware River, the Delaware and Raritan Canal and the Camden and Amboy Railroad. The Trenton mills immediately went to work on a contract to produce 2,000 tons of rails for the Camden and Amboy Railroad, employing nearly 500 men and consuming 87 tons of coal and 62 tons of pig iron daily in the production of 50 tons of rails.

Heirs of the original owners of the Andover Iron Works conveyed the 60-acre Andover mine lot in Sussex County, NJ, abandoned for half a century, to Peter Cooper and Sons, of Trenton, on 6 June 1847 for $6,000.[52] The new owners employed fifty men in raising ore under the superintendence of Augustus G. King, of Stanhope. While they contemplated whether or not to

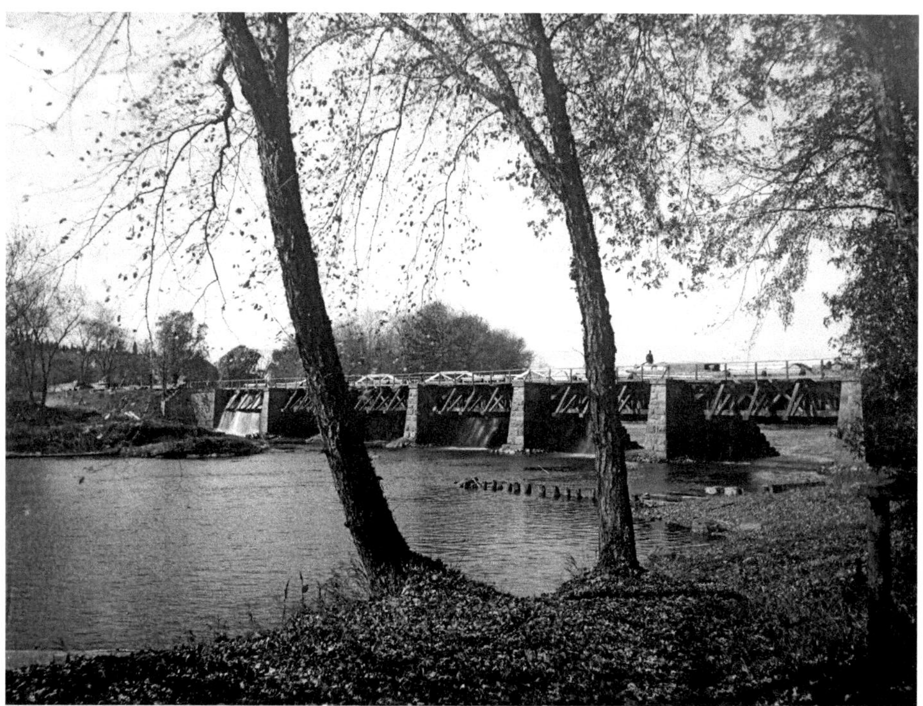

Aqueduct spanning the Pompton River at Mountain View, NJ, *c.* 1900. (*Detroit Publishing Company, Library of Congress*)

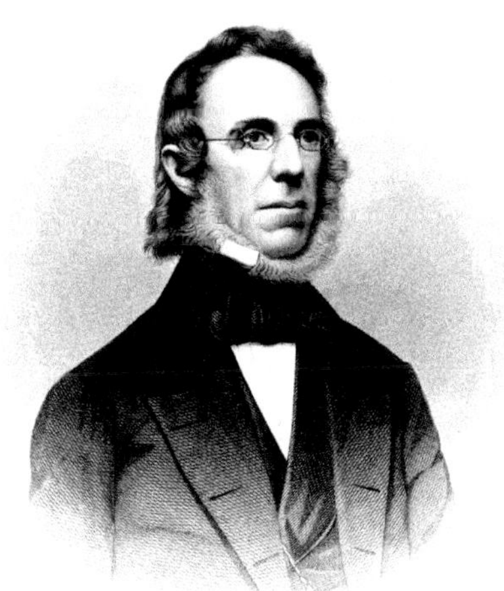

Portrait of Peter Cooper, engraved by John Chester Buttre. He ran the first American locomotive on the Baltimore & Ohio Railroad in 1830. (*Library of Congress*)

build furnaces near the mine, its output was carted in wagons over the Morris Turnpike to the Morris Canal at Waterloo. From this point the ore was boated to the Thomas Furnaces in Allentown, PA, for smelting. Pig iron was then shipped to the Trenton Ironworks for conversion into railroad iron. Peter Cooper, Edward Cooper and Abram Hewitt, proprietors of the Trenton Iron Company, erected Andover Furnace, consisting of two stacks at Phillipsburg, NJ, in March 1848. By 30 October 1848, the Trenton Iron Company was 'turning out one thousand tons of rails per month [...] of the very best quality, made exclusively from the famous Andover iron.'[53]

Each month wagons hauled 500 to 800 tons of Andover ore along the Morris Turnpike, a task requiring no less than 150 to 200 teams of two to four horses each. Every available beast and stable within a 15-mile radius was pressed into service. Paying a toll of $1 per ton for traveling the 6 miles of turnpike between the Andover mine and Waterloo, the Trenton Iron Company decided to reduce its cartage costs by building a mule tramway about 7 miles in length with a 3-foot gauge. Even more ambitiously, they applied in November 1847 for authorization to build a railroad from Newton, by or near the Andover mines, to the Morris Canal, at or near Stanhope. The legislature

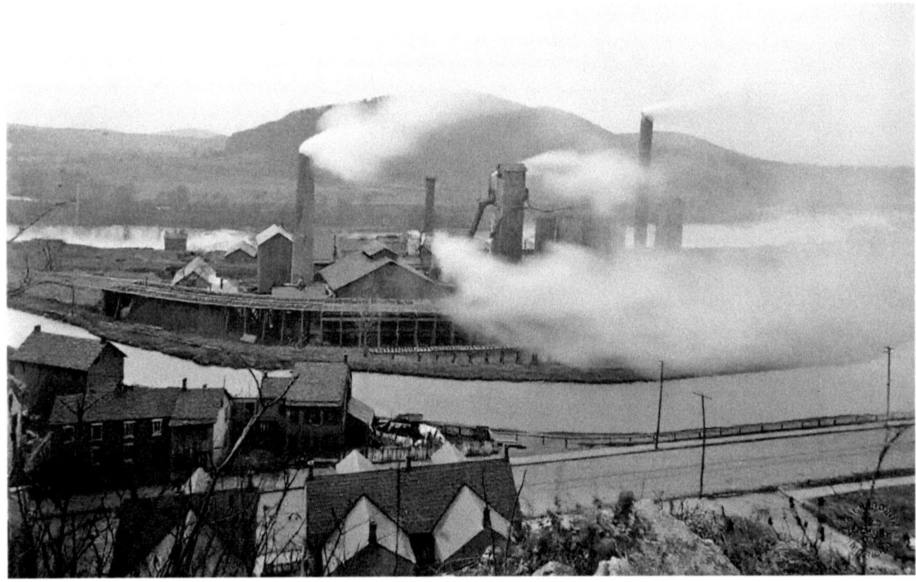

The Trenton Iron Company built the Cooper Anthracite Steam Furnaces, about a mile below Phillipsburg, NJ, in 1847–48 to smelt ore from the recently re-opened Andover mine. One furnace stood 55 feet tall and a second 42 feet tall; the boshes measured 18 feet in diameter. A third furnace was added in 1852. Employing about 300 men in 1860, Cooper Furnace consumed 60,000 tons of ore and 60,000 tons of coal in the annual production of 25,000 tons of pig iron. The furnaces were sold to the Andover Iron Company in 1867. (*Historic American Engineering Record, Library of Congress*)

chartered the Sussex Mine Railroad on 9 March 1848, naming Peter Cooper, Abram S. Hewitt, Edward Cooper, David Ryerson, Nathan Smith, Andrew A. Smalley, John Wills and Alexander McKain as its incorporators. Fearing the loss of income, even at a reduced rate of toll, the Morris Turnpike countered with a proposal to build a plank road at an estimated cost of $1,500 per mile. When subscription books opened on 9 January 1850, Cooper and Hewitt subscribed nearly all the stock for the Sussex Mine Railroad. Peter Cooper, of New York, Nathan Smith, of Waterloo, Abram S. Hewitt, of North Trenton, James Hall, of Trenton, and Ira C. Kent, of Greenwich, Warren County, were elected directors. A substantial 'T'-rail was used to complete the line within a year, allowing the Trenton rolling mills to procure ore deliveries for less than $2.50 per ton. Thomas Hewitt, brother to Abram S. Hewitt, moved from New York City to become superintendent of the Andover mine and later the railroad.[54] He resided on the farm later owned by Charles A. Gardner, near the outlet of Gardners Pond. The mule railroad was completed in May 1851 at a cost of $60,000 on a dirt bed without cinders and with iron rails mounted atop timber sleepers, approximately 4 inches square, laid on wooden ties. Horsepower drew small ore cars called 'jimmies', each holding 6 to 8 tons, which hauled 200 to 300 tons of ore daily to the canal. Three or four mules pulled each loaded car from the mine to the Whitehall Summit, whence two mules took it the rest of the way to the canal bank at Waterloo. A round trip took about five hours.[55]

The re-opening of the Andover Mine brought substantial business to the Morris Canal, but the steady westbound traffic in ore tested the durability of the planes, which could only pass one half of a section boat, carrying 25 tons at a time at a velocity of 100 feet per minute. Lock planes could only pass them in counter balance, when both ascending and descending boats were loaded with 50 tons each. Even in good working order, the planes could only pass two boats hourly in each direction, resulting in a detention of half an hour at each plane. Multiplied by twenty-three (that is, the number of planes along the route), the delay amounted to eleven-and-a-half hours per trip or an estimated two days in making a round trip between Newark and Easton. Mechanical failures, most notably the breakage of old and worn parts, added an additional two days' delay per trip. These detentions amounted to a third of the time required to pass a boat over the whole line of the canal. Proprietors of the Lehigh Coal and Navigation Company were of one mind with the iron interests.

> [...] all that is wanted, in order to command for the [Morris] canal a very large through trade, is such an improvement, and of their machinery, as shall enable the coal scows of the Lehigh to pass, without detaching the sections of which those scows are composed. This improvement, there is reason to hope, may be effected in time to accommodate the business of 1848.[56]

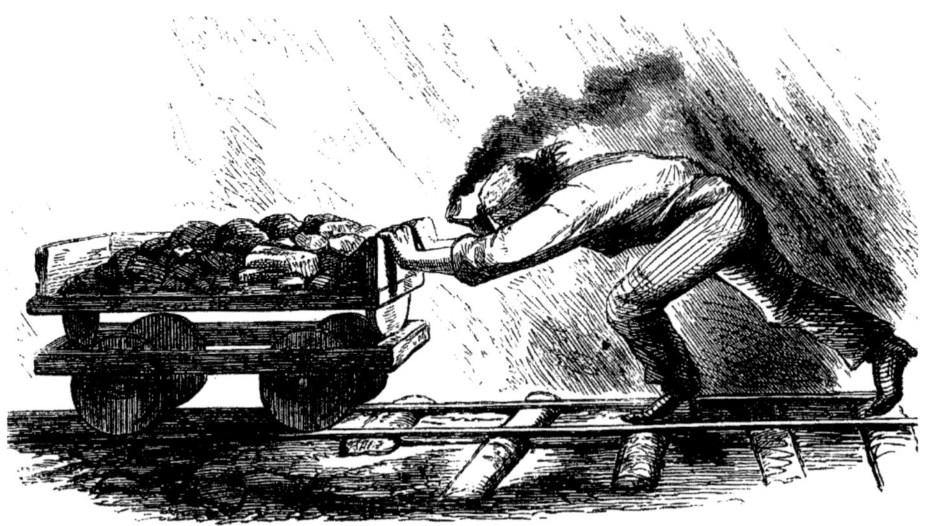

'Artist-Life In The Highlands of New Jersey', *Harper's New Monthly Magazine* (April 1860). Iron miner pushing an ore car.

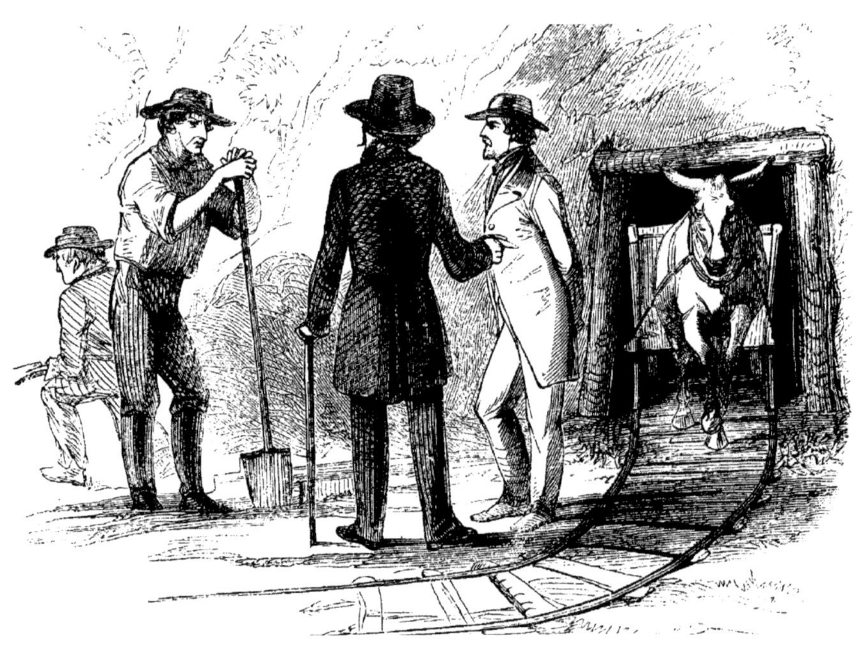

'Artist-Life In The Highlands of New Jersey', *Harper's New Monthly Magazine* (April 1860). Mule-drawn ore car exits the audit of Sweed's Mine, situated on the Morris Canal about a mile east of Dover, NJ.

In 1847, round trips between the Lehigh coal mines and Newark over the Morris Canal averaged twenty-one days. Once the canal was re-opened again to Jersey City, it would add another day.[57] However, of the 61,951 tons of Lehigh coal that entered the western terminus of the canal during the boating season of 1847, only 17,885 tons reached Newark. Over the course of the same season, the Delaware and Raritan Canal delivered more than 27,000 tons of coal to Newark. Coal deliveries along the interior line of the canal, however, were insufficient to pay for repairs and to reward stockholders on their investment. Obviously, the Morris Canal was not a competitive coal carrier to tidewater, due to the limited capacity of its inclined planes.[58] Something needed to be done.

On 6 July 1847, the sprocket chain broke at Plane No. 6 West, near Port Colden, precipitating Captain Frederick Fliger's canal boat into the water with such great force as to break the boat cabin, drowning the father, mother and three children of a family of German immigrants who were traveling west from Paterson. Consequently, the Morris Canal Company decided on 6 August 1847, to substitute new machinery of a stronger and more powerful kind at Port Colden. Moreover, all lock planes then in use were to be converted to summit planes, where section boats would pass over a hump, elevated about 18 inches above the surface of the water in the upper level, instead of passing through a lock at the head of each plane. Summit planes were able to pass boats more expeditiously, required less water to operate and were cheaper to construct and maintain. The company also decided to use two tracks rather than one at Port Colden, thus doubling capacity. The mechanical apparatus was to be made sufficiently strong to pass both sections of a boat loaded with 70 tons at a velocity of at least 300 feet per minute.[59]

At first, canal engineers considered purchasing a turbine from Merrick and Town, of Philadelphia, for $1,000, but eventually settled upon a more powerful 'Scotch Motor' for $1,700. A 6½-ton cylinder to wind wire rope was substituted for the sprocket wheel and chains, but an accident at the foundry destroyed the first mold and core. Finished too late in the season for water transport, it required a wagon of wider tread than usual and a team of fifteen horses to deliver, costing the company $25 per day simply for the driver. In consequence of the injury done to some public bridges and the delay caused in obtaining permission to cross others, civil process filed against the teamster further held up delivery for several days, during which time it rained heavily, making the roads nearly impassable. Even with the constant assistance of eight men, it took five days to cover the last 15 miles of the journey.[60] It ultimately cost $826 to move the cylinder into place, whereas water transport to accomplish the same task would have cost a mere $100. While the first wire rope arrived in Philadelphia at the cost of $1.25

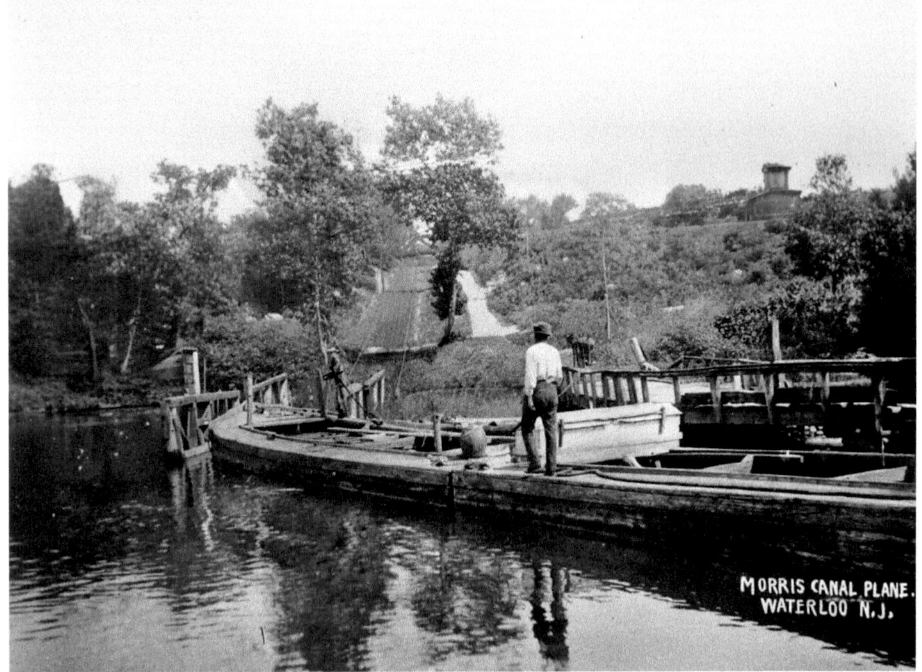

Partially missing image from a real photo postcard, *c.* 1900, of a section boat crossing the Lock Pond and entering the submerged cradle car at Plane No. 4 West at Waterloo, NJ. Note the water barrel and feed chest amidship. (*Author's collection, courtesy of John Zeek, 1979*)

per 100 lb, a freshet carried away 100 miles of the Juniata Canal, just as the remaining wire ropes arrived in Hollidaysburg, PA. Consequently, they had to be returned to Pittsburgh and transported overland to Chambersburg, continuing thence by railroad to Philadelphia at an added cost of $334. Arriving in Philadelphia just as the canals were closing, the wire cable had to be delivered overland.

J. L. Bevins and Company received the contract to rebuild the Port Colden plane on 7 August 1847, but never responded. Consequently, another contractor began work on 23 August, but difficulty in securing possession of the necessary land for the site of the new wheel pit caused further delay. The contract was virtually abandoned in the middle of September and only day work proceeded under supervision of canal foremen and engineers. To make matters worse, a large break in the foot of the plane on 8 October carried away much of what had already been accomplished. Work resumed after a week of repairs. Workmen were unable to finish the stonework of the wheel pit because the large quadrant pipe, which passed under the masonry, cracked due to a flaw in its manufacture. This took another week to repair. The company increased wages to entice a sufficient force

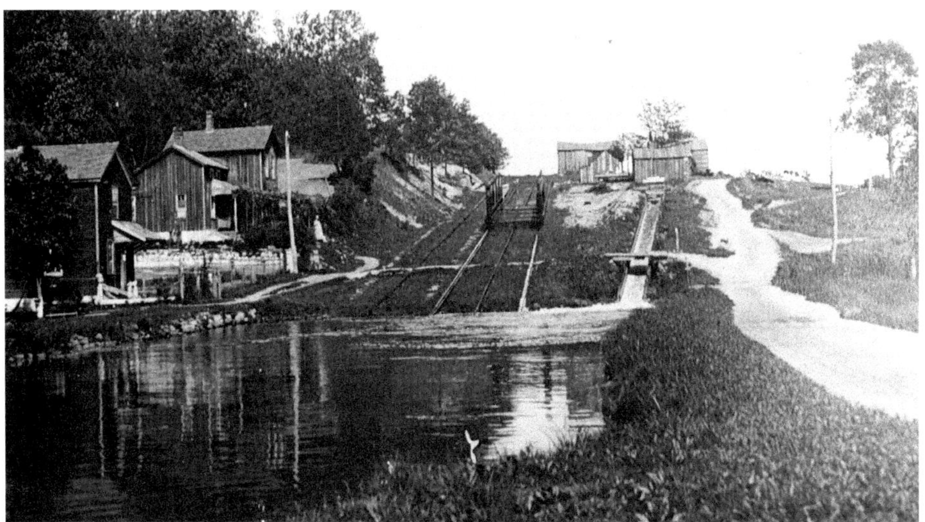

Plane No. 6 West at Port Colden. (*Historic American Engineering Record, Library of Congress*)

of machinists and laborers to work not only in daylight, but also at such work as could be safely done at night. Working in the inclement months of November, December and January, masonry could only be laid in the middle of the warmest days and immediately covered with straw, earth or water, to protect it from frost.

It ultimately cost $27,168 to reconstruct Plane No. 6 West at Port Colden—nearly $6,000 more than originally estimated due to unforeseen circumstances. The first test of the new design came on 27 January 1848, with one section of a boat carrying 25 tons on one track and an empty section on the other. After several successful trial runs, two sections of a boat, each loaded with 25 tons, were placed on a single plane car, with an empty section riding the other car. Finally, the empty section of boat was removed and the load increased in the section boat to 70 tons. According to contemporary report, 'that boat was then passed repeatedly up and down the plane, with great apparent ease, and without employing more than half the power that had been provided.'[61] Most satisfactorily, the boat passed up the plane, overcoming a change in elevation of 51 feet in 3½ minutes. In the end, canal engineers hoped the new design would be capable of passing at least six boats in each direction per hour when loaded with 70 tons each, or when all or any part of them were empty (which was quite as many as could previously be passed through a single lift lock in the same amount of time). Thus the new model plane would be three times as capacious as existing summit planes and more than four times that of lock planes. Being cheaper, lighter and more durable, wire rope would replace sprocket chains.

The Morris Canal floated 108 boats, including 'flickers', during the boating season of 1846.[62] Sixty-four additional boats were purchased in 1847. The following season, arrangements were made for running sixty scows, besides boats engaged in the local trade, more than doubling the number of available craft. To keep up with its competitors, the Morris Canal Company envisioned spending $300,000 in 1848 to complete the enlargement between Newark and Jersey City; to reconstruct the remaining ten planes west of the summit; to strengthen the ten old lock planes and the two summit planes east of the summit; to build the new aqueduct over the Pompton River; to raise the banks (where it had not been done) so as to hold 5 feet of water; and to deepen the ferry across the Delaware River to 5 feet at low water.[63]

The model inclined plane at Port Colden gave timely hope to increasing the canal's capacity. It took only a glance over the shoulder to see railroads fast gaining ground. General Mahlon D. Dickerson broke ground for the extension of the Morris and Essex Railroad from Morristown to Dover on 8 April 1846. Track-laying commenced on 23 October 1847. The first train arrived at Rockaway on 1 July 1848, and, on 29 July, directors of the Morris and Essex Railroad made an inaugural excursion over the 13-mile extension, which cost $20,000 per mile to build. Soon six stage lines accommodating passengers from Morris, Sussex and Warren Counties connected with the new depot at Dover. The 35 miles of track between Newark and Dover competed with the canal as it traversed the heart of one of the richest mineral regions in the country. Freight and passenger trains began running between Dover and tidewater at Jersey City on 9 October 1848. The company next secured a charter supplement, authorizing an extension from Dover to any point on the Delaware River between Belvidere and the Delaware Water Gap. In April 1851, the Morris and Essex Railroad took measures to extend their rails from Dover to Hackettstown, via Stanhope and Waterloo, at which latter place the line would intersect with the proposed Sussex Railroad, near Inclined Plane No. 4 West.

The anthracite coal trade experienced enormous growth in the quarter century ending in 1850, doubling every five or six years.[64] Coal consumption would rise dramatically over the next decade, due to a growing number of sea-going steamers and a steady increase in household and manufacturing demand.[65] The Lehigh Canal was capable of moving 2 million tons annually to Easton, with all lock chambers below Mauch Chunk able to pass two boats loaded with 70 tons each in one lockage. Construction of an outlet lock on the Delaware Division Canal at Wells Falls allowed coal to flow through the feeder of the Delaware and Raritan Canal, thereby materially shortening the southern route to New York City. This forced the Morris Canal not only to increase capacity, but also to speed up the eastbound transit of coal. For the time being, as railroads struggled to extend their reach and capacity, the

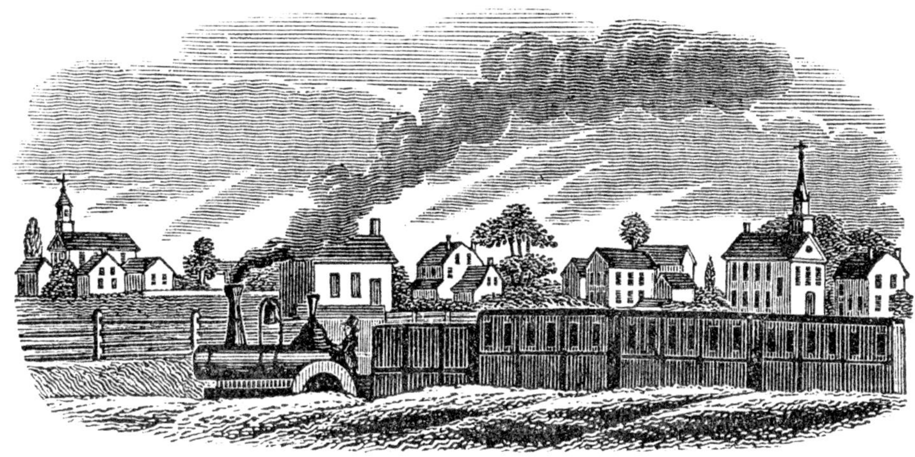

View in Madison.

This 1844 woodcut prominently features the Morris and Essex Railroad passing through Madison, NJ, 4 miles south-east of Morristown. (Barber and Howe, *Historical Collections of the State of New Jersey*, 1844)

Morris Canal remained the only carrier of Pennsylvania coal across northern New Jersey, resulting in winter fluctuations in supply and price. With no practical alternative, the Lehigh Coal and Navigation Company contracted with the Morris Canal to carry any quantity of coal it could accommodate. Pushed to capacity, however, the Morris Canal boated about 100,000 tons of coal in 1850. In 1851, one writer noted,

> The Lehigh Canal has some exit for its coal, by the Morris Canal, across New Jersey; but the difficulties of transfer from one canal to the other, at Easton, as well as of the defective lockage along the line of the canal itself, have heretofore rendered the Morris Canal almost a nullity, so far as the coal trade is concerned. These difficulties have been, to some extent, removed, and the Morris Canal, it is hoped, will hereafter be a sharer in this important business. There are, however, no data on which any accurate estimate of its business can be made. Its friends suppose that it may be able to carry as much as 400,000 tons.[66]

To pay off debts and fund enlargement, the Morris Canal and Banking Company secured passage of an act on 9 February 1849, authorizing issuance of 11,750 shares of preferred stock at $100 per share ($1,175,000) and consolidation of the original 41,000 shares into 10,210 shares, holding their previous nominal value ($1,021,000).[67] As part of the agreement, all profit would go to 'preferred' shareholders until 10 percent per annum was paid,

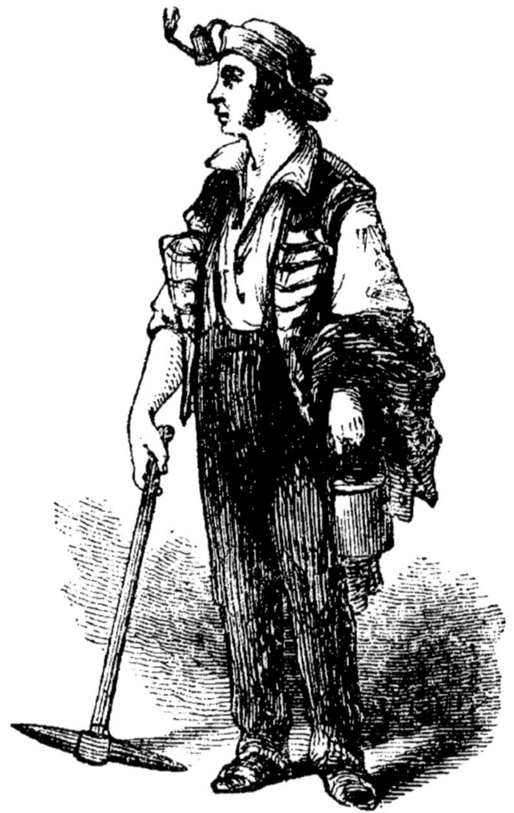

'Coal-Miner', *Harper's New Monthly Magazine* (September 1857). Note the tin lamp on hat and lunch pail.

after which 'consolidated' shareholders would participate in profits. In return, the company surrendered its banking privileges.[68] With Ephraim Marsh as president, stockholders approved the re-financing plan on 18 May 1849, and shovels hit the ground the following summer. To speed the carriage of iron ore westward to the Lehigh Valley, engineer William H. Talcott advertised for bids covering the grading, masonry and carpentry work on ten inclined planes along the Western Division on 14 May 1850; these 'to be constructed on the same plan as Plane 6, west.'[69] To facilitate estimates, water was drawn out of the canal at the head and foot of Plane No. 6 West 'from 10 o'clock A. M. till 3 P. M. to give contractors an opportunity to examine the work to be constructed in the bottom of the canal.'[70]

On 27 May 1850, the Morris Canal Company's dam at Cranberry Lake burst in the neighborhood of the Iron Hotel, above Waterloo, opening a breach 250 feet long and allowing 15 feet of water to drain from two lakes about 1 mile long, each averaging ½ mile wide.[71] Water rushed with great force over the turnpike road, obliging teamsters to retreat precipitously to the neighboring heights for safety. The deluge covered the entire flat below the turnpike tollgate, carrying away everything in its path. In its progress down Dragon Brook and Lubber's Run towards the canal, the surge of water tore away John Smith's forge dam at New Andover. The old gatehouse filled with 4 feet of water, soaking 300 bushels of corn belonging to Samuel H. Allen. Using nets and seines, locals caught a great number of fish of all sizes, from pike and perch down to minnows, in the bed of the drained pond. A storm on 15–16 July 1850 caused the Delaware River to rise 7 feet higher than any previous summer record. A break in the Lehigh Canal above Easton, 3 or 4 miles in extent, prematurely ended navigation for the entire season. Consequently, hundreds of boatmen and their horses went over to the Delaware and Hudson Canal in search of employment.

In June 1850, workmen began removing mud and gravel from the section of canal between Newark and Jersey City to enlarge its dimensions. Contracts to rebuild ten planes on the Western Division for $327,987 were awarded on 11 July 1850.[72] James Finlay, of Cold Spring, NY, was engaged to provide the new jet-reaction turbines, called 'Scotch motors', each with four arms of 6-foot radius. Contracts were awarded to Evans Thompson for machinery, to David W. Wetmore, of New York, for railroad iron, and to John A. Roebling for wire rope.[73]

In reconstructing planes on the Western Division, engineers salvaged the best parts of the old machinery to strengthen planes on the Eastern Division, enabling them to lower both sections of a boat, when loaded with 65 or 70 tons, and to raise a boat loaded with 40 tons.[74] The cost-saving measure would not allow boats to pass over the old planes as quickly as over the new ones, 'yet it could be done in less than half the time now employed.'[75] Thus strengthened, 'four boats loaded with 65 or 70 tons, could be passed eastwardly per hour, and the same number westwardly, when not loaded with more than 40 tons each.' It was believed the improvements would increase the capacity of the canal from 240,000 tons to 624,000 tons per season. On 14 June 1851, the *Sussex Register* pronounced the Morris Canal to be 'in good working order throughout the whole line and full of business.' Improvements to the machinery of its planes had 'materially enlarged its capacity, and afforded increased facilities for the rapid and systematic transportation of freight.' The canal was expected

> [...] to do double the amount of business it has heretofore been capable of transacting. Boats can now pass over the planes in five minutes with 60 tons cargo, whereas, before, it required half an hour to pass a plane with 50 tons cargo [...] many, who in former years, had reason to seek other modes of freighting, are now glad to avail themselves of the superior facilities, which the Canal affords.

In a boost to business, the New Jersey Exploring and Mining Company shipped 50 tons of zinc ore daily from Lake Hopatcong to its furnaces and mills in Newark for manufacture into white and brown paints. On 25 June 1851, general superintendent and chief engineer William H. Talcott, of Jersey City, advertised for boatmen, promising steady employment throughout the season. He believed the new planes would now allow canal boats 'to make average trips from Jersey City to the Coal Mines and back in 20 days.'

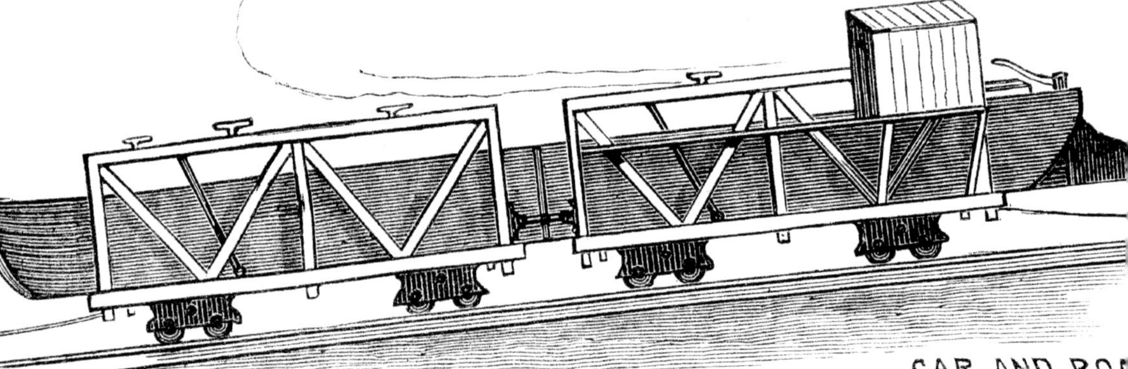

The timber-frame plane car was made in two sections, shackled together, to accommodate hinged section boats. (*Scientific American*, 20 May 1882)

5

A Paying Proposition

Notwithstanding the short time the Morris Canal was operational during 1851, a greater amount of tonnage was carried than in any previous year: 281,707 tons as compared with 239,682 in 1850. The directors felt the increased capacity more than justified the $50,000 spent on improvements, and they expected business to grow on account of the rapidly increasing consumption of coal, which already crowded all avenues of transportation.[1] When the canal opened in April 1852, it could finally claim to be a canal in reality rather than simply a play-thing for directors, who previously gave more attention to its banking privileges than its operations. By October 1853, thirteen out of twenty-three inclined planes had been rebuilt on the new plan. In that month, chief engineer and superintendent William H. Talcott invited Henry Poor, editor of the *American Railroad Journal,* to view the double-tracked Newark Plane, which used 3-inch rails on a 12-foot gauge.[2] The plane car consisted of a strong timber frame with high stanchions, riding on sixteen wheels and outfitted with brakes. It was made in two sections, shackled together, to accommodate hinged boats. More durable, easier to load and unload, but requiring less timber to obtain equal stiffness, the section boats were originally introduced for use on the Lehigh Canal. The wire rope, used to pull the boat in its car along the track, measured $2\frac{9}{16}$ inches in diameter and weighed 9 lb per foot. Although one English wire rope remained in use at Newark, John A. Roebling, of Trenton, manufactured the remainder. The wire rope passed around horizontal sheave-wheels at the head of the plane, mounted strongly enough to resist the pull of the turbine. The ropes were fastened at opposite ends and on opposite sides of a 12-foot-diameter drum, which wound and unwound the cable in a continuous spiral groove on its surface. A clutch on the turbine's jackshaft reversed the drum's motion, 'so as to work either up or down the plane without the friction and strain of an endless rope.' A smaller wire rope, connecting the outer ends of the two wire ropes, was used to draw the boat out of the upper level onto the summit of the plane. The winding drums, measuring as much as 10 or 12 feet long, were cast in a single piece in dry loam. The spiral groove on the outer surface was produced in the mold,

> […] a smooth circle equal to the diameter of the rim at the bottom of the groove being first 'swept out,' and a cutter or shaper, carried on a stiff arm secured to a large revolving nut and fixed screw of proper pitch being afterwards carried around until the proper groove was formed upon the whole face of the rim.[3]

Five drums were manufactured in Paterson, two in Rockaway, and six in Philadelphia. A pinion, working just within the rim rather than the central shaft, was used to apply power, thus reducing torsion. With 75 percent efficiency, the 'Scotch Motor' (also known as Whitelaw-and-Stirrat's reaction wheel) provided 400 hp on a 55-foot fall of water.[4] The turbine employed four curved arms with an extreme radius of 6 feet each, the overall diameter being 12 feet. The jets, known as 'orifices of escape', comprised 'vertical parallelograms, each fifteen and a half inches high, and three and a half inches wide.'[5] During the three minutes it took to ascend the 70-foot Newark plane, the turbine discharged 6,000 cubic feet of water per minute under a full head, but not more than 3,500 cubic feet per minute were usually required. A single operator could stop the machinery with a brake, 'combining the toggle joint and friction strap.' With full view of the operation from his elevated tower, the plane tender could easily work the gate wheel, the reversing lever for the main clutch and the brake wheel.

Henry Poor admired the smooth transit of a boat over the Newark plane:

> The boat coming along the lower level, enters between the stanchions of the submerged truck, fastens a single hawser, and without stopping its motion settled upon the truck as that is drawn out of the water; it continues up the plane at from four to five miles per hour, goes over the summit, the truck descending to the bottom of the canal,—the boat floating off by the impulse acquired,—the horses, who have been trotted up the hill, are again hitched on, and the boat is away upon another level![6]

The editor recommended those interested in witnessing the plane's operation to 'visit on Monday morning, when the boats which collect on Sunday at Bloomfield, on the 17-mile level, are descending to tidewater.'

Despite growing competition from railroads, traffic expanded. At the close of navigation in December 1853, the Morris Canal boasted receipts totaling $187,000. Of this amount, about $67,000 went to working expenses; $30,000 to interest on funded debt; and $70,000 to the payment of a dividend on

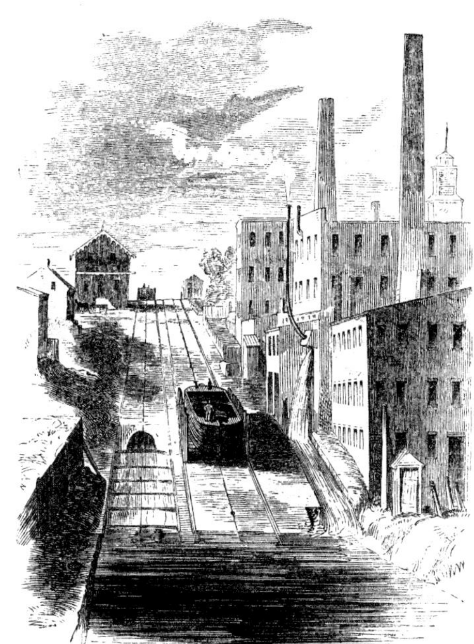

INCLINED PLANE ON THE MORRIS CANAL.

This drawing of an 'Inclined Plane on the Morris Canal' from *Ballou's Pictorial Drawing-Room Companion*, 14 April 1855, depicts Plane No. 12 East in Newark, NJ.

preferred stock. This left a surplus of about $20,000. On 28 March 1854, boatmen on the Lehigh Canal and the Delaware Division of the Pennsylvania Canal struck for a rate increase, making coal scarce at Newark and unavailable in many small towns along the Morris Canal. Receipts for the boating season of 1854 amounted to $246,615—a 30-percent advance over the income for the previous year. The earnings were not only sufficient to pay all current expenses, interest on the bonded debt, dividends on preferred stock and the cost of permanent improvements, but also to pay off the company's floating debt. The canal carried 543,269 tons of freight, including 284,506 tons of coal.

Extension of the Morris and Essex Railroad westward from Dover to Hackettstown was completed in January 1854. With the opening of navigation in April 1854, Andrew Smalley, of Stanhope, advocated freighting on the Morris Canal, noting the price of canal freight was $2.50 per ton, or 'about half the rate charged by the railroad, saying nothing about breakage and wet weather and no Depot.' Augustus G. King opened a canal freighting line between Stanhope and Newark on 1 April 1856. At this time, a host of teamsters, woodcutters, charcoal burners and miners populated the mountains and woodlands about Sparta, where bloomeries manufactured wrought iron for wagon tires, blacksmith iron and anchors. Wagons hauled anchors over the Woodport turnpike from Sparta to Lake Hopatcong, a distance of 12 miles. Canal boats then delivered them to the freight depot at Dover.

Waterloo, nestled along the Musconetcong River at the foot of Allamuchy Mountain, is perhaps the best-preserved example of how proximity to mines and the confluence of waterpower, roads, towpath and railroads proved advantageous to trade. General John Smith conveyed the Andover Forge Farm, which he purchased in 1812, and several adjacent tracts to sons Nathan and Peter Smith in 1840. By this time, they had refurbished an old stone barn into a dwelling, a dwelling and out-kitchen into a tavern, a charcoal house into a gristmill, and built a store on the canal bank at the foot of a lock and inclined plane. As loyal Democrats, they not only supported Texan independence, but also its annexation to the United States. Consequently, Nathan Smith chose the name 'Waterloo' for his thriving inland canal port, to honor the frontier village in Texas which became the capital of the Republic of Texas in October 1839 (only to be promptly renamed 'Austin'). Nathan Smith was a self-taught mechanic, who not only built and operated grist-and-sawmills, but also patented an 'Improvement in the Self-Acting Brake for Inclined Planes' on 28 November 1842, saying, 'What I claim as my invention, and desire to secure by letters patent, is the combination of a weight or spring, supported by the back chain, when in action, with the brakes of a car, in the manner and for the purpose set forth.'[7] He was also an adept politician, being elected to the General Assembly in 1841 and to the State Senate in 1843. On 11 February 1848, Senator Nathan Smith

> [...] presented the memorial of the Trenton Iron Company and the petition of David Ryerson and other citizens of the County of Sussex, praying for the passage of an act to incorporate a company for the purpose of constructing a railroad from the Andover mines, in said county, to some convenient point on the Morris Canal, with permission to extend the same to the village of Newton.[8]

Securing the terminus of the Sussex Railroad for Waterloo instead of Stanhope was his final notable achievement. He died suddenly at Waterloo on 6 March 1852, at only forty-six years of age. Losing her twin brother, Stephen O. Hart, only five days later, Nathan's disconsolate widow Matilda 'committed suicide by hanging herself in her bedroom' at Waterloo on 16 June 1852.

Younger brother and partner Peter Smith picked up the reins, advertising the rental of his 'large stone Flouring Mill and stone Store House, situated at Waterloo, Sussex County, NJ' on 17 December 1853. He announced:

> The Flouring Mill is situated in a flourishing part of the farming country and consequently has a large run of customer work, besides that it is one of the best locations for retailing on the Morris Canal, which gives the stand an excellent opportunity to do a large business without the expense of carting

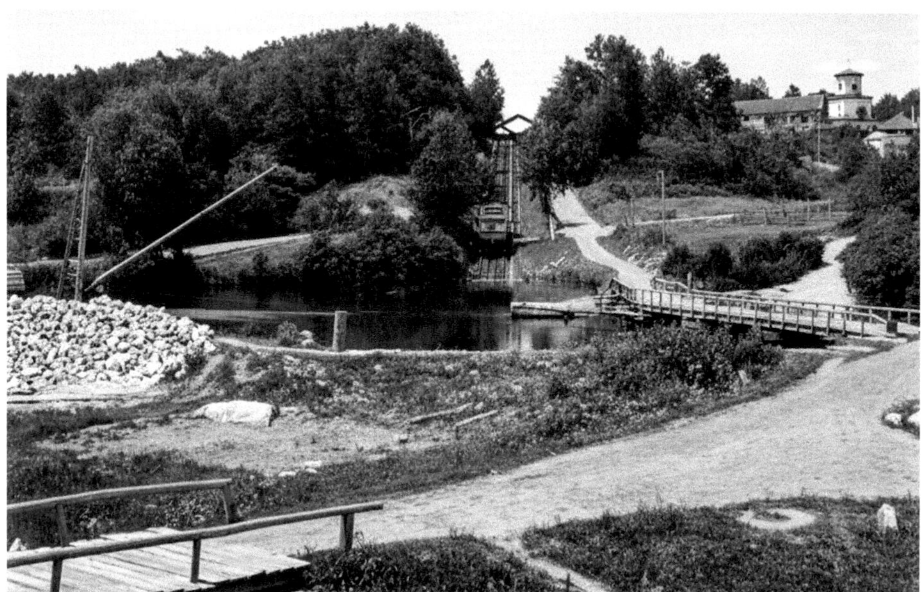

This image of Inclined Plane No. 4 West at Waterloo, NJ, dates to about 1880. Nova Scotia gypsum is heaped on the banks of the Lock Pond in the left foreground. Schooners conveyed gypsum rock from Nova Scotia to Newark, where it provided a return load for canal boats carrying coal eastward. A derrick unloaded the gypsum from boats, just beyond the Waterloo lock. An old ore car from the Sussex Mine Railroad conveyed the gypsum to the Smith Brothers' plaster mill, where it was ground into a soil application. (*Originally from the collection of Peter Louis Smith*)

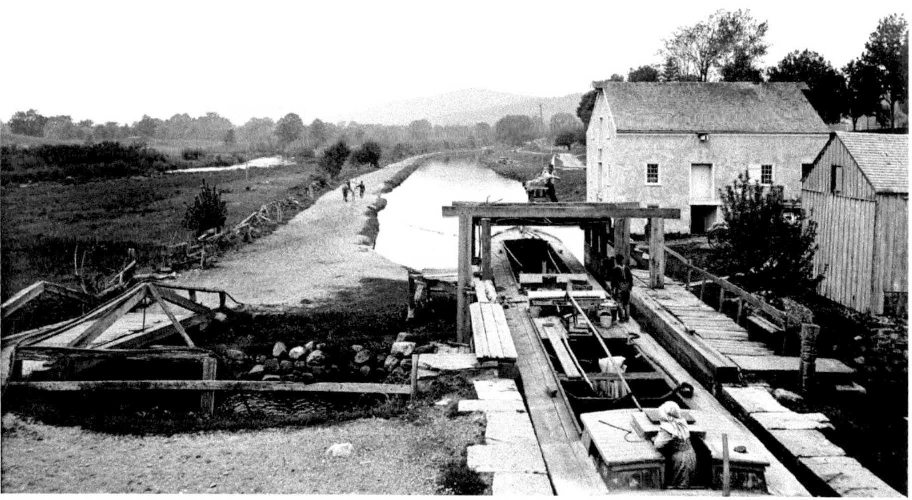

A combination lock-and-aqueduct crossed the mill tailrace at Waterloo, NJ. Smith's store stands on the canal bank. This image (*c.*1900) also depicts the embankment and abutments that marked the southern terminus of the original Sussex Mine Railroad, whereby ore cars crossed over the road on a trestle to drop their contents through chutes to canal boats. (*Detroit Publishing Company, Library of Congress*)

and keeping teams. It is also situated at the outlet of Warren county and therefore, there is an excellent chance to purchase grain. The Store House has also a decided advantage as it is situated immediately on the bank of the canal and at the foot of a Lock and Plane, which always detains and gives the boatmen an extra chance to trade without extra detention. The boatmen's trade is one of the best in the country and always cash.

Peter Smith's store was outfitted with 'all necessary hoisting machinery' for storing goods.

Whereas Waterloo thrived on the transshipment of iron ore, Shippenport prospered as an entrepôt for wood products, especially tan bark. William Green Jr auctioned valuable real estate at Shippenport, situated at the summit of the Morris Canal and Morris and Essex Railroad, on 20 November 1855. The premises comprised a sawmill, two dwelling houses, a blacksmith shop and store on the canal bank. The sawmill was equipped with an upright saw

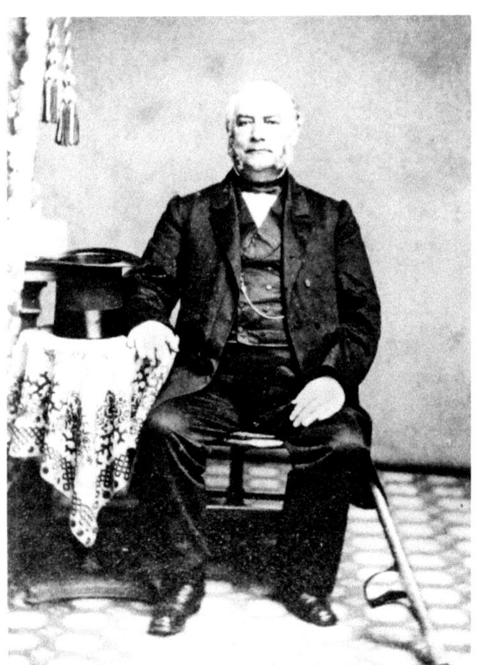
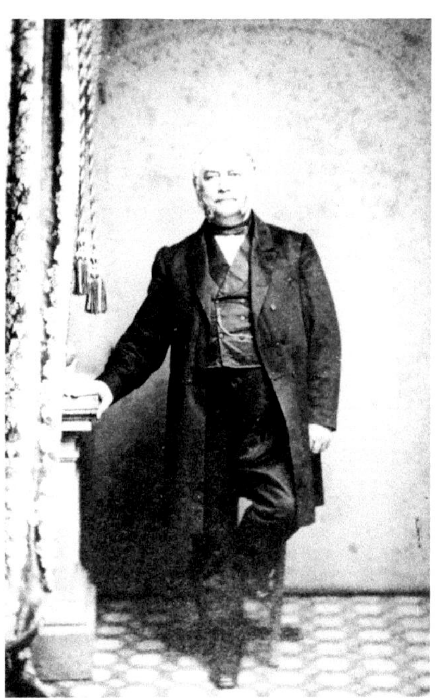

These likenesses of Peter Smith (1808–1877), of Waterloo, NJ, were taken when he was elected to the State Senate in November 1861. He was photographed both wearing and seated alongside a homemade walking aid. After accidentally cutting a tendon of his left leg with a corn knife as a young man, he ever afterward walked with a homemade contraption made of a cane with an attached step that raised his foot up several inches off the ground. This cane came up alongside his hip and there was a hole in the top for his belt to pass through. And so he learned to walk despite his disability, and once even jumped into the canal with this cumbersome device to rescue his son Peter D. Smith from drowning.

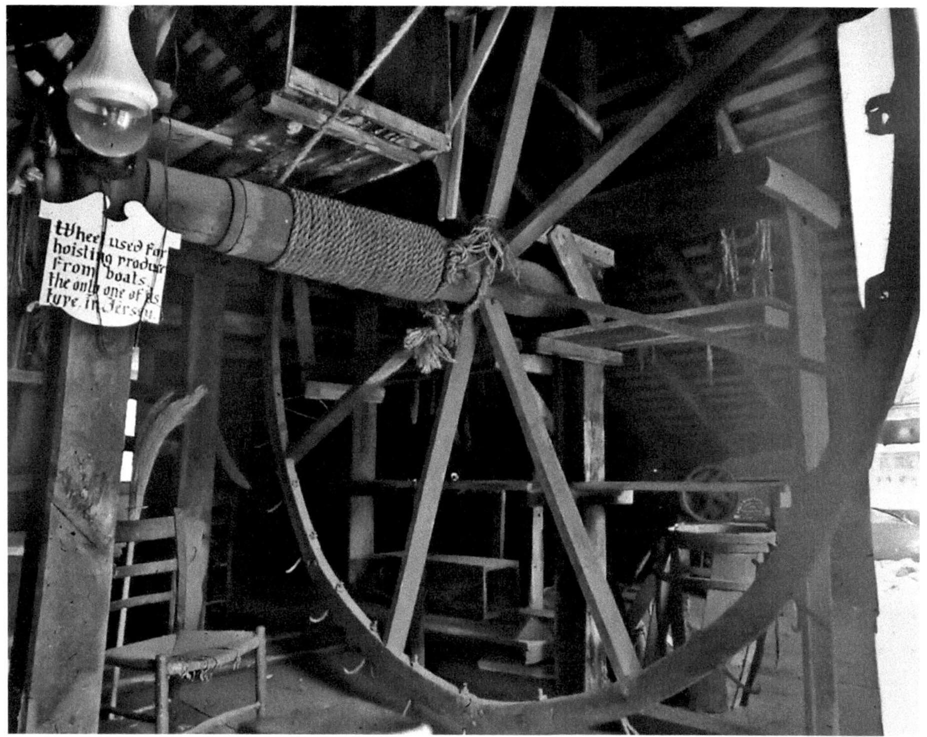

Hoisting machinery in the third story of the canal store at Waterloo, NJ. The open door overlooking the canal is partly visible in the upper right. (*Photograph by Kevin Wright, 1978*)

for timber and four circular saws for curved-sawing wagon sills, felloes and plough beams. A new shingle machine produced 600,000 shingles yearly at a cost of about $3 per thousand. A new bark mill could grind 10 tons of bark daily at a cost of 40 cents per ton. The location was one of the best in New Jersey for purchasing bark, about 1,000 cords of bark having been sold in the neighborhood the previous year at $7 per ton. It cost $2 per ton to transport bark from Shippenport to Newark for use in the leather-harness industry.

To accommodate eastbound coal traffic, planes on the Eastern Division were rebuilt between 1852 and 1860. By the start of the 1856 boating season, fifteen planes had been reconstructed, including Plane No. 12 East at Newark, rebuilt as a double plane in 1855 at a cost of $33,890. Work proceeded on the remaining eight. Round-bowed section boats, ranging in capacity from 60 to 69 tons, were introduced in 1847 when the waterway was deepened to 5 feet. Captains purchased these boats for $550 on an installment plan, paying 20 percent of their income for two years (approximately $20 per trip), then 15 percent (approximately $15 per trip) until the purchase price was paid. Boats usually paid for themselves after four or five years. Boatmen owning their own boat received $1.45 per ton for coal carried from Mauch Chunk to Jersey City. Crews consisted of a captain, bowman and driver. In 1855, it cost $49 to feed and shoe a horse for the seven-month boating season. Horses were fed straw, cut hay, oats and cracked corn, sometimes with rye or wheat bran admixed. A trained pair of mules, accustomed to canal work, was worth about $275 in 1860. The Morris Canal Company provided free stables along the route. Boat captains generally paid farmers to care for their animals during winter.

John I. Blair—for whom Blairstown in Warren County is named—opened the Warren Railroad on 27 May 1856, connecting the Delaware, Lackawanna and Western Railroad (DL&W), 5 miles below the Delaware Water Gap, to the New Jersey Central Railroad at New Hampton Junction, thus opening a through-route to tidewater for Pennsylvania coal.[9] Blair perpetually leased the 18 miles of new track to the DL&W, which immediately built trestlework, chutes and machinery for transferring Scranton coal from railcars to canal boats at Washington, New Jersey. They offloaded 21,558 tons of coal at the Washington basin in 1856 and would have sold much more 'if the sizes wanted could have been supplied.'[10] Anticipating a large increase in business at this point, the railroad company announced its intention on 23 January 1857,

> [...] to construct, during the coming spring, a piling-ground similar to that at Ithaca, with the addition of pockets, from which boats can be loaded with dispatch, as we find this an important inducement for them to stop and take in loading. The sales for the year at this point are estimated at from thirty to forty thousand tons.[11]

By 1860, one-third of all the coal entering the Morris Canal came through Port Washington.[12]

The Mount Hope Mining Company built another important feeder in 1857, opening a gravity railway on a 40-inch gauge.[13] Six ore trains carrying about 250 tons passed daily between Mount Hope and the Morris Canal at Rockaway, whence it was transshipped to Scranton, Pennsylvania. Despite the influx of ore and significant improvements to its facilities, the Morris Canal hovered on the cusp of obsolescence, looking over its shoulder as the Lehigh Valley Railroad neared completion in 1855, forming a junction with the Central Railroad of New Jersey at Phillipsburg.

Water was let into the upper level of the canal on 20 March 1857, and a canal police force began patrolling the waterway to detect and prevent thefts of coal and iron. A break in the Morris Canal at Paterson on 7 May 1857, caused all water to be drawn from the 17-mile level. A break at Waterloo on 30 May 1857 flooded 100 acres and business was suspended for a week between Waterloo and Saxton Falls. Responding to an increase in eastbound coal freight, the Morris Canal Company advertised on 25 July 1857 for

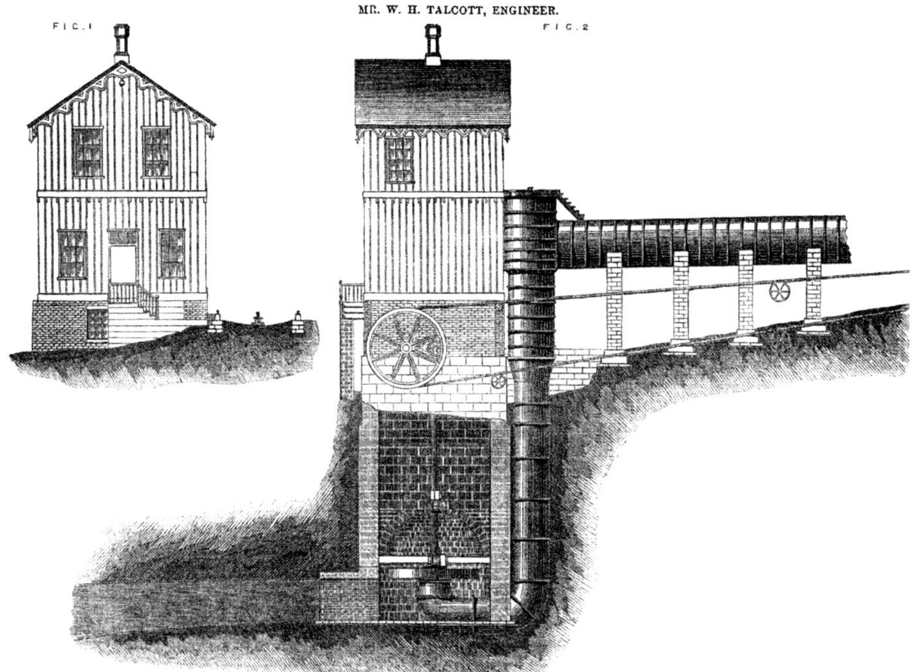

'Inclined Planes of the Morris Canal, New Jersey, USA, Mr W. H. Talcott, Engineer', from Colburn, *Engineering, An Illustrated Weekly Journal, From July to December 1868*, Vol. 6. This illustration shows the inclined plane at Newark with its subterranean turbine for working the winding drum.

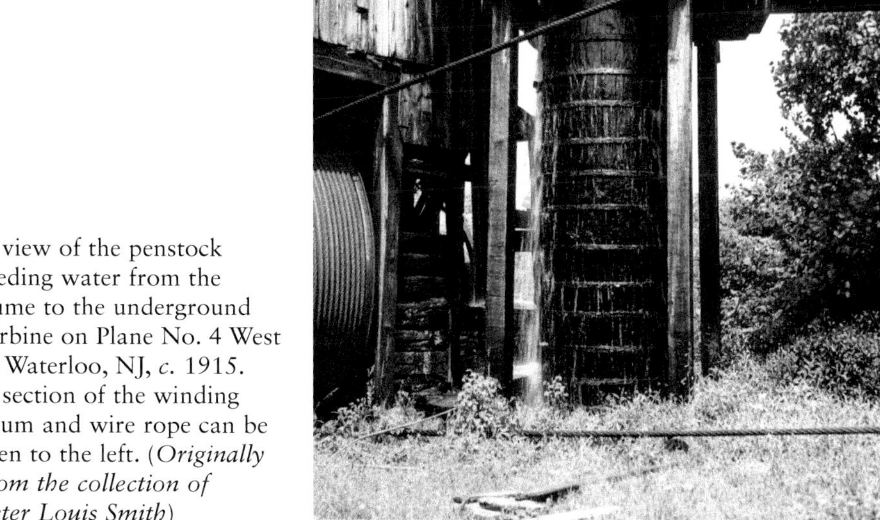

A view of the penstock feeding water from the flume to the underground turbine on Plane No. 4 West at Waterloo, NJ, *c.* 1915. A section of the winding drum and wire rope can be seen to the left. (*Originally from the collection of Peter Louis Smith*)

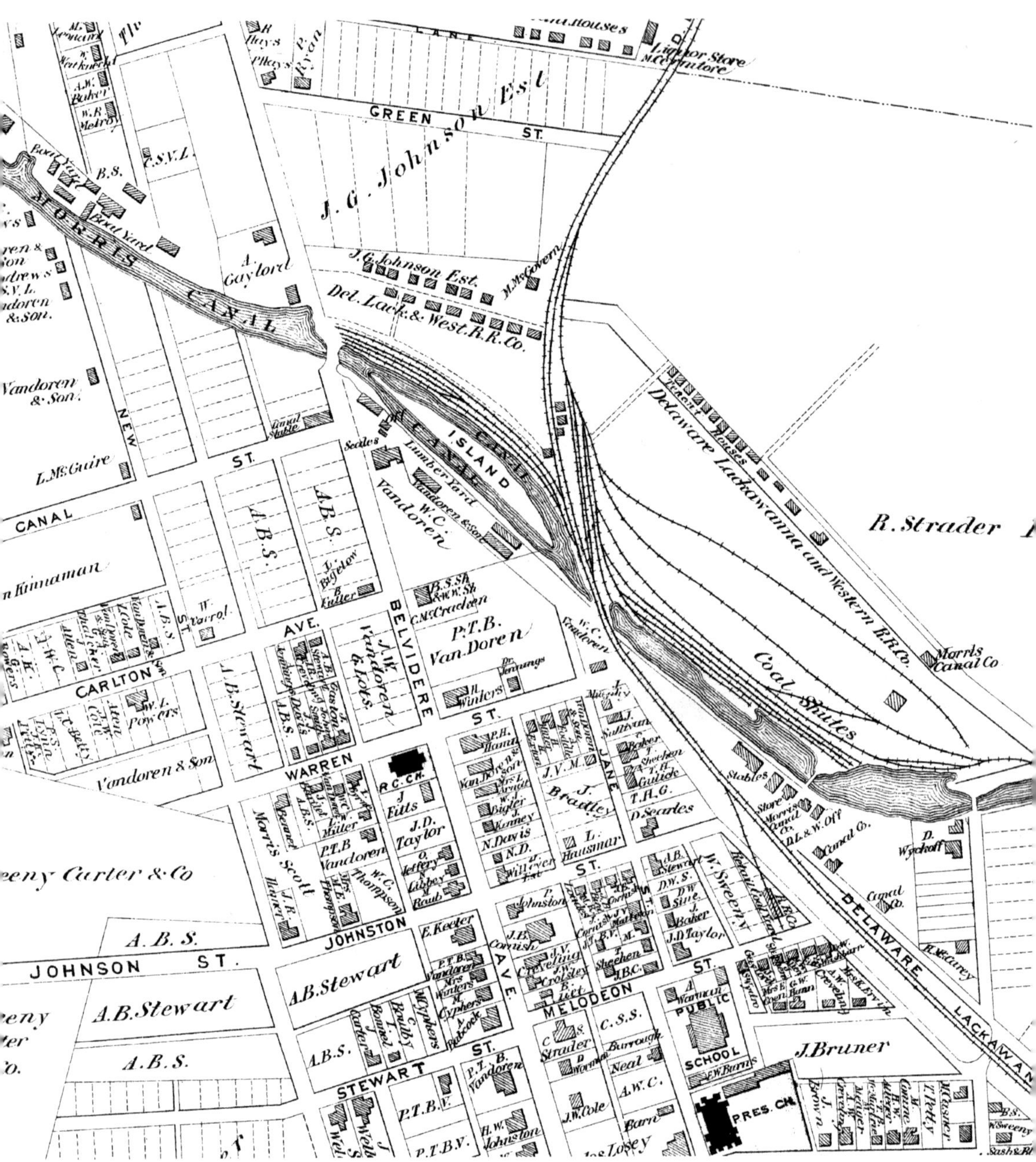

Port Washington, Washington, NJ, from the *County Atlas of Warren*, New Jersey (1874).

Opposite: Map of the Canals and Railroads for Transporting Anthracite Coal from the Several Coal Fields to the City of New York (Baltimore: Hunkel & Son, 1856).

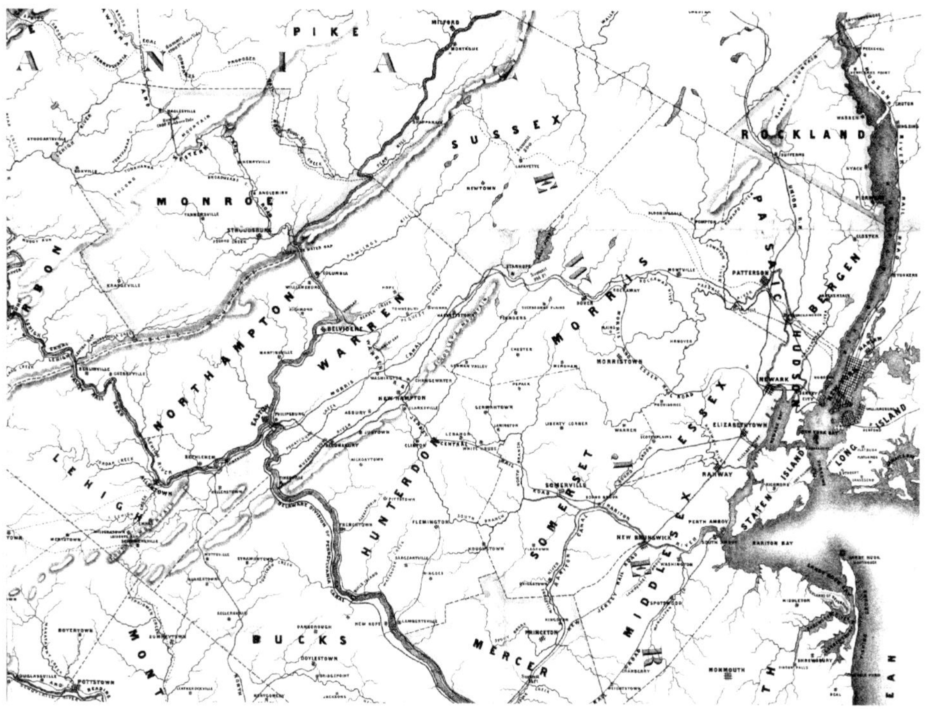

laborers at Dover, Rockaway and Denville to rebuild Inclined Planes Nos. 4, 5, 6, 7 and 9 East. On 24 August 1857, failure of the Ohio Life Insurance and Trust Company triggered a financial panic, bringing down many Wall Street brokers, paralyzing manufacturing interests and throwing men out of work. Sixteen New York banks suspended specie payments on 13 October 1857, followed by banks in Sussex, Warren and Morris Counties. Having manufactured 130,000 kegs of nails and 15,000 kegs of railroad spikes the previous year, the Boonton ironworks shut down on 24 October 1857, throwing 1,200 men out of work. The ranks of unemployed in Philadelphia numbered 40,000. On 10 November 1857, state and federal troops were summoned to control bread riots in New York City.

Unable to earn sufficient revenue to meet expenses, the Morris Canal almost entirely suspended operations, discharging about 400 boatmen.[14] The company's receipts for the boating season amounted to $53,726 on 1 November 1857, a decrease of $23,352 from the previous year.[15] By the time a sudden cold snap froze the canal and halted navigation on 25 November 1857, it had carried 536,362 tons of freight, including 298,011 tons of coal—down from the 563,386 tons of freight, including 311,929 tons of coal, the previous year. It was drained in March 1858 to clean and repair for re-opening on 1 April. Boatmen took notice when Salmon Vanderen advertised *Jack Black Warrior* for stud service during the season (5 April to

5 July) at the low price of $6. This was probably the first advertisement for 'Mules, mules, mules' in the Sussex County newspapers. In less than a decade, mules replaced horses as the draught animals of preference on the towpath. While horses lasted only a year, mules could work up to eight years and cost only two thirds as much to keep.

Other forms of locomotion were also tested. In connection with notice of a steamboat trial on the Erie Canal, the *Paterson Guardian* reported, 'a regular built propeller, driven by steam,' was placed on the Morris Canal on 23 July 1858. This steamboat traveled 2½ miles per hour. Although the Morris Canal Company declared a semi-annual dividend of 5 percent on its preferred stock in 1858, receipts declined $36,528 in comparison with the previous year, reflecting the economic recession. The boating season ended on a note of tragedy when, on 1 December 1858, the canal bank near Drakeville (Ledgewood) burst at 5 a.m., unleashing a torrent of water. A house occupied by the Hulbert family was washed from its foundation, drowning a mother and three children in their beds.

Morris Canal boatmen banded together in April 1859 to demand $1.15 per ton of freight to Paterson, $1.20 to Bloomfield, and $3 per day after lying forty-eight hours in tidewater. Strikers blocked the canal with their boats at several strategic points. Business came to a standstill. When Stephen Ryerson attempted to get through the blockade at Paterson with a boatload of lumber and without paying the advance, he was pelted with stones before police rescued him.[16] That summer, workmen constructed a lock near the Plank Road Ferry in Newark and deepened the canal between the Passaic and Hackensack Rivers to increase its capacity.

Lashed to a 'flying ferry' and propelled by the current, canal boats crossed the Delaware River between Easton and Phillipsburg—a distance of about 600 feet—guided on a cable suspended about 20 feet above the river.[17] Slackwater pools were used to cross the Musconetcong River twice (at Waterloo and at Saxton Falls) and the Rockaway River twice (at Powerville and Dover). The canal crossed the Pompton River on a long wooden aqueduct and the Passaic River at Little Falls on a substantial masonry one.[18] Mules walking across bridges towed boats across the Passaic River, beyond Newark, and the Hackensack estuary. Steam tugboats pulled canal boats across New York Harbor and hauled large quantities of iron ore, firewood and coal across Lake Hopatcong. Over 200 road bridges, mainly of wooden king-post truss design, with a standard headway of 10 feet, crossed over the canal.

The canal carried 638,019 tons of freight, including 365,861 tons of coal, in 1859. The annual report for the fiscal year ending on 29 February 1860 showed the company spent $149,478 on permanent improvements, including reconstruction work on five inclined planes. After eight years, work on the last plane on the Eastern Division was completed, facilitating passage of seventy-

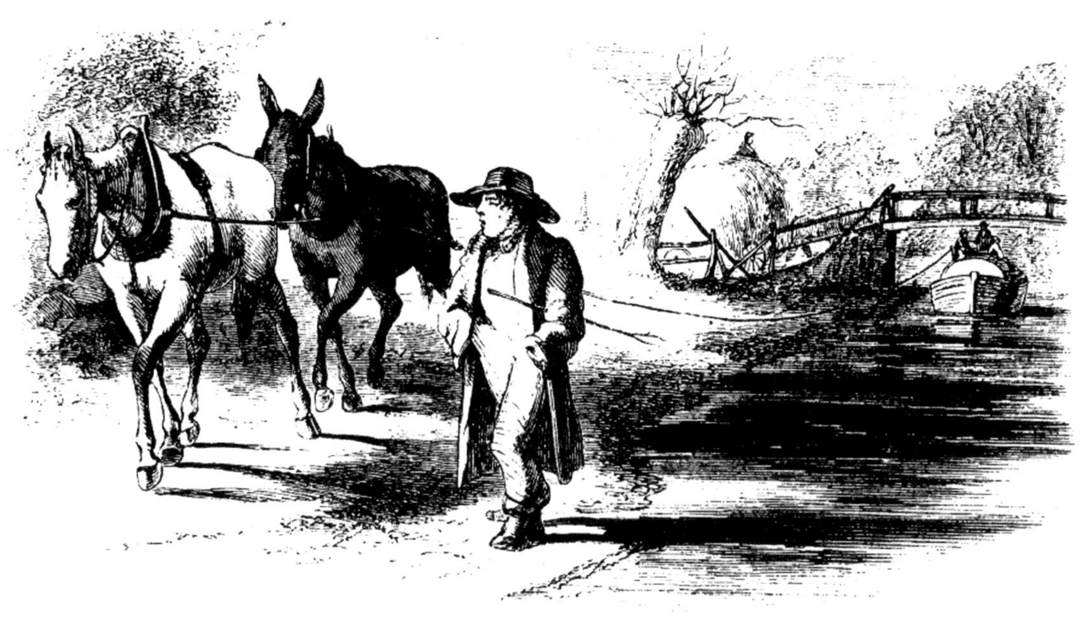

'The Team' from J. R. Chapin's 'Among The Nail-Makers' depicts a fourteen-year-old German boy driving a horse and a mule for the canal boat *Sarsey Fanney*. The driver has tucked his switch under his arm and withdrawn his hands into the sleeves of his overcoat on a chilly October morning. A hay wagon crosses a canal bridge. (*Harper's New Monthly Magazine*, 1860)

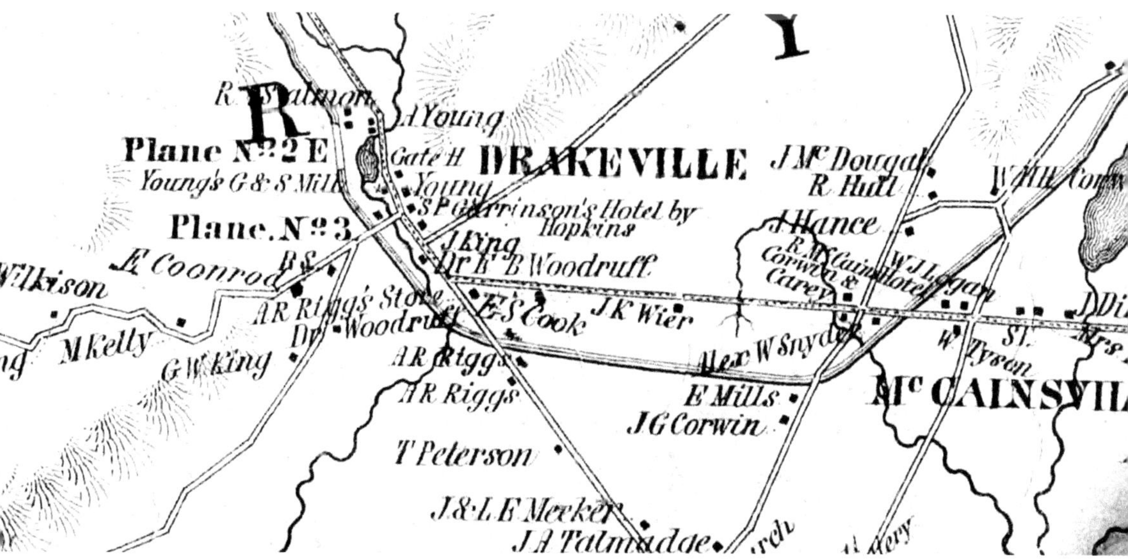

Drakeville, *Map of Morris County, NJ* (1853). Inclined Planes Nos. 2 and 3 East were adjacent in Drakeville, now Ledgewood, N.J.

ton boats. The twelve planes on the Eastern Division cost $351,114 to rebuild, or $29,259 per plane. The company spent $17,000 on repairs in 1859, largely to deepen the canal, 'including dredging between the Passaic and Hackensack Rivers, and towing the boats around while the work was being done.'[19] The company built a new lock where the canal connected with the Passaic River at Newark and constructed a powerful pump to supply the canal with water at low tide between the Hackensack and Hudson Rivers. New piers, wharves and basins were built at Jersey City. Chief engineer Talcott could finally report,

> [...] the inclined planes are all rebuilt upon the improved plan; several locks have been extensively repaired, and all are in good working order. There is full five feet of water in all the levels. The navigation between Newark and Jersey City has been made equal to any part of the canal, and the improvements at Jersey City greatly facilitate and encourage the reshipment of coal at that point.

The shipping basin at Jersey City, begun in 1859, was eventually

> [...] enclosed on all sides by a substantial *crib work*, thereby securing still water for handling coal on the south side of the company's coal piers; increasing the storage room, and otherwise facilitating the trade of the canal.[20]

To the consternation of Jersey City officials, the canal company built a pier 1,000 feet long into the bay. The basin at Washington Street, Jersey City, was dredged in April 1860 to enable large-draft vessels to enter and load from canal boats. Increasing the tonnage of boats from 50 to 70 tons reduced coal freights from $1.43 to $1.00 per ton between Mauch Chunk and New York City.

The reconstructed planes employed a reaction turbine, capable of generating at least 163 hp, set in a deep well beside the plane.[21] It wound and unwound wire cable around a spiral-grooved drum, 12 feet in diameter, raising or lowering boats in 'cradles' on 12-foot gauge railways at about 3.41 miles per hour if ascending, and 4.55 miles per hour if descending. Accommodating hinged section boats, heavy timber cradle cars were made in two sections, each 36 feet long, coupled with iron hinges to allow vertical adjustment in crossing the summit. Each section of the cradle car was mounted on a truck with four pairs of double-flanged iron wheels, 30 inches in diameter. Boats floated into these cradle cars and were fastened to stanchions on the timber frame. The turbine turned a vertical shaft. Grooved wheels and rollers, set between the rails, supported the heavy wire cable, which turned around sheave-wheel guides at the head and foot of each plane. The winding drum's direction of revolution was reversible. Cables, 2⅛ inch in diameter, manufactured by John A. Roebling of Trenton, lasted on average about four years. The plane tender directed affairs from an operating house set above the turbine and machinery, moving levers in response to signals from a brakeman riding the plane car. It took an average of eight minutes to pass a plane. In 1876, the monthly salary of a plane tender was $37, of a brakeman $34, and of a lock tender $31. Three inclined planes were double-tracked, allowing for simultaneous passage of boats in opposite directions.

Section boats eventually grew to 88 feet in length and weighed 20 tons. The stern was decked for 8 feet to provide a cabin for the boatman. Hinged amidships to pass the summit humps, boats carried 70 tons with a draught of 3 feet, 9 inches. Built of Georgia yellow and white pine, they had a life expectancy of five to seven years. Each cost about $700 to build in 1861 and were sold or leased to their captains. Two or three horses or mules towed a boat, covering 15 to 20 miles per day. In 1862, it cost 11 cents per mile to tow a loaded boat and 7 cents for empty boats. The average expense to run a boat was estimated at $3 per day.[22] Because the waters from its summit reservoirs flowed westward towards Phillipsburg and eastward towards Jersey City, canal boats progressed at 2 miles per hour when traveling against the current, placing a considerable strain on the mules, and 3 miles per hour when running with the current.[23] The Morris Canal Company purchased and installed one of the first platform scales manufactured by Francis M. Strong and Thomas Ross, of the Vergennes Iron Company in Vermont, at Plane No. 6 West at Port Colden.[24] It had a capacity of 400 tons with a platform measuring 30 by 70 feet. The toll collector kept a register of the weight of each boat.

Company president Ephraim Marsh and superintendent William H. Talcott embarked on a four-day excursion from Phillipsburg to Jersey City with thirty invited guests on 16 July 1860.[25] Besides enjoying the scenery at a leisurely pace and observing the reconstituted inclined planes, these voyagers also watched a flourishing two-way waterborne trade. The correspondent for the *Public Ledger* duly reported,

> Of the number of coal boats passing through the Canal from the Anthracite regions in Pennsylvania, five-sixths, or perhaps, six-sevenths, return freighted with the rich iron ores, which have been discovered all along the line of the work, and which are so essential in the manufacture of the best quality iron, now so abundantly produced in the Lehigh Valley.

He also remarked upon the 'large and highly valuable wharf property at Jersey City.'

In July 1860, *Harper's New Monthly Magazine* featured the Morris Canal in an illustrated article entitled, 'Among the Nail-Makers'. The literary tour

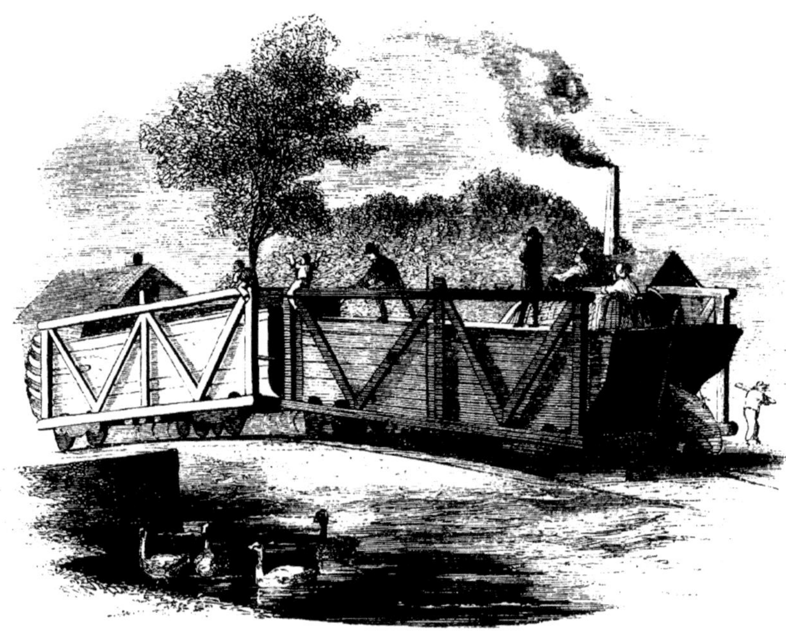

Captain Blivens's boat, the *Sarsey Fanney*, crossing the summit of Plane No. 4 East at Baker's Mills (Wharton, NJ). The rudder blade has been raised out of harm's way. (*Harper's New Monthly Magazine*, 1860)

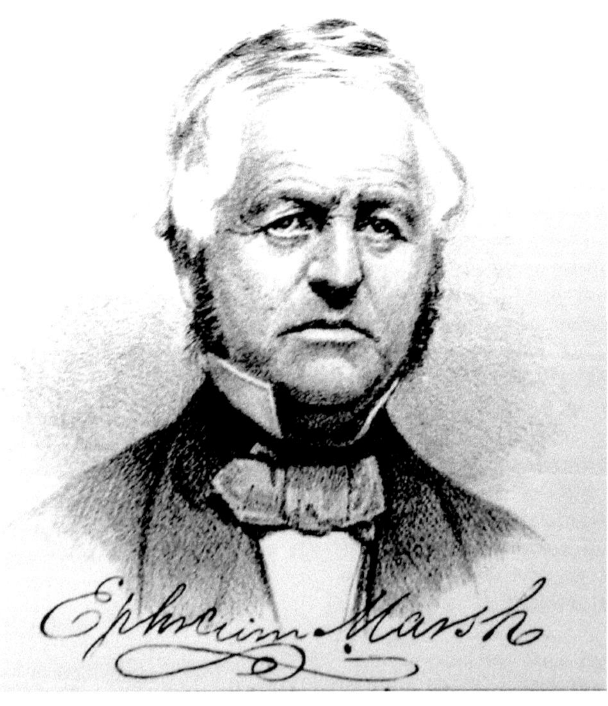

Portrait of Ephraim Marsh. (*History of Morris County, New Jersey 1739–1882*, 1882)

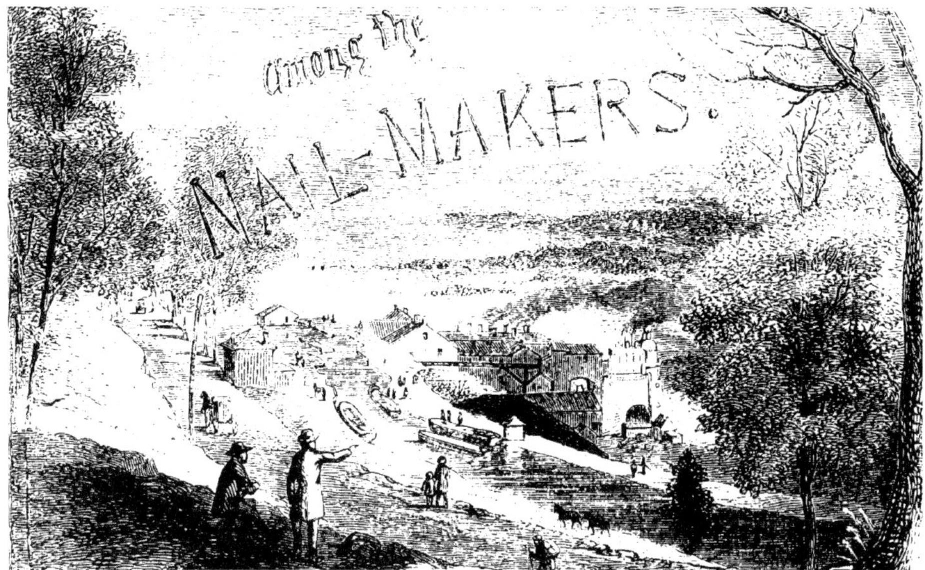

In October 1859, illustrator and author John R. Chapin, of Rahway, NJ, traveled by canal boat with a load of iron ore from McCainsville (Kenvil) to Fuller and Lord's ironworks and nail factory in Boonton, NJ. His title illustration for 'Among The Nail-Makers', published in *Harper's New Monthly Magazine* in July 1860, depicts the Boonton Ironworks and the summit of Inclined Plane No. 7 East.

focused upon the nail works at Boonton Falls, known as the Fuller, Lord and Company's Ironworks, which embraced a blast furnace, rolling mill and nail factory, employing 600 workers in the manufacture of 1,200 kegs of nails daily and consuming 25,000 tons of coal annually.[26] Describing a colorful cast of towpath characters, artist and author John Reuben Chapin noted,

> The Morris Canal affords an invaluable means of transit to the Highland region of New Jersey, without which its mineral wealth would be entirely undeveloped; and would, like the miser's hoarded gold, rust in its rocky coffers for want of use. Like a broad river, it offers a channel for the internal commerce of the mining and agricultural districts, its benefits ramifying right and left for many miles, every highway and country road forming a tributary, over whose dusty or muddy surface teams loaded with the produce of the farm or the mine, the mill or the forge, are hurrying to and fro like a colony of ants busy in laying in their winter's store. The transportation of ore from the various mines in its vicinity to the numerous forges ... and mills along its banks, as well as to the manufacturing region of Pennsylvania, and the conveyance of the large quantities of coal and limestone used in the manufacture of the iron, employs large numbers of boats, the greater number of which never pass further eastward than the plane at Boonton.[27]

On 24 July 1860, the Philadelphia *Public Ledger* enthused,

> One important advantage enjoyed by the Morris Canal results from the fact that its business is largely confined to the line of the work, and is therefore, in a great measure, free from competition that is so frequently found ruinous to rival lines for the same trade.[28]

While there was a considerable through-traffic, especially in coal, to tidewater, 'much more than the usual portion of its trade is distributed along its line.'

With the opening of the American Civil War, a vast number of horses, mules, wagons, canal boats, locomotives and freight cars were needed to meet the burden placed upon all lines of transportation. The Western Division opened for navigation on 18 March 1861, and the Eastern Division a week later. On 4 June 1861, the largest canal boat ever run on the Morris Canal took 81 tons of coal from Washington in Warren County to Jersey City. At their annual meeting on 19 June 1861, directors of the Morris and Essex Railroad noted work on their proposed extension to Washington, NJ, was postponed due to the outbreak of war.

The whims of nature still ruled. Dover was inundated on 2 November 1861, when a torrential rain and windstorm caused a dam owned by the Morris and Essex Railroad to burst. The highest tide recorded in twenty-one years put parts of Jersey City and the Newark Meadows under 3 feet of water. At 9 p.m., William, John and Welch Bird, sons of Joseph Bird, attempted to cross the Morris Canal on a footbridge at Baggot's Lock, located at Guinea Hollow between Waterloo and Hackettstown. In the darkness, William took a misstep and fell into 6 feet of water. Welch plunged in after him and John shouted for help. Their parents rushed from the house to their rescue, but Mr Bird was delayed in lighting a lantern and getting a pole. The boys were unable to climb up the smoothly planked sides of the lock and the pole brought by their father was what got Welch out. But badly bruised by his fall, William was unable to grasp the pole and drowned. He was twenty-one years old. A small boat from the Musconetcong River was floated into the lock to rescue his body.

The canal closed for the season on 13 December 1861, having carried 619,369 tons of freight.[29] Superintendent Talcott noted the ongoing expenditure for lengthening locks authorized in July 1860.[30] During the winter of 1859–60, five locks were lengthened and another eight the following winter. These thirteen locks were grouted with hydraulic cement, re-floored and new gates and wickets were installed. To prevent frost from damaging the new mortar, each lock was housed and artificially heated for a period of four to six weeks.[31] The lift lock at the outlet of the Stanhope reservoir (Lake Musconetcong), originally built of wood in the winter of 1845–46, was rebuilt of stone and its chamber lengthened. In all, seven lift locks (Nos.

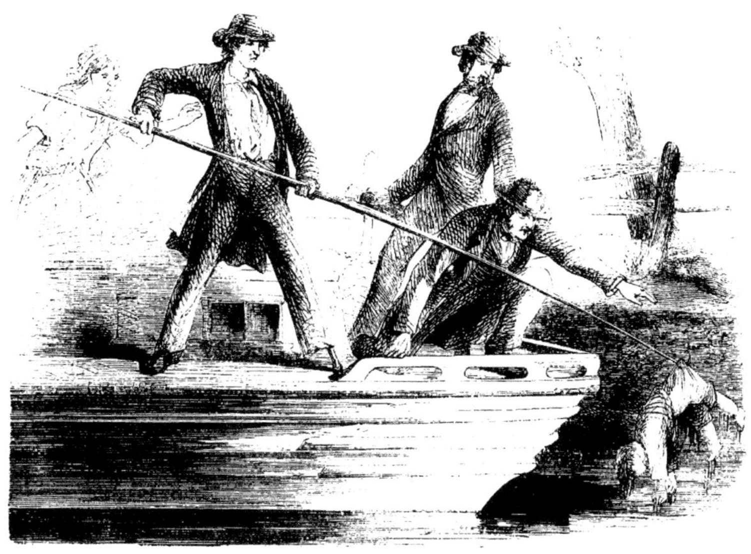

Illustrator John R. Chapin (*Neutral Tint*) takes the tiller as his brother Snell helps Captain Blivens fish his two-year-old son from the canal with a setting-pole and boat hook. Dressed in bed-gown and quilted calico skirt, Mrs Blivens stands behind her husband. The canal boat *Sarsey Fanney* (perhaps a colloquialism for *Sassy Fanny*) may have been named for Blivens' wife. (*Harper's New Monthly Magazine*, 1860)

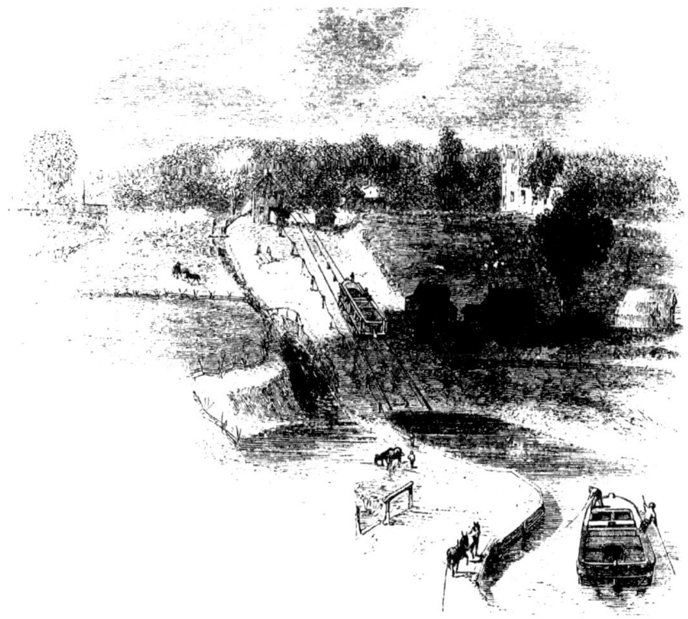

'The Plane At Rockaway', from 'Among The Nail-Makers', *Harper's New Monthly Magazine* (1860).

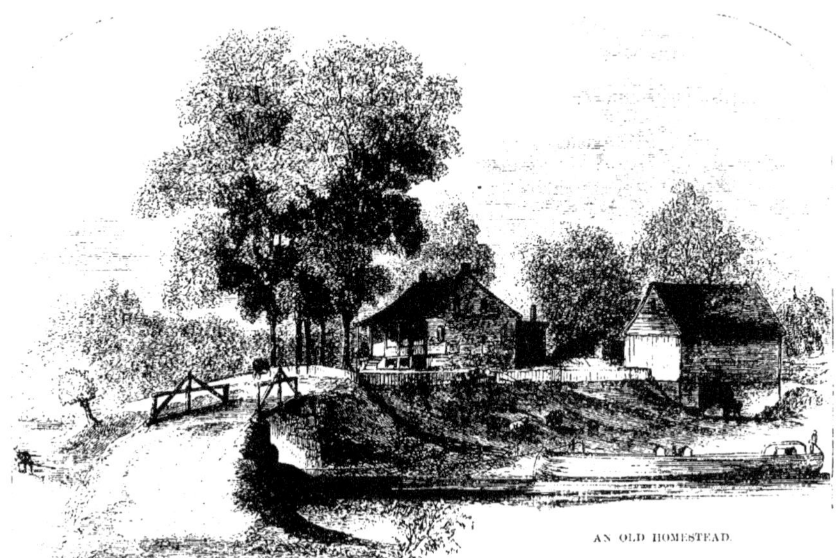

An old homestead where the road (County Route 513) crosses the canal within sight of Rockaway, possibly the residence of Rev. Barnabas King, pastor of the Rockaway Presbyterian Church, on West Main Street. (*Harper's New Monthly Magazine*, 1860)

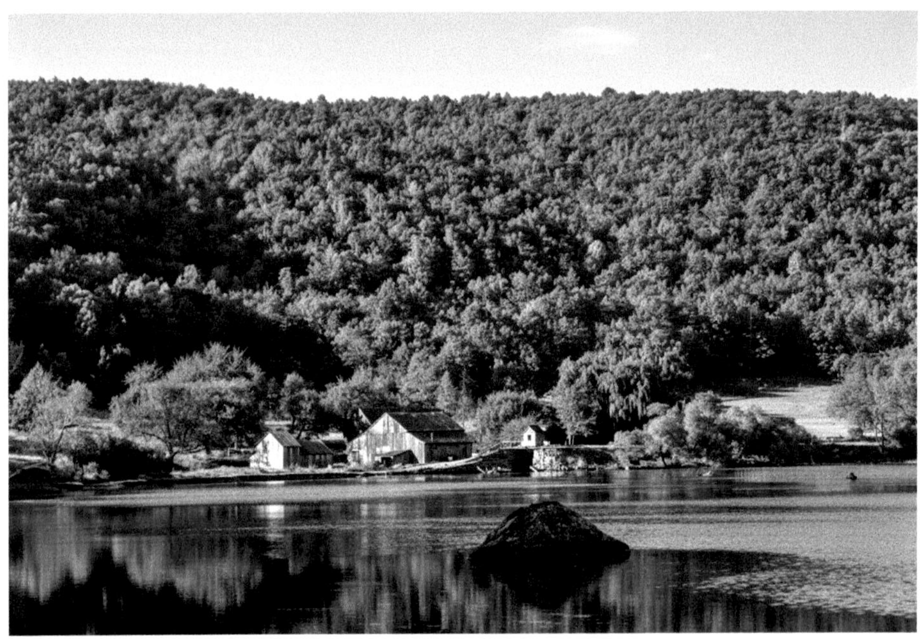

The canal entered the impounded Musconetcong River (Saxton Lake) through a lock along Waterloo Road at Guinea Hollow in Allamuchy Township, originally known as Baggot's Lock. Note the footbridge across the lock. (*Historic American Engineering Record, Library of Congress*)

2, 3, and 4 West, and Nos. 2, 3, 11 and 12 East), the guard lock at Saxton Falls and the tide lock at Jersey City were lengthened to 100 feet clear in the chamber.[32] Sixteen lift locks, four guard locks and two tide locks remained to be lengthened before 'the full benefit of this improvement' could be realized.[33]

Talcott reported the annual cost per plane increased by 22 percent, from $1,106 to $1,351, likely due to the increased tonnage carried on the canal. He also noted no provision was made during the original construction of the stone aqueduct over the Passaic River at Little Falls to prevent water from finding its way into mortar joints and seams, causing injury when it froze. Repeated year after year, this process resulted in accumulated damage that seriously endangered the stability of the masonry structure.

> To prevent further injury from this cause, the water-way of the aqueduct has been lined since the close of navigation with pine plank, and made perfectly water-tight by the use of concrete and grout between the lining and the masonry, and by caulking and paying the joints of the planking.[34]

The company also built a new bulkhead or pier, 300 feet long and 120 feet wide, on the east side of the basin in Jersey City.

To save 'half a mile of difficult and tedious navigation' and 'one third of a day in each round trip,' Talcott strongly recommended altering the line of the canal at Dover to make it 'comparatively straight, and easy to navigate,' substituting one inclined plane for five locks.[35] In that vicinity, Locks Nos. 3 and 4 were situated about a mile apart, while the next three locks were so close together that boats practically ran out of one and into another. Though Talcott estimated the cost of this improvement at $60,000; it would result in savings of $11,000 per season, given the current trade on the canal, and, with a trade equal to the canal's full capacity, 'at least $25,000 per season.'[36]

On 12 March 1862, the *Sussex Register* took note when an iron drum weighing 13 tons, cast by the Novelty Works in New York, was placed in position in the center of Plane No. 3 West at Mount Olive, near Stanhope, for hoisting up canal boats. With the resumption of navigation on 1 April 1862, the *New Jersey Herald* noted,

> [...] this route is fast becoming a favorite one for the transportation of coal, for the trade of New York City and eastern parts. The coal trade of the canal for 1861 was about 400,000 tons—upwards of 150,000 tons being taken through to New York and upwards of 115,000 tons being shipped from their wharves at Jersey City. The coal is from the Lehigh and Scranton regions, the Scranton being loaded on the line of the canal at Washington, NJ. The whole tonnage of the canal last year was upwards of 600,000 tons.

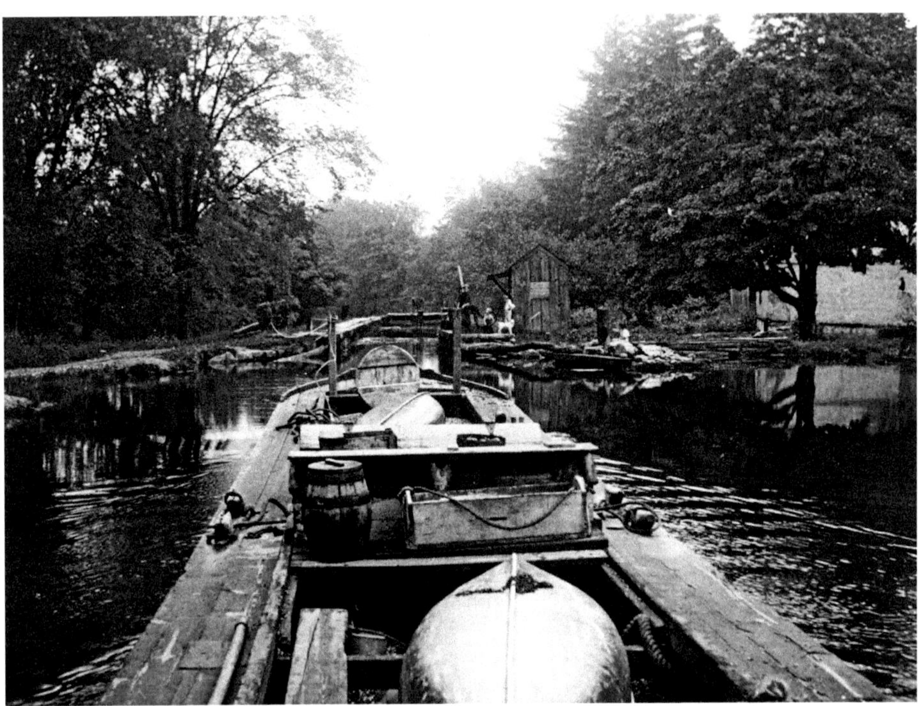

A boat approaches Lock No. 2 East in Wharton, NJ, also known as 'Bird's Lock'. (*Historic American Engineering Record, Library of Congress*)

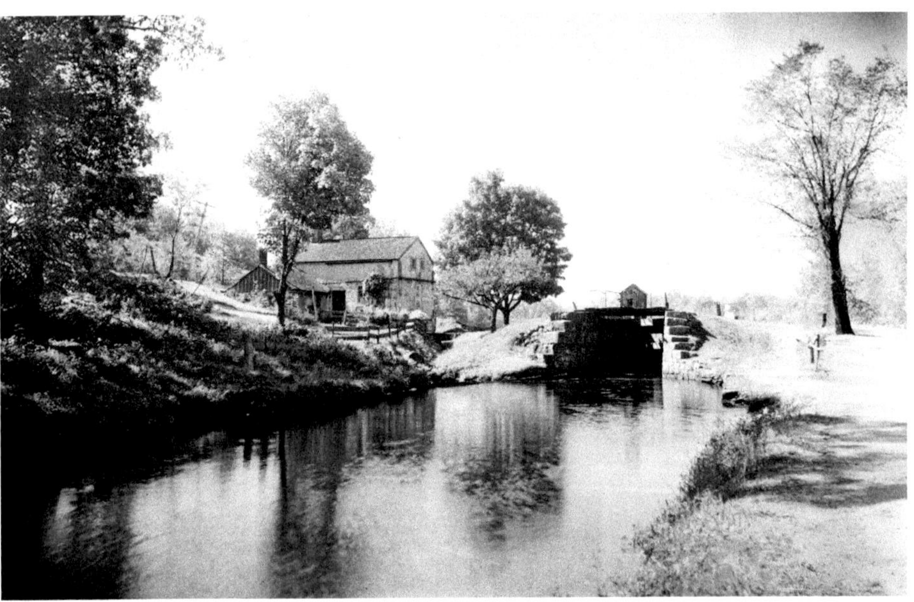

This photograph, taken by Newark photographer George S. Richardson *c.* 1905, shows Lock No. 2 East in Wharton, NJ. The lock tender's house is wrapped with a cable from one of the inclined planes to bind its deteriorating walls. (*Library of Congress*)

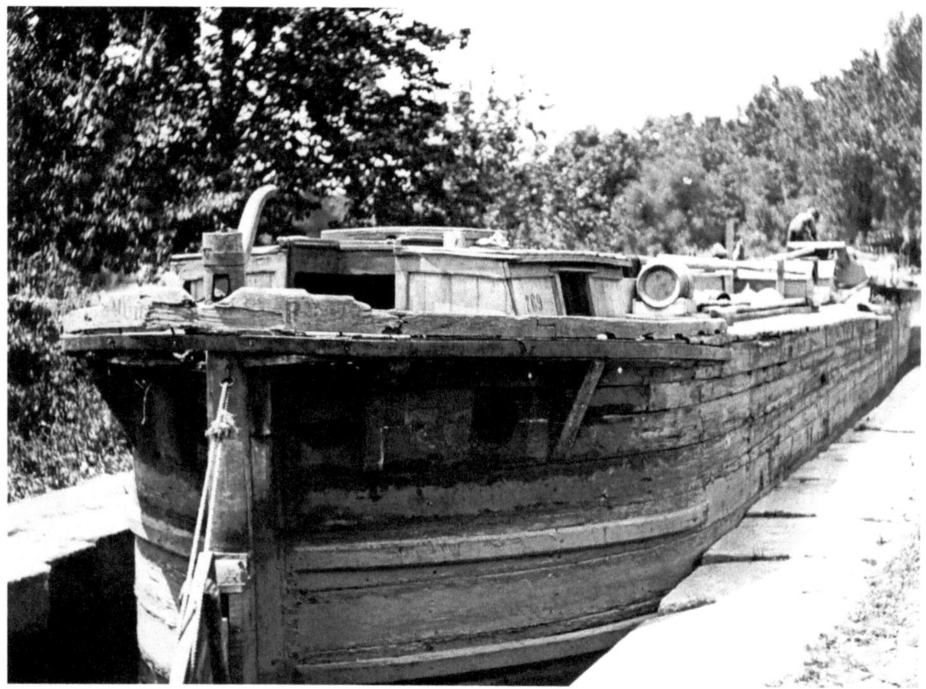

Boat No. 769 passes a lock near Boonton, NJ, *c.* 1890. (*Detroit Publishing Company, Library of Congress*)

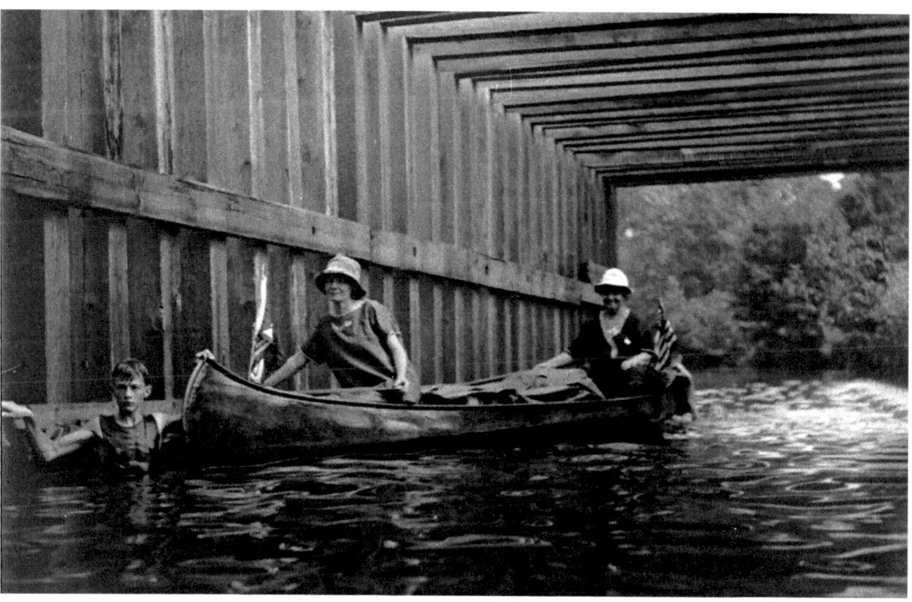

This view of canoeists inside the Little Falls aqueduct shows planking installed to prevent damage to the masonry from seepage and freezing. (*Historic American Engineering Record, Library of Congress*)

When all the improvements that are contemplated are finished, 1,500,000 tons can be transported easily.[37]

But, in May 1862, the annual report of the Morris Canal Company reflected a decrease in trade, due to a prostration of the coal and iron interests subsequent to the outbreak of Civil War.[38] Income from tolls and other sources was $201,848, down from $355,710 the previous year—the heaviest income ever received to date. Despite the dip in profits, the Morris Canal carried 620,369 tons of freight and brought nearly $17,000 more in revenues than it had in 1858. The *Herald* concluded: 'All things considered, the year's results should be a source of gratification to stockholders and to all interested in the securities of the company.' The editor pointedly admired 'its machinery for ascending to or descending from the levels, being the most simple, complete and expeditious of any canal of anything like the same length in the world.'[39]

A deluge of rain swelled streams and destroyed many bridges on 4 June 1862. The Great Freshet was especially ruinous in the Lehigh region, where floodwaters reached 27 feet high on the Mauch Chunk dam. The northernmost dam at White Haven burst in the dead of night, releasing a torrent that tore canal boats from their moorings, swept away bridges, uprooted trees, undermined foundations and drowned sleeping residents, together with their livestock. The high canal lock at Mauch Chunk, which withstood the Great Freshet of 1841, gave way, engulfing at least fifty canal boats and their occupants. Boats loaded with coal were later found high and dry on mountainsides. The *Friends' Intelligencer* described 'ruined fields of grain, stranded boats upon three great rivers, tottering and deserted houses, and at least one hundred dead bodies, dashed by a wild current against mountain rocks or floating logs.'[40] The Delaware River rose 17 feet above its previous high-water mark, submerging the lower portion of Easton and its canals. Floodwaters reached the second stories of buildings in Glendon, PA. The Lehigh Iron Company, the Carbon Iron Works, the Lehigh Valley Works, and Cooper's Furnace shut down and a scarcity of coal threatened operations at the Allentown Works and Thomas Iron Company.

Although embankments, dams and locks on the Lehigh Canal were ruined for miles, the Lehigh Valley Railroad was not seriously injured. The Morris Canal escaped direct harm from the storm, but it suffered with other canals in the loss of boats and business. Coal prices remained high until the Lehigh Canal was restored to operation between Easton and Mauch Chunk in October 1862.[41] Thereafter, a steady increase in supply reduced prices by New Year. The Morris Canal, with 1,000 boats in service between Jersey City and Phillipsburg, hired men in November to break ice in an effort to stay open as long as possible. The final report for the fiscal year ending on 28 February 1863 noted completion of the work of rebuilding the planes on the plan adopted in 1850 at a cost of $679,101.[42] Planes Nos. 6 and 9 West and Plane No. 12 East were reconstructed with double tracks at a cost of $101,128 and the remaining twenty planes with a single track at a cost of $577,973. Shipping facilities at Port Delaware and Port Washington were also improved. The canal carried 612,018 tons in 1862.

Business was brisk the following season. By 1 September 1863, receipts ran $40,000 ahead of the previous year. Coal was going up in price because of the difficulty of obtaining men to work the mines in wartime; laborers were scarce, even at $1.50 per day, and machinery was rapidly taking the place of men called into military service. The boating season ended on 15 December 1863, and the annual report stated that traffic showed 'a very gratifying increase over that of last year, which was larger than the year before.' Receipts for the fiscal year amounted to $65,207, an increase of $26,178 over the previous year. The company earned $211,772 in 1863, an increase of $44,432 over the previous year. These earnings paid for increased expenses, the interest on bonds, a 10-percent dividend on preferred stock and a 3½-percent dividend on common stock, leaving a balance of $16,490. The canal carried 718,519 tons in 1863, an increase over the previous year of 6,501 tons. But there were ominous clouds on the horizon. On 17 June 1863, directors of the Morris and Essex Railroad, meeting in Newark, decided to extend their line

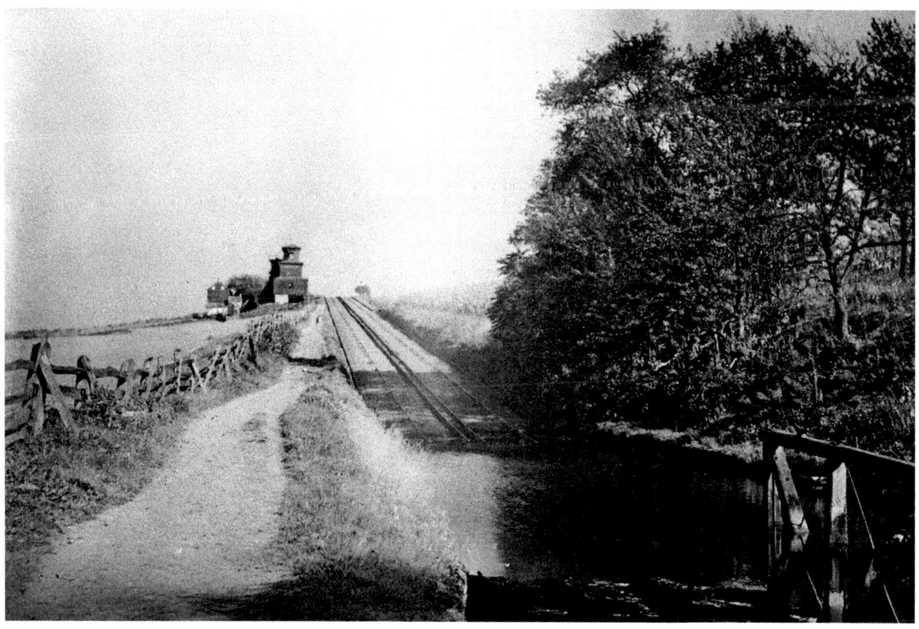

Inclined Plane No. 9 West at Port Warren was the longest inclined plane on the Morris Canal and one of three double-tracked planes. (*Historic American Engineering Record, Library of Congress*)

to Phillipsburg, offering direct competition for the canal's trade. Work on the Morris and Essex extension commenced at Phillipsburg on 10 May 1864.

Expending $48,559 on permanent improvements in 1863, the company enlarged the lift lock at the head of the Pompton Feeder to allow boats to reach the Ryerson Ironworks, 2 miles up the Pompton River. An outlet lock was constructed into Mill Creek at Jersey City, thereby increasing facilities for passing boats to and from New York Bay. Work resumed on lengthening locks to accommodate longer boats and increased tonnage; this effort was suspended at the outbreak of war after only nine locks were completed, leaving twenty-two lift and guard locks to be enlarged. Chief engineer William H. Talcott urged the substitution of an inclined plane for three lift locks west of Port Washington and another for two lift locks near Dover, so as to 'do away with the necessity of lengthening five locks, and reduce the number to be lengthened east of Port Washington to thirteen.'[43] He also recommended deepening the canal to hold 6 feet of water, thereby enabling boats to carry 100-ton cargoes. In his opinion, these improvements could not be delayed any longer as the Morris and Essex Railroad, once extended to Easton would become a competitive carrier of coal and iron ore, forcing the canal to reduce tolls to the lowest possible rates, despite the increasing cost of labor and materials.

After a dry winter, Lake Hopatcong stood 5 feet lower in March 1864 than it was ever known to be in spring. Two days of heavy rains caused a bad break in the canal between Waterloo and Hackettstown on 16 May 1864, carrying away part of the railroad embankment. The canal operated for 261 days between 23 March and 10 December 1864, carrying 723,927 tons of freight—an increase of 5,408 tons over the previous year. Although partly offset by an increase of 4,982 tons from the Scranton region, the Lehigh coal trade was down 24,574 tons from 1863. The decline in coal tonnage was attributed to a scarcity of miners during wartime, but railroads were clearly making inroads. On the other hand, ore tonnage exceeded that of 1863 by 32,257 tons. This partly reflected the recent construction of a 3½-mile, horse-powered railway, which transferred ore from the Trenton Iron Company's Hibernia mine to canal boats at Rockaway for shipment to their furnace in Phillipsburg. Four trains of eight cars each conveyed 160 to 180 tons of ore daily during summer months.

The annual report for 1864 included memorials to president Ephraim Marsh, who died suddenly of heart failure at his son's residence on Schooleys Mountain on 28 August 1864 aged sixty-eight years, and to the company's late secretary, Lewis N. Condit. Chief engineer William H. Talcott was elected president and civil engineer John Dod Ward, of Jersey City, became vice-president and general manager.[44] John Rogers, cashier of a Burlington bank, became secretary, and Alexander Peter Berthoud accepted the office

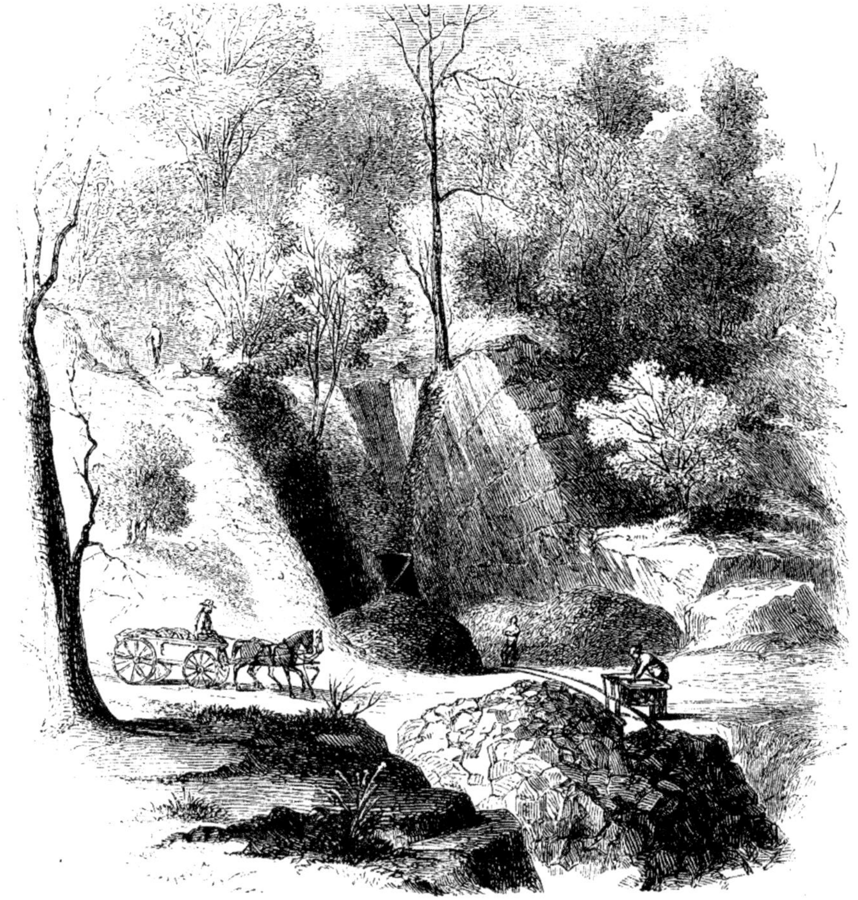

'Entrance To Hibernia Mine' from 'Artist-Life In The Highlands of New Jersey', *Harper's New Monthly Magazine* (April 1860)

of assistant engineer and superintendent. Income from all sources amounted to $590,392, leaving $353,935 in net earnings after meeting expenses. The company paid a 10-percent dividend to stockholders. Projecting a large business, the company prepared to open navigation with a thousand boats.

Proprietors of the Glendon Ironworks in Pennsylvania incorporated the Ogden Mining Railroad and Manufacturing Company on 19 February 1864. They employed 150 men and horses to grade a 9.86-mile railway connecting the Ogden mine atop Sparta Mountain to Nolan's Point on Lake Hopatcong, where there was a sufficient depth of water to accommodate canal boats.[45] Commencing operations in the spring of 1866, the Ogden mine railroad was built and equipped at a cost of $452,993 to haul iron ore from the Ogden, Weldon, Ford and Schofield mines. Difficulty in descending the steep grade of Sparta Mountain deterred extension of the Ogden Mine Railroad to

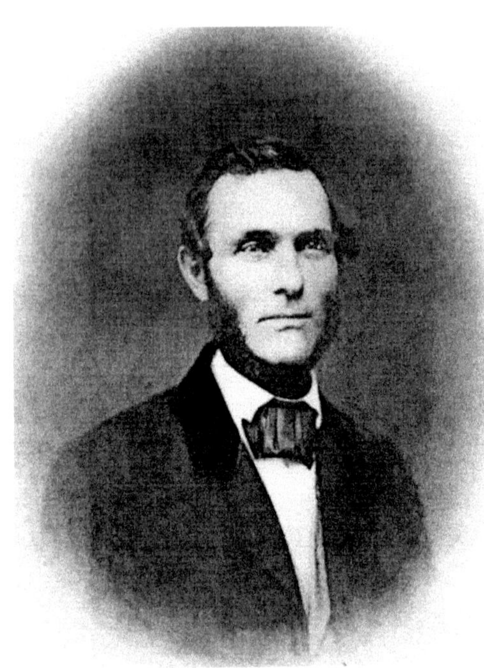

Left: Portrait of William H. Talcott. (Talcott, *Talcott Pedigree in England and America From 1558 to 1876*, 1876)

Below: Portion of *Map of the Rail Roads of New Jersey, and parts of adjoining states* (Philadelphia: James McGuigan, 1869). (*Library of Congress*)

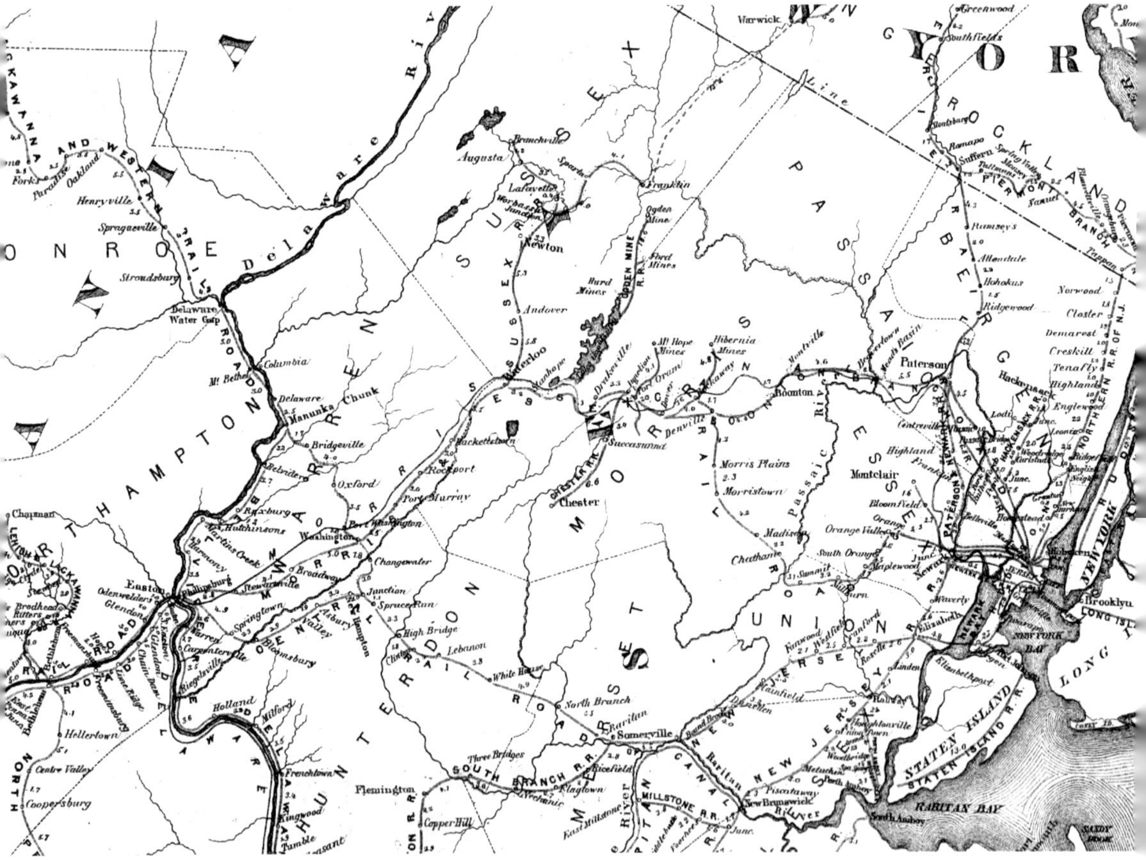

Franklin and Ogdensburg or its connection to the Morris and Essex Railroad. Mules, however, carted bulk ore from Franklin and separated zinc ore from Sterling Hill (Ogdensburg) up the mountain, using stone steps or terraces, for transshipment over the mine railroad.

Years after the fact, one elderly Sparta resident recalled seeing a fleet of as many as fifteen canal boats anchored to the roadstead in Woodport, where Lehigh and Scranton coal was unloaded for Franklin, Ogdensburg and Sparta.[46] Local farmers in need of coal took on a load of ore at the zinc mines, which they carted to Woodport or Henderson Rocks on Lake Hopatcong to exchange for coal. Boats floated the Passaic Company's ore from Nolan's Point to Jersey City for processing into white oxide of zinc to manufacture paint.

Northern industrialization during the Civil War proved profitable for the Morris Canal. After an expensive program of enlargement, total tonnage rose, due largely to increasing transport of coal and iron ore. About 500 tons of iron ore from the Mount Pleasant Mine, belonging to Fuller, Lord and Company, of Boonton, was carried by railroad monthly to the Morris Canal at Port Oram—named for mine superintendent and storeowner Robert F. Oram—a village of nearly a dozen houses that came into existence during the war.[47] On 14 June 1865, Israel D. Condict, of Millburn, NJ, president the Musconetcong Ironworks, announced construction of a large cupola furnace at Stanhope to make Bessemer steel. He also owned the rolling mill at Rockaway, which employed fifty to seventy-five men.

Prosperity proved all too brief as railroads, heretofore feeders of the canal, became fierce competitors. At the annual stockholders meeting in Hoboken on 14 June 1865, the Morris and Essex Railroad Company announced contracts to purchase twenty-eight locomotives and 400 eight-wheel coal cars in anticipation of coal traffic on their extension to Phillipsburg. Two cars loaded with coal at the Mauch Chunk mines passed over the Morris and Essex Railroad to Hoboken on 15 November 1865. The Atlantic and Great Western Railway Company, which leased the Morris and Essex Railroad, contracted for grading the Boonton Branch between Denville and Bloomfield on 30 January 1866, further threatening the Morris Canal with a loss of trade.

On 1 January 1866, the Morris Canal Company declared a dividend of 5 percent on preferred stock and 6 percent on consolidated stock.[48] The canal opened on 29 March 1866, and boating proceeded without major incident until July, when the turbine at Plane No. 9 East broke, suspending navigation at that place for seven days. Stockholders and others interested in the economic future of the Morris Canal embarked on an exploratory trip on 24 July 1866, in a canal boat under command of Commodore Frederick Engle, superintendent of the Philadelphia Navy Yard, especially fitted for their use. A pair of fast trotting mules provided motive power. The party consisted

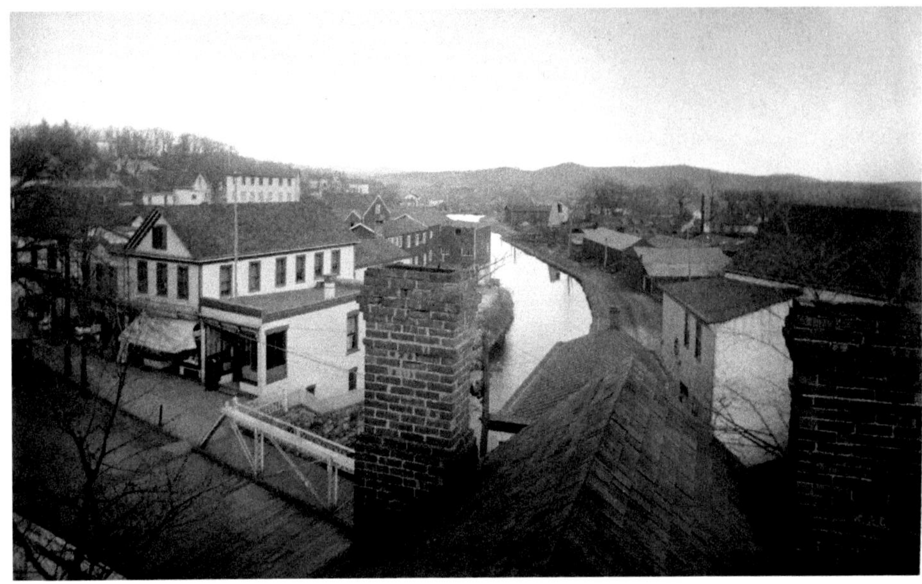

This photograph was taken from the belvedere of the Rockaway Hotel at the intersection of Wall and Main Streets in Rockaway, NJ. Dock Street and Friendship Place now occupy this portion of the canal bed. With the addition of modern storefronts, these commercial buildings still stand on the east side of Wall Street, including the post office, alongside the canal. The low building, just below the hotel's roofline, was a drugstore. Behind it, the shed addition to the white, framed building housed the stage and scenery of the Opera House, located on the second story of the general store on Main Street. The Union Foundry and Machine Shop can be seen on the bank of the canal in the distance. (*Historic American Engineering Record, Library of Congress*)

of Asa Packer, of Pennsylvania; former United States Senator John C. Ten Eyck; former Assembly Speaker John M. Hill; Colonel Cornelius Stewart, of Warren County; F. Wolcott Jackson, general superintendent of the New Jersey Railroad; his brother John P. Jackson, of Newark; and a large company of gentlemen from Philadelphia and New Jersey. Starting from Phillipsburg, they anchored for the night at Hackettstown, making a side trip to Schooley's Mountain. The next morning 'the excursionists made their way up through the rocky fastnesses along the canal, over the planes, and into Lake Hopatcong, whose romantic coves and wooded islands furnished them with an idea of the beautiful in Jersey scenery that few of them anticipated.'[49] They stayed in Dover that evening, after touring mines and factories along the route. The Lehigh Coal and Navigation Company leased the Delaware Division Canal in August 1866.

In October, a large reservoir constructed on Garret Mountain for the Paterson waterworks suddenly gave way, washing out a section of the canal below that took four days to repair. By the time the canal closed on 12 December 1866 it had carried 889,220 tons, about 15 percent more than the previous year.[50] The extension of tracks and chutes at Port Delaware, commenced in 1865, was completed, creating facilities to load fifty boats of 62 tons each daily.[51] While gross earnings of $616,350 exceeded any former year of operation, net earnings of $275,970 reflected 'a reduction in the rates of toll made necessary by reductions in the rates of competing coal-carrying companies.'[52] President William H. Talcott recognized,

> The Morris and Essex Railroad was completed so far as to commence carrying coal and ore in the early part of last year. This road will now become a strong competitor for the way trade hitherto transported on the canal, particularly that of coal and iron ore, dividing this trade with the canal, and very likely compelling the work to be done at rates less remunerative than heretofore.[53]

During the previous year, Bessemer steel rails, instead of iron rails, were substituted for renewals on the planes at a cost of $9,000. Aqueducts over the Peckman River, near Little Falls, and over Hurd Brook at Dover were widened. Eleven thousand dollars was spent to erect houses for the use of locktenders, brakemen and ferrymen.

Street and navigational access to docks grew contentious as Jersey City's shoreline now began to 'fill' with piers, rail yards and waterfront industries.

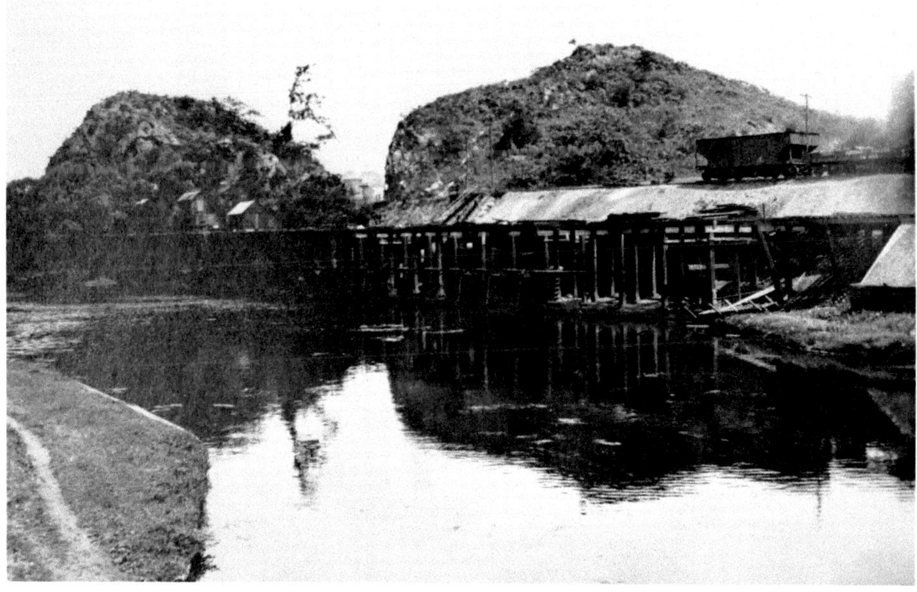

The Lehigh Valley Railroad made a deep cut through Mount Parnassus in Phillipsburg to allow passage for its tracks. Just beyond lay the coal chutes on the Morris Canal at Port Delaware. (*Historic American Engineering Record, Library of Congress*)

The Sugar House Company claimed the Morris Canal Company infringed upon their property rights in 1859 by constructing a pier from Washington Street, constricting access to what had been Communipaw Cove. To settle the dispute equitably, the New Jersey legislature leased land underwater in Jersey City to the Morris Canal Company for $20,000 in annual rent on 14 March 1867, but provided for open navigation through a channel of specified width. The Morris Canal's Big or South Basin became a tidewater inlet, 900 feet wide and 1,735 feet long, adjacent to the canal's terminus on the Hudson River.

Severe winter weather and the backwardness of spring delayed opening the canal about one week later than usual in 1867. The great demand and high prices paid for labor drew off many boatmen, making it impossible to keep all the company's boats manned and running. A great depression in coal markets and railroad competition for way-trade 'resulted in high freights and low tolls, and in a corresponding reduction in the receipts of the company.'[54] The transfer of coal at Port Delaware declined 5,584 tons by railroad and 34,085 tons by canal, but increased by 5,451 tons at Port Washington, resulting in an overall reduction of 34,218 tons of coal freighted. Ore shipments decreased by 615 tons over the previous year to 289,550 tons.[55] The Morris Canal freighted 822,741 tons of cargo in 1867, representing a 7½-percent decrease from the previous year. It earned $134,995 above expenses for repairs, navigation and management. With railroads and canals of greater capacity competing for the anthracite trade, William H. Talcott warned, 'it cannot be expected that the Morris Canal can retain its share of the coal trade without corresponding enlargement and improvements.'[56] Supervisors continued to lengthen locks by 10 feet whenever a lock required general repairs. Consequently, seventeen locks were enlarged, leaving fifteen to be rebuilt at an estimated cost of $30,000. A 15-percent increase in the tonnage of boats was projected upon completion of the work. To further increase capacity, two 'Osgood's Patent Underwater Excavators' were dredging the canal, deepening its water while raising the height of the banks.[57]

William H. Talcott, president of the Morris Canal Company, died at Jersey City, aged sixty, on 8 December 1868. He was a founder of the Thomas Iron Company and interested in the furnaces being built at Port Oram (Wharton, NJ) at the time of his death. He was also a founder of the American Society of Civil Engineers. One eulogist noted that when Talcott first arrived as Western Division superintendent in 1845, the Morris Canal

> [...] was little more than a ditch of no profit to anyone. Under his management it developed into one of the principal coal-carrying companies of the country, and, although it had a competing railroad on each side, paid regular dividends upon both preferred and common stock. The system of inclined planes used upon the canal in their improved form was the creation

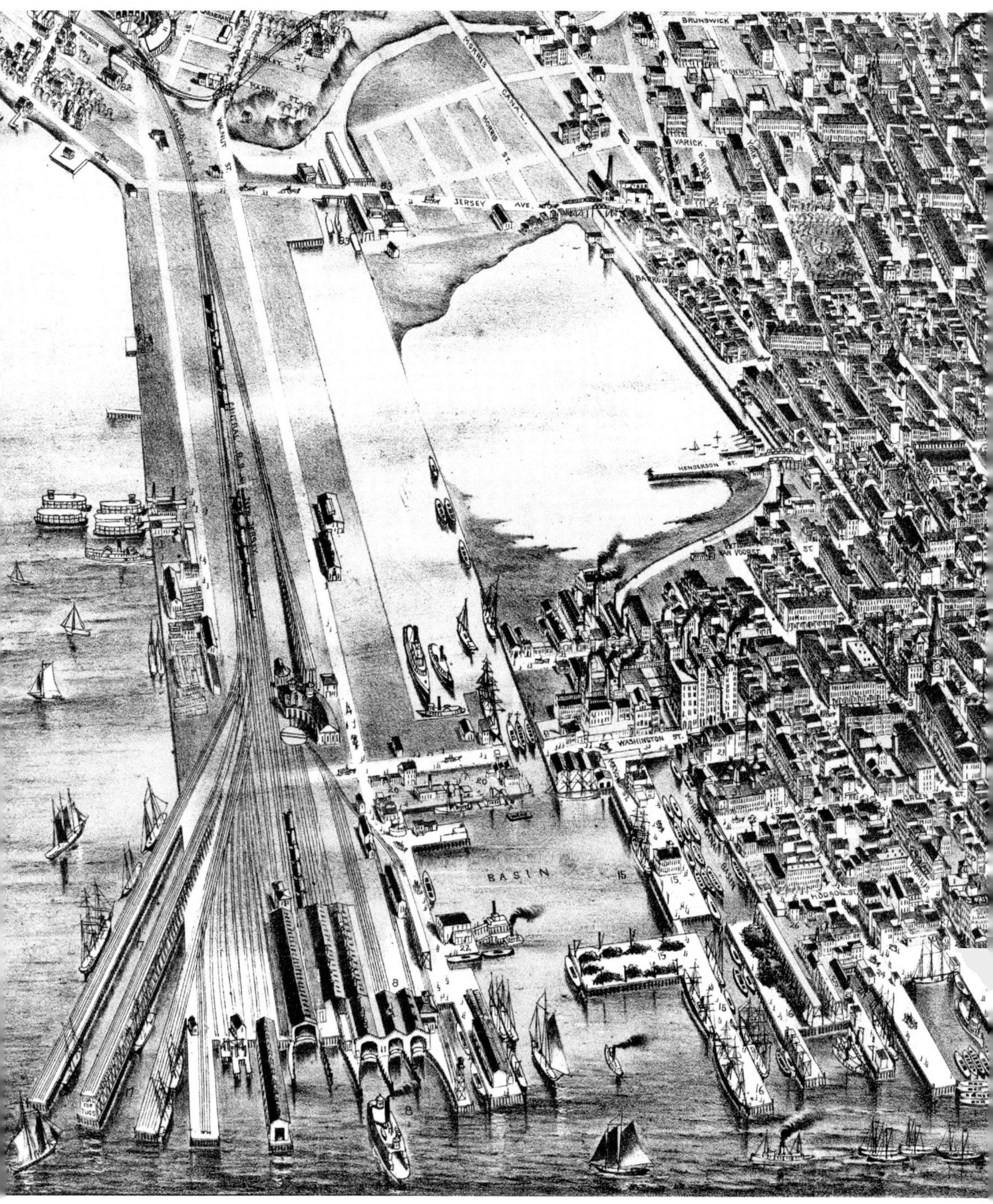

This 1883 panoramic view shows: (15) 'Morris Canal Docks, Lehigh Valley R. R. Co., Lessees'; (16) 'Lehigh Valley Coal Co.'s Pier'; (17) 'Communipaw Coal Co.'s Pier'; (21) 'Havemeyer Sugar Refining Co.'s Works'; and (22) 'J. McCarthy & Bro., Floating Dry Docks, Morris Canal Basin'. From *Jersey City, NJ* (Boston: O. H. Bailey & Co., 1883).

of his brain, and was absolutely essential for the successful operation of the canal. They attracted the attention of engineers, not only throughout the United States, but in foreign countries.[58]

Jacob F. Randolph, longtime vice-president and superintendent for two years, succeeded him.

The Morris Canal operated from 1 April to 8 December 1868, carrying 744,412 tons—a decrease of 78,507 tons attributed to growing railroad competition and a seven-week coalminers' strike over reduced wages in a glutted marketplace.[59] Over the course of the 1868 boating season, the Lehigh Canal supplied 161,828 tons of coal, the Lehigh Valley Railroad delivered 107,387 tons at Port Delaware and the Warren Railroad delivered 80,977 tons at Port Washington, making a total coal tonnage of 350,172 tons. Of 269,672 tons of ore transported on the canal, the Lehigh Valley received 120,603 tons, while 56,044 tons were transshipped at Port Washington, leaving 93,025 tons to way-trade. Forced by competition to lower its rates, the annual report for the fiscal year ending 27 February 1869 showed net earnings of $187,090, a decrease of $26,176 from the previous year. Since Bessemer steel rails laid at two planes in the winter of 1856–57 showed little signs of wear, the company purchased and installed 100 tons of steel rails on two planes and part of a third. The Delaware, Lackawanna and Western Railroad leased the Morris and Essex Railroad in December 1868, agreeing to complete the Boonton Branch as soon as possible.

The canal opened on 25 March 1869 after a busy winter season when Lock No. 13 (later 14) East at Beavertown (Lincoln Park) was almost entirely rebuilt and the locks at Dover thoroughly repaired.[60] A coal miners' suspension of work starting on 7 May 1869 halted coal shipments for ten weeks, compelling many boatmen to find other employment. When coal traffic resumed on 1 July, the company had to purchase and lease mules at an attractive rate per trip to induce boatmen to return. In June 1869, the directors traveled over the canal from Jersey City to Easton in a steam tug named the *Gussie*. En route, president Jacob F. Randolph entertained them at his Bloomfield residence. They stayed for successive nights in Dover and Hackettstown, arriving at Easton on 25 June 1869. This experimental voyage was intended to show how, in time, steam tugs might substitute for mules.

On 4 October 1869, a great freshet opened five breaks within the distance of 3 miles from Port Delaware. The largest rupture, about 500 feet in length, occurred ¾ mile from Andover Furnace in Phillipsburg and washed out 800 feet of the towpath embankment, excavating the bottom of the canal to a depth of 10 feet. It took two weeks and an expenditure of $18,621 to repair. While coal shipments from Port Delaware resumed on 19 October 1869, damages on the Lehigh Canal prevented shipments from that source until 19

November. Shipments of ore to the Lehigh furnaces were cut off, resulting in an overall decrease of 50,000 tons. In 1869, the Morris Canal received 78,787 tons of coal from the Lehigh Canal; 134,570 tons from the Lehigh Valley Railroad at Port Delaware; 68,269 tons at Port Washington; and 11,417 tons of bituminous coal and 11,322 tons of anthracite, shipped westward from Jersey City and Newark, for an aggregate of 804,365 tons. Of the 227,696 tons of ore shipped that year, 93,574 tons crossed the Delaware River to the Lehigh Valley; 47,809 tons were transshipped on the Delaware, Lackawanna and Western Railroad at Port Washington; and 85,318 tons were way-trade along the canal. After the canal closed on 5 December 1869, a mild winter enabled the company to enlarge its basin to twice its former width for nearly a half mile at Port Delaware, allowing more boats to receive coal from the Lehigh Valley Railroad. To ward against future shortages and inconveniences to customers, the Morris Canal Company began to stockpile 50,000 tons of coal under the trestlework there.[61]

The canal resumed business on 28 March 1870. That September, the *American Railroad Journal* reported,

> The bond and shareholders of the Morris Canal will be glad to learn that the work has been put in most excellent order along the whole line—and added to this the President of the Company has paid off the last note against the Company, and it is now free from debt, a thing that has never occurred before since its organization.[62]

The canal carried 707,572 tons before loading was discontinued at Mauch Chunk on 25 November, at Port Delaware on 3 December, and at Port Washington on 7 December.[63] Owing to another coal strike, business was lighter than usual in 1870—only fifty canal boats passed through Stanhope daily, whereas sixty-five boats per day was the average in a busy season. Transportation rates were reduced on 1 December 1870 to $1.06 per ton between Phillipsburg and tidewater, a decline of 64 cents per ton over the previous year. Therefore, although the canal carried 57,373 tons more than in 1869, receipts were $39,696 less. The opening of the Boonton Branch of the Delaware, Lackawanna and Western Railroad to Paterson threatened a further loss of trade in 1871.[64] To remain competitive, work progressed on deepening the canal to 6 feet to accommodate passage of 100-ton cargoes. One hundred tons of steel rails were installed on four more planes and connections were made with all the railroad companies at Phillipsburg. The canal company also purchased 275 young mules and horses for towing boats.

Combining with coal companies to form monopolies, railroads were able to double their carrying charges, thereby doubling the price of anthracite coal to consumers.[65] They also began to buy up canals to reduce or eliminate

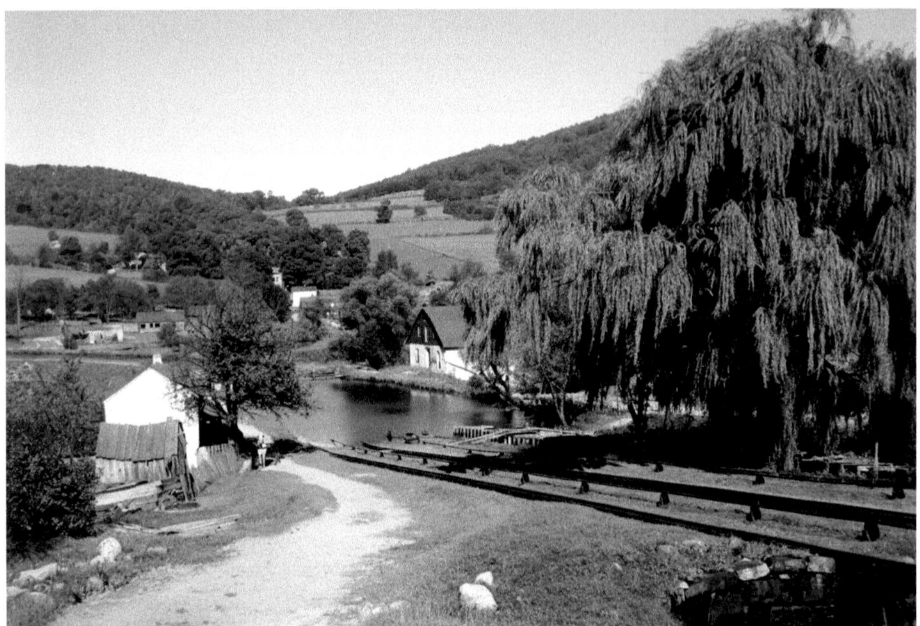

Harvey S. Cole's Feed Mill on Pohatcong Creek at the foot of Inclined Plane No. 7 West at Bowerstown, a mile north-west of Washington, NJ. The belfry of the schoolhouse is visible in the distance. (*Historic American Engineering Record, Library of Congress*)

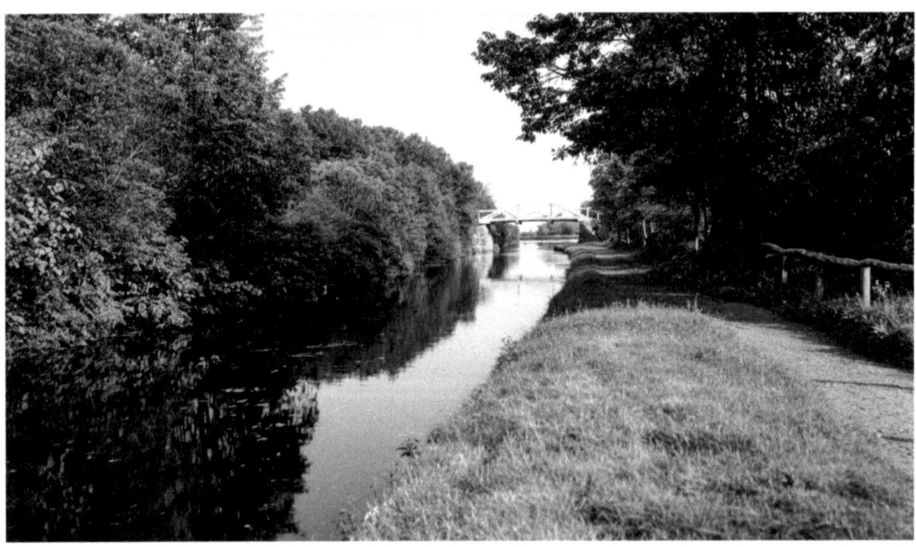

A mule driver on the towpath heard a rumbling noise as a whirlpool suddenly formed in the canal near Broadway in Warren County, NJ, on 19 June 1871. He only got several yards past the spot when a sinkhole 40 feet in diameter opened in the bottom of the canal, stranding his boat. Fifty men were employed to repair the breach, which emptied 1½ miles of water from the 7-mile level. (*Historic American Engineering Record, Library of Congress*)

competition, especially for the New York market. The Delaware, Lackawanna and Western Railroad and the Central Railroad of New Jersey independently offered to guarantee 7-percent dividends in perpetuity on preferred stock of the Morris Canal Company and 3-percent on consolidated stock in exchange for a long-term lease. The directors of the Morris Canal Company, however, agreed on 20 February 1871 to lease the canal to the Lehigh Valley Railroad for 999 years, on a guarantee of a 10-percent dividend on preferred stock and 4-percent on consolidated stock, subject to ratification by a majority of stockholders.[66] At this historic juncture, the directors closed their books with a testament to their accomplishments:

> In view of the probabilities of our works passing into other management, and of being enlarged and thereby made a still more important avenue of trade, it is proper here to make record.—That the present Morris Canal and Banking Company, organized in 1844 by the purchase of the works and franchises of the old company, has thus far performed the purposes which are laid down for it in the preamble to its charter, viz: 'To secure to the State a great public work, to be a great public benefit and advantage to the people of New Jersey.'[67]

6

BACK NUMBER

Whatever management by a railroad company portended, canalers continued their seasonal routine along the meandering channel, struggling from one level to the next. Five hundred boats plied the Morris Canal in November 1871, each about 80 feet in length, 12 in width and 6 in height, capable of transporting between 60 and 75 tons of cargo.[1] Most carried coal from Phillipsburg to Jersey City, some returning westward with loads of iron ore. A crew of three was ideal, allowing 'one at the helm, one at the horse, and one to wait on the other two.'[2] Two persons generally sufficed with either a captain hiring a boy at $15 a month and board, or, more commonly, two captains partnering to crew a boat. In the latter case, one tended the horse on the towpath as the other steered, exchanging stations every 5 miles. With that said, it was not at all uncommon for a captain and his wife to run a boat with their children, especially if they owned their own boat and horses. Such independent canalers received $1.10 per ton for freighting coal between Phillipsburg and Jersey City. Those who hired company boats but used their own horses occasionally took their families with them, though they often made other arrangements. While they received the same percentage as boat owners for transporting ore and coal, they paid 20 percent of tonnage in boat rental fees. The canal company also hired men at $50 a month and boys at $12 to $20 a month to run boats. The boys got free board, while hired men spent on average $20 per month for board. Under such terms, a reliable man with an iron constitution, spared from injury or sickness, could save nearly $30 a month over the course of a boating season.

The Morris Canal Company provided convenient stables, such as the large one built at Stanhope in July 1871 to accommodate thirty-six mules, leased for navigation purposes. It was built within sight of the massive new Furnace No. 2 of the Musconetcong Ironworks, reputed to be the largest such plant in the United States. Spurs of the Morris Canal and the Morris and Essex Railroad, both elevated about 35 feet above the furnace's hearth, approached its north side, depositing materials to supply the furnace on a stock bank some 15 feet lower. The furnace was built to produce from 325 to 350 tons of iron per week, requiring the handling and loading of 1,500 tons of materials weekly, or more than 100 tons every twelve hours.

A correspondent for the *New York Evening Post*, writing in November 1871, described those who lived on the canal as

[...] a class by themselves. Some are respectable people who seek this employment because it pays them better than any other business in which they can engage with as little capital. Others are from the cities, or without any homes, and they boat because they can do nothing else. These, at the approach of winter, disappear like grasshoppers or bears or other hibernating

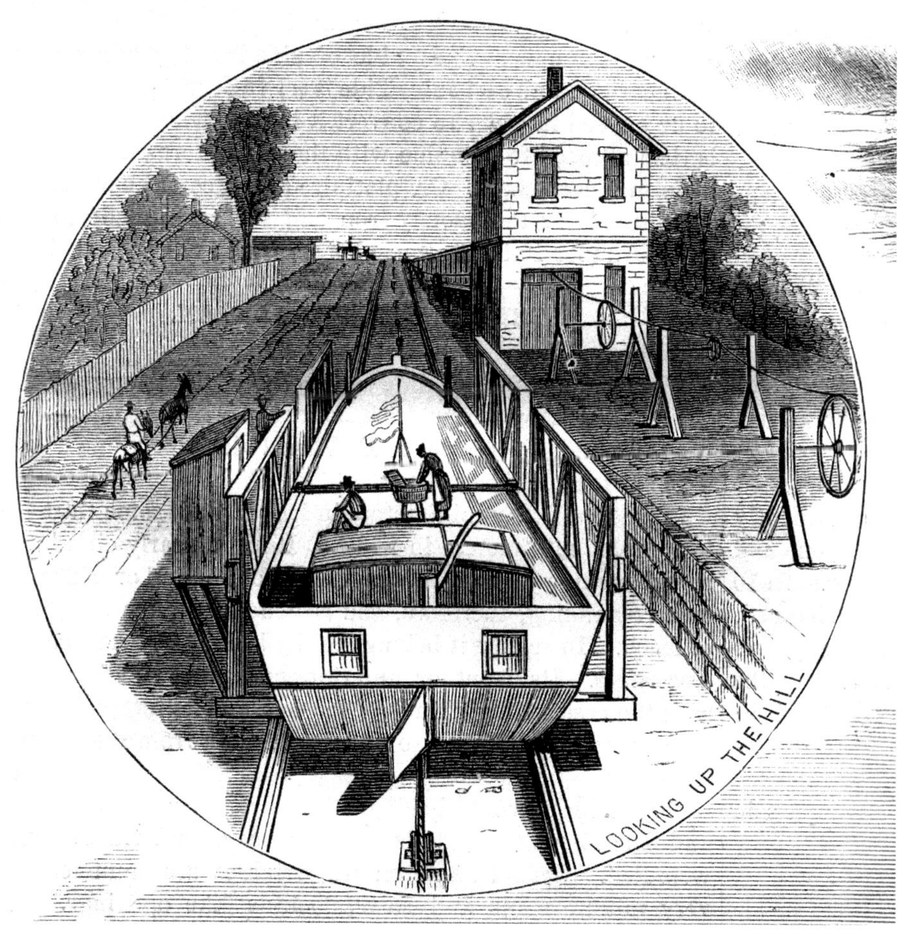

Women with washtub and laundry hanging out to dry on a boat ascending the Bloomfield plane. (*Scientific American*, 20 May 1882)

creatures; but at the approach of spring come out from their hiding places ready for another season of canal life.[3]

Hundreds of canal boats tied up for winter in the basin at the foot of Henderson Street (Marin Boulevard) in Jersey City with a plank walk placed rail-to-rail amidships providing access to land. Captains and their families inhabited nearly half of the mothballed fleet. Boats were thoroughly cleaned, stores for winter brought aboard, and children sent to three nearby schools.[4]

It was by no means an easy calling: boatmen were 'obliged to work all the time in all weather—in the hottest suns and the hardest rains—and, unlike most laboring classes, they must work from four or five o'clock in the morning till nine at night; and they do it all summer long.'[5] There were few diversions, except for 'the bouquet of wild flowers in the cabin and in the music they bring out of the long tin tubes with which they give to the lock-tender their signal of approach.'[6] The routine was invariably disagreeable and monotonous, yet, as our correspondent noted in 1871, 'it has such an air of independence and ease that those who get weary of it and quit it, often return to it of choice.'[7]

Captain and crew habitually awoke an hour and a half before sunrise, sitting down to a 'hard chuck' breakfast of coffee, baker's bread, butter and potatoes.[8] Once the animals were fed, utensils were cleaned and stowed away so as to get underway by 5 o'clock. If a family crew included children big enough to work, then they drove the horses; otherwise, the mother and father alternately performed this task. There was no dinner stop at midday, as horses and mules were fed from a basket of oats hung over their ears and under their snout. The crew's standard midday fare consisted of coffee, salt pork, boiled potatoes and beans. Supper was much the same as breakfast.

To gain firsthand experience of canal life, the correspondent for the *New York Evening Post* boarded the *Skipping Fawn* for a short trip.[9] Its crew consisted of the captain, his wife, thirteen-year-old son and eleven-year-old daughter. While aboard, the reporter observed the girl driving the horses—she having just relieved her brother of this task. Mother was busy with her sewing as her husband steered. He was not likely capable of walking the towpath for any stretch, having served three years in the Union Army before his wounded leg was amputated after the Battle of the Wilderness. In such condition, he was otherwise unemployable,

> [...] and hence he was driven to this kind of life. But having his family with him, his new life was not so unpleasant or unprofitable as he at first supposed it would be.[10]

Hiring a boat until saving enough to buy his own, he was thus able to make money 'faster than he could at any other business.' He routinely took on a

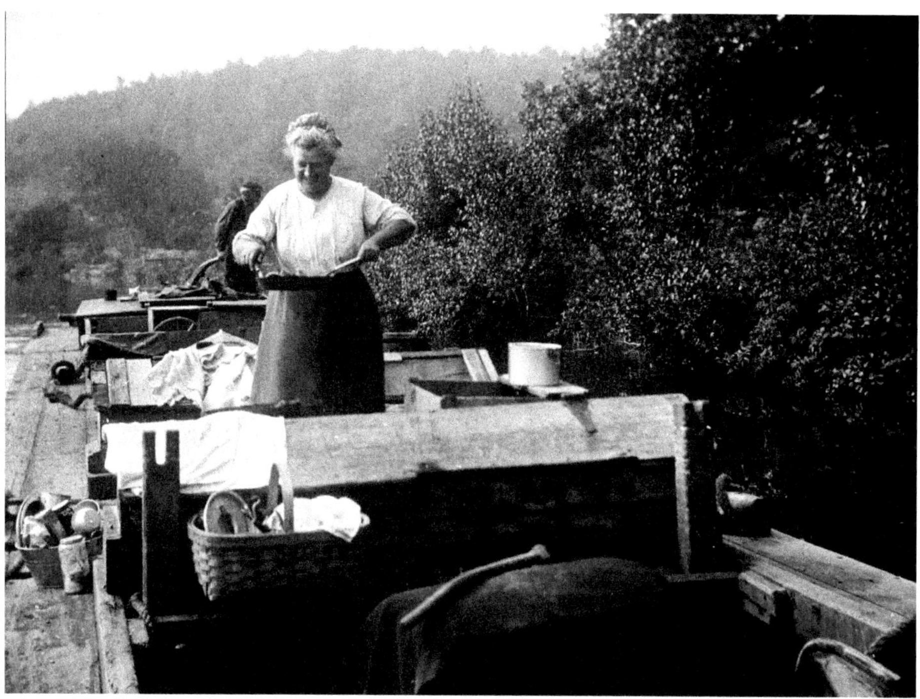

The captain's wife prepares a meal. (*Historic American Engineering Record, Library of Congress*)

load of coal at Phillipsburg on Mondays or Saturdays, delivering it to Jersey City at $1.10 per ton. On a 75-ton load, he earned $82.50. He might pick up a backload on the return trip, but like most who owned their own boats, he thought it paid 'better to return immediately to Easton to ship another load of coal.'[11] With a fair degree of luck, a boatman could complete two trips monthly, netting $165. Deducting 20 percent for necessaries and 30 percent more for provisions, a boat owner thereby set aside $82.50 in profit.

But it did not take a prophet to read the handwriting on the wall: once the Morris and Essex Railroad reached Phillipsburg in 1865, the Morris Canal proved inadequate to carry the necessary volume of business to remain competitive. The introduction of steel rails, which lowered the rates of railroad transportation, hastened its decline. Traffic and income for the canal culminated in 1866 at 889,220 tons and $616,350, declining to 707,572 tons and $391,549 in 1870. In contrast, the shipment of anthracite coal by all avenues of transport grew from an average of 12,000,000 net tons in 1863 to over 17,000,000 in 1869. While output declined to 15,600,000 tons in 1870, it recovered to 19,000,000 tons in 1871.[12]

As authorized by charter amendment in January 1871, the Morris Canal Company leased the canal with its corporate franchises, rights and privileges to its main coal supplier, the Lehigh Valley Railroad, on 17 April 1871. By offering generous terms to the canal's stockholders, the Lehigh Valley Railroad thus gained control of the canal's valuable waterfront property in Jersey City, opposite Manhattan, and instant parity with its main competitor, the Central Railroad of New Jersey. On 17 June 1872, *The Manufacturer and Builder* observed,

> Notwithstanding that water transportation is the cheapest, there are such drawbacks in canal navigation that the railroads have not only successfully competed with canals, but taken the trade entirely from some of them. So the canals along the Lehigh River, above Mauch Chunk, have been abandoned and allowed to fall in ruins, the railroads there doing all the transportation. The Morris and Essex Railroad has taken all the trade of the Morris Canal, which has been a bad investment all along, for reason of its small capacity and system of inclines in place of locks.[13]

From all sources, the Lehigh Valley Railroad carried 3,877,179 tons of coal in 1872.[14] Its total coal tonnage for 1873 exceeded 4,000,000 tons.[15] The Lehigh Coal and Navigation Company discontinued shipping coal over the Morris Canal, once it was leased to the Lehigh Valley Railroad, thenceforth feeding waterborne coal exclusively to the Delaware and Raritan Canal via the Delaware Division Canal. The Central Railroad of New Jersey leased the Lehigh Canal in February 1874.[16] The large business of transshipping coal and iron ore between the Delaware, Lackawanna and Western Railroad and canal boats at Port Washington, NJ, also dwindled away as 'the Lehigh Valley [Railroad] raised the tolls to such an extent as to make transportation that way prohibitory.'[17]

New rancor developed when John B. Haight, tax collector for Jersey City, assessed the Lehigh Valley Railroad for $6,500 in taxes on the canal's tidewater basins. Protesting on the Lehigh Valley Railroad's behalf, the Morris Canal Company argued before the Court of Errors and Appeals in March 1873 that the canal was a tenant of the state and therefore not liable to taxation.[18] Legal contention over taxability on lands formerly underwater drove the railroad company to seek abandonment of the Morris Canal.

A winnowing of luxuriant economic growth seemed overdue. For as long as anyone could remember, natural occurrences of waterpower and proximity to raw materials dispersed manufacturers across the countryside, but that was changing. Steam power gave birth to large mechanized factories dependent not on waterfalls, but upon canal- and rail- transported coal. By now, the expanding web of canals and railroads exchanged raw materials and finished goods in a national market place, increasingly dominated by giant corporations, holding companies, combinations and trusts. Growing urban populations offered a steady supply of factory workers.

The Civil War raised industry and high finance to a scale capable of fielding vast armies over half a continent. To meet and manage the Federal Government's huge military expenditures, Congress established a national banking system. While state banks remained local engines of finance, many—including those at Paterson, Jersey City, Newark, Hackettstown, Newton, Phillipsburg and Washington (NJ)—obtained national charters in 1865. Under such stimulation, the economy feverishly overheated. Government printing presses spewed forth 'rag money', energizing consumers and manufacturers. Mines and furnaces worked overtime, rolling out iron for thousands of miles of 'wild cat' railroads.

> [Workmen] carried pockets full of greenbacks, lived luxuriously and shouted for [President] Grant; young men without means purchased farms at exorbitant prices; incompetent and unprincipled favorites were placed in positions of trust and Credit Mobilier, Emma Mine, Crooked Whiskey and District of Columbia Rings were run direct from the National Capital, if not from the White House itself.[19]

The bubble burst when Jay Cooke and Company, the Government's preferred banker, announced insolvency on 18 September 1873. The consequent stock market crash brought general ruin in its wake.

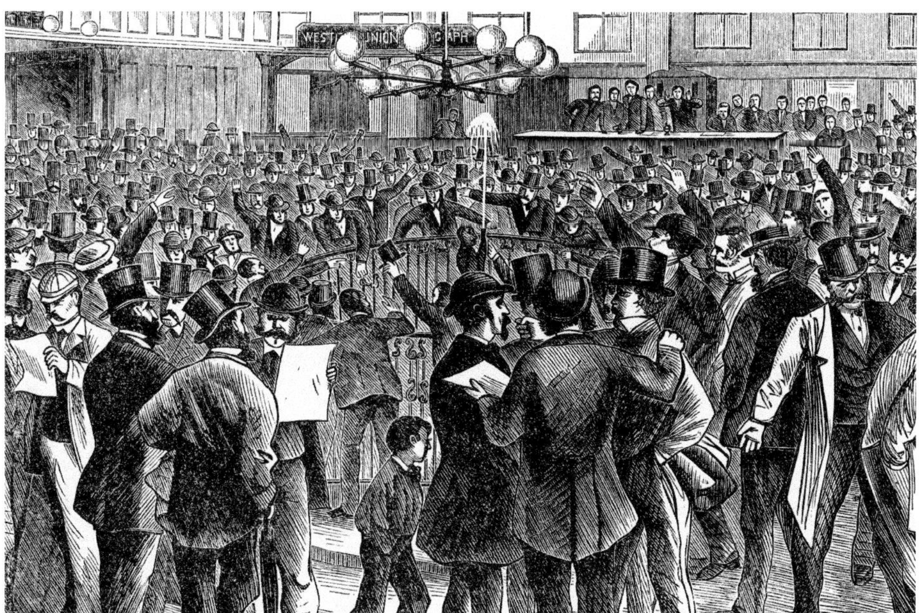

Scene in the New York Stock Exchange during the 'Railroad Panic' of September 1873. (Northrop, *The Student's History of the United States*, Vol. 2, 1901)

While former panics came and went within a few months, these hard times lengthened into the Long Depression. Outmoded industries suddenly fell by the wayside and many old channels of commerce were drained of their former trade. Factories stopped, laborers went begging for bread and property suddenly sold 'at prices far below the assessed value.'[20] Farms along the eastern seaboard, including those in northern New Jersey, depreciated in value from 30 to 50 percent as railroads brought the great western plains, suited to mechanized agriculture, under cultivation. Significantly lower production and transportation costs gave western farmers an advantage, even when selling in eastern markets. And although laborsaving machinery enabled one man to accomplish the same work previously requiring three men, increasing numbers of rural laborers abandoned farm life to become wage earners in manufacturing cities only an hour away.

Despite the economic downturn, the Lehigh Valley Railroad completed the Easton and Amboy Railroad between Phillipsburg and Perth Amboy in 1875 after three years of construction work. This line was subsequently extended from South Plainfield to Jersey City, thus nullifying the Morris Canal as a through-carrier to tidewater. For the remainder of its days, the canal was wholly subsidiary to railroad interests. While it continued to supply towpath industries along its winding route, thriving inland ports began a slow, but steady, decline. The canal's valuable right-of-way and water privileges now became the object of commercial interest and legal dispute, especially given the rise of industrial cities on its banks.

To supply 120,000 customers, the Newark Water Works pumped three million gallons of water daily in 1874 from the tidal Passaic River, an unhealthy source, badly polluted with sewage and industrial waste.[21] Given the low elevation of its intake, Newark spent about $50,000 annually to pump water through its mains; Jersey City spent nearly $120,000 annually to do the same. Since Newark already obtained a portion of its water supply from the Morris Canal, entrepreneurs tried to purchase or lease it "as a conductor for furnishing pure water" from Greenwood Lake and Lake Hopatcong, part of the first scheme to tap Highland reservoirs for municipal water supplies. John P. Culver, chief engineer of the Jersey City Water Works, also eyed the Morris Canal for a gravity supply of potable water. The New Jersey legislature accommodatingly authorized Newark and Jersey City to purchase the canal for this purpose in 1873 and the Morris Canal Company offered to sell the Eastern Division from Lake Hopatcong to Jersey City for $4.5 million. It was thought that a single aqueduct, 4 feet in diameter, could deliver a constant stream of Highland water through the canal's long level between Mead's Basin (Mountain View) and Bloomfield, where it could be partly diverted to the Jersey City reservoir on Schuyler's Hill. As an added bonus, canal abandonment would not only eliminate a public blight in urban areas, but it would release the lands it occupied for more profitable uses. To appease those who received coal deliveries along the towpath between Easton and Paterson, proponents of this first abandonment plan recommended keeping the Morris Canal operational west of Mead's Basin (Mountain View). Even this offer, however, did not overcome resistance from those who depended on the canal for their livelihood. There was life in the old waterway yet and twenty-five boats were reported in various stages of construction at the boatyard in Washington, NJ, in January 1876.

Despite setbacks, the economy began a slow but steady recovery. Many could sense its strengthening pulse in mining villages along the canal's banks, heralding an increase in freight. In a stab at modernity, the Morris Canal Company installed a 12-hp Baxter steam engine on a canal boat at its Washington boatyard in May 1878. Its trial run in June, heavily laden with coal, met with mixed reviews: fear the propeller would produce a harmful wake against the towpath embankment proved unfounded, but the two-blade propeller proved insufficient, requiring the substitution of a four-blade model. Long grass growing in the canal limited its average speed to about 3 miles per hour. The most important question, however, remained unresolved: was steam power cheaper than mules? The company seemed to think so, for, in September 1878, they announced plans to build twenty-five steam canal boats at Washington, NJ, on the Baxter design.

Peter F. Hart, of Newark, also experimented with steam power in July 1878, making three trips in a canal boat (named for himself) outfitted with a steam engine weighing 1,500 lb. Each trip only cost $15. Hart made several improvements to his steam canal boat over winter and took his boat from Waterloo to Bloomfield the following July, covering 45 miles in one day; the same trip took several days by mule power. The Morris Canal Company, however, refused to pay tonnage for running the boat up the Hackensack River, where he was usually consigned with loads. Consequently, after only two weeks, Hart removed the engine and sent the boat to Phillipsburg, where it was made available for mule power. Apparently, no one controlling the canal's destiny was much interested in schemes for its modernization. Although coal companies agreed to provide a full share of traffic, business and income on the Morris Canal dwindled away.

A drought raised new concerns about diverting water from Highland watersheds. After a dry summer, mills ran less than half time in August 1879. The water level in Lake Hopatcong was so low in November that the mining company stopped loading canal boats and large piles of ore quickly accumulated along the Ogden Mine Railroad. By December, a scarcity of water and the onset of freezing weather blockaded the Morris Canal, halting seventy-two boats below Stanhope. Over fifty canal boats passed the Waterloo lock on 6 December 1879. A week later, navigation closed and the canal was drained for repairs.

Signs of a general business revival appeared in the late spring of 1879. *The New Jersey Herald* reported on 25 June 1879:

> Business is steadily improving; evidence accumulates that in all parts of the country hopefulness and consequent cheerfulness prevail. The shaded side of the last sad cycle is giving place to brighter phases and better times. The quickened step of businessmen evinces purpose and rekindled ambition. Miles of moving railway trains, the hum of machinery, long processions of mechanics, artisans, and laborers, rested and ready at the shrill call of the time whistle, all betoken the very presence of the long expected good time.

Reports from the iron trade were encouraging: over fifty furnaces that had been out of blast for a long time returned to work in May 1879.

As the New Jersey Zinc Company prepared to resume mining at Ogdensburg in 1879, mine superintendent John George contracted with the Sussex Railroad to transport 100,000 tons of zinc ore on the Morris Canal to Newark, using a chute constructed at Waterloo to transfer ore from rail cars to canal boats in the Lock Pond, loading four boats daily. Boatmen worked early until late, making as many trips as possible as navigation was to be suspended in the middle of November. By the time the Ogden Mine Railroad shut down for winter, it also carried the largest tonnage in its history. Consequently, freight carried on the Morris Canal rose from 408,046 tons in 1879 to 503,486 tons in 1880, when it earned $315,677 in gross income. In March 1881, the Morris Canal Company decided to acquire fifty new boats. At the same time, the DL&W planned to lower freight rates on coal as soon as navigation resumed for the season.

The New Jersey Central Railroad Company negotiated a perpetual lease of the Ogden Mine Railroad in November 1881 at a rental of 5 percent on its capital stock. To form a connection with their High Bridge Branch at Port Oram (Wharton, NJ), engineers surveyed a line of track from Port Oram through the Berkshire Valley to a point at the base of Mase Mountain, where they proposed to build an inclined plane. Completion of this new rail connection obviated the necessity of transferring ore from the mine railroad to boats at Nolan's Point for transshipment on the Morris Canal, allowing these productive mines to ship ore directly in rail cars to furnaces in Pennsylvania.

Although the Morris Canal never met operating expenses after 1877, it was not a dead number quite yet: upwards of 350 boats and 800 horses worked the boating season of 1882, moving 459,846 tons of cargo. When navigation closed in December 1882, almost 1,250 men were, as usual, left unemployed. Their combined wages, averaging $12 per week, totaled nearly $540,000. The Morris Canal Company was assessed for 316 boats, 20 scows, 2 dredge boats, 26 mules and harness, 26 horses and harness, 19 wagons and 12 carts

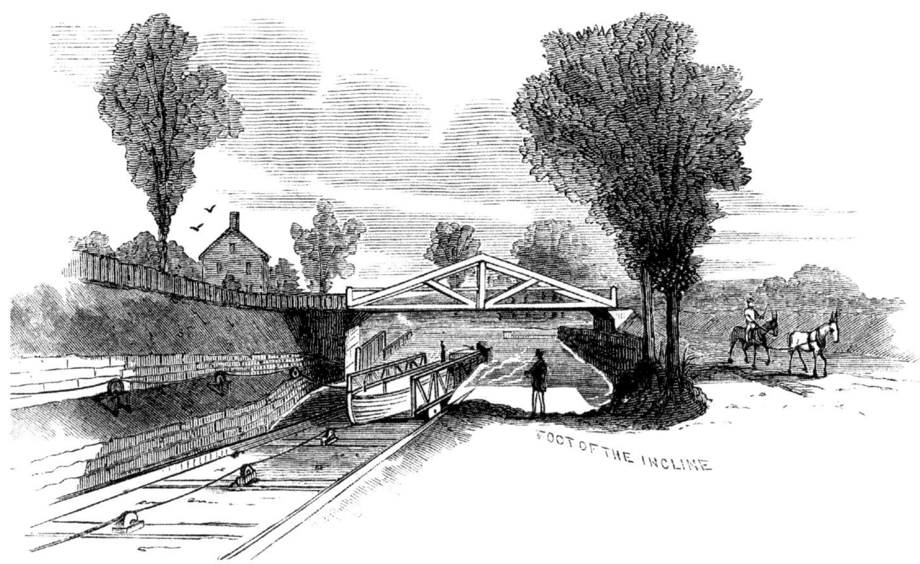

This view of the foot of Inclined Plane No. 11 East in Bloomfield was drawn from the grounds of the historic Collins House and shows the Baldwin Street bridge crossing over the canal. Preservationists are currently working to save the Collins House, its oldest section having been built in 1790 by Revolutionary War veteran John Collins. (*Scientific American*, 20 May 1882)

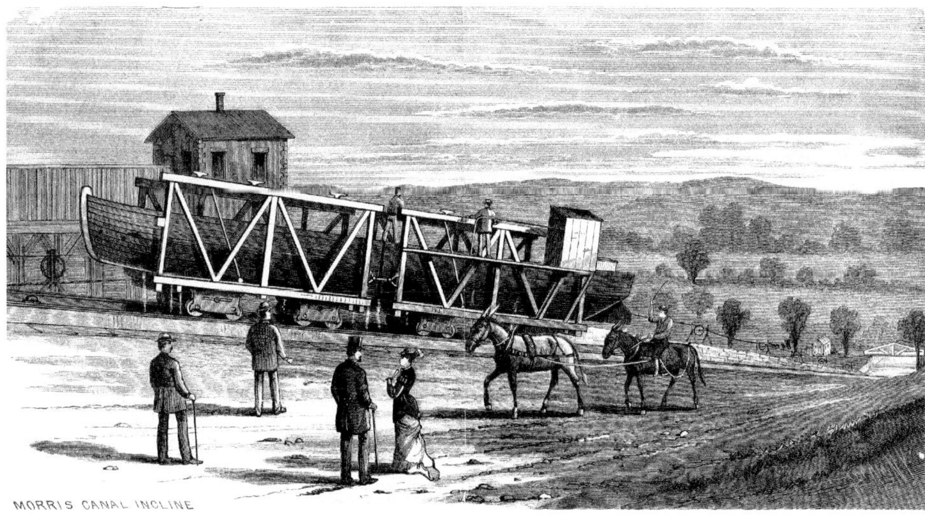

'Hydraulic Lift of the Morris Canal at Bloomfield, NJ', *Scientific American*, 20 May 1882. The brakeman has a small shed and a hand-railed walkway on the plane car. Here he appears to converse with the boat captain.

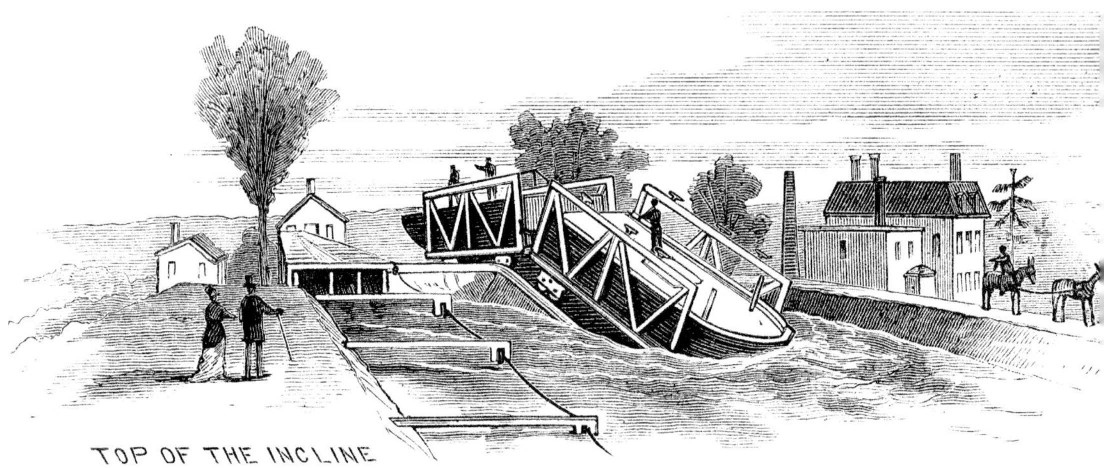

'Top of the Incline', *Scientific American*, 20 May 1882. Hinged midsection, the plane car carrying separated sections of a canal boat bends over the summit of Plane No. 11 East at Bloomfield, NJ. The flume conveying water to the powerhouse is on the left (east). A blacksmith and carpentry shop is visible to the left (east) of the powerhouse. The smokestack of the Weymouth Paper Company is visible to the right (west).

in 1884.[22] Freight declined from 423,495 tons in 1883 to 372,049 tons in 1888.[23]

The Morris Canal carried 413,073 tons in 1889. Despite optimism, the Lehigh Valley Railroad, lessee of the canal, contracted with the East Jersey Water Company in 1889 to use the canal's water privileges and right-of-way to deliver 27,000,000 gallons of water daily from the Clinton, Oak Ridge and Macopin reservoirs to Newark by 1 May 1892. Opponents derided the agreement, insinuating the Lehigh Valley Railroad hoped to secure 1,600 feet of waterfront on the Hudson River, worth millions of dollars, while profiting from the sale of the canal's right-of-way for railroad and traction purposes. Ultimately, the East Jersey Water Company did not use the canal, instead funneling water from the Macopin intake through a steel conduit, 48 inches in diameter and 21 miles long.[24] Due to a rise in business, the canal company ordered twenty-five new boats in 1889.

The Lehigh Valley Railroad paid the capitalized sum of $357,142 to buy out the annual rental fee of $20,000, which the Morris Canal Company agreed to pay the state in March 1867 for its lease of the Big Basin in Jersey City. The Board of Riparian Commissioners then sold the state's reversionary interest in the Big Basin to the Lehigh Valley Railroad for $48,000. This enabled the company to build its terminal on an adjacent mud flat, but the court of chancery declared this deed invalid in 1911, giving impetus to the railroad's cries for canal abandonment and its demands for at least a partial refund of taxes paid on the property.

By 1891, mining interests in Morris County were waning and 200 miners were discharged at Hibernia. The vein of ore at Mine Hill, near Stanhope, gave out in March 1891. The William Wright Farm, near Stanhope, containing about 60 acres and a valuable iron ore deposit, sold for $2,000 in June 1891. Mines near Stanhope closed and the furnace at Port Oram was blown out in June 1892. Franklin Furnace shut down four different times for various reasons before being abandoned in October 1893, due to competition from Lake Superior ores. Franklin Furnace was demolished in 1905 and its machinery sold for scrap. The commercial world was astonished when the Glendon Iron Company, whose furnace at Easton was one of the country's largest, fell into receivership in March 1896. The company also operated extensive mines at Hibernia in Morris County. The Andover Iron Company, situated along the Morris Canal in Phillipsburg, decided to go out of business in March 1901 and looked to sell its properties in Warren, Sussex and Morris Counties. The Singer Sewing Machine Company, of Elizabethport, largest manufacturer of its kind in the world, purchased the Stanhope furnace of the Musconetcong Iron Company in September 1902, including water rights to Roseville and Wright Ponds.

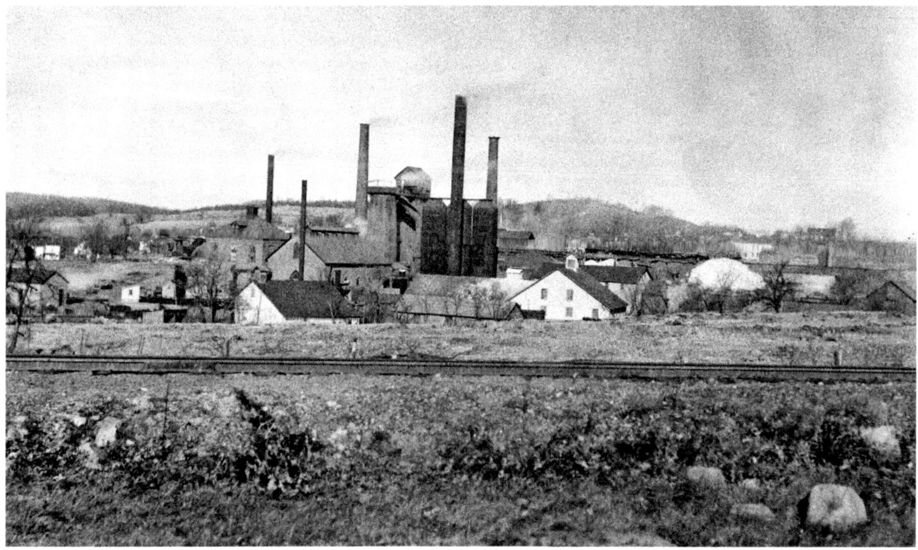

This view of the Musconetcong Iron Works shows three gas stoves standing beside the one remaining furnace and casting house. The United States Mineral Wool Company was organized in 1894. Its carpentry shop, storage house and foundry occupy the right foreground. Starting from about 1875, furnace slag and limestone were converted into mineral wool for fireproof insulation. The Singer Sewing Machine Company, of Elizabeth, purchased the Stanhope furnace in 1902 and built a three-story, concrete-block and steel foundry measuring 100 by 200 feet in 1906. (*Historic American Engineering Record, Library of Congress*)

The Morris Canal opened in March 1891 with 200 new boats. Boatmen petitioned for an increase of 13 cents per ton of freight. During 1892, the canal shipped 243,560 tons of coal from Port Delaware in 2,365 boat trips. In that same year, the Delaware, Lackawanna and Western Railroad carried 9,327,446 tons of coal over its lines. The so-called 'Cleveland Panic' of 1893 threw 3,000,000 men out of work. Consequently, the 1893 boating season was very unprofitable. In January 1894, the canal company owned 317 boats and, anticipating a modest increase in trade, ordered ten new ones since none had been built in the past two years—a boat with a careful captain lasted about fifteen years. The canal struggled back to life in 1894, but boating was suspended for a few days in August due to the small amount of coal dumped at Port Delaware. In that year, a flood swept away the dam that allowed canal boats to ferry across the Delaware River between the Lehigh and Morris Canals—it was never rebuilt.[25]

The Morris Canal had more applications for boats in April 1897 than there were boats to use. By the time they were frozen out for the season, boatmen collected $8,000 in premiums, based on 3 cents for every ton of coal delivered at points west of Paterson and 5 cents for each ton delivered east of that point. The Lehigh Valley Railroad again complained in 1898 that the canal was obsolete: the largest canal boats carried 70 tons and consisted of two sections, which had to be separated at twenty-three inclined planes in their five-day journey between the Delaware and Hudson Rivers. A single locomotive pulled 2,000 tons of coal over the same distance in five hours.

Residents of Jersey City tenement houses routinely dumped refuse into the canal, whose surface was covered with a green scum.[26] As health officials feared the spread of disease, canal officers sent scows up and down the waterway in July 1898 to pick up fifty-eight dead dogs. Boats had to be poled underneath the Centre Market between Broad and Mulberry Streets in Newark, through waters fouled by the sewerage of the markets and the drainage of the streets.[27]

In the final year of the nineteenth century, the annual production of anthracite coal reached 76,300,000 tons.[28] Coal and ore shippers, however, patronized railroads as much quicker and cheaper, all-weather carriers. Abram S. Hewitt, long an ardent advocate of canals, wrote the New York Committee on Canals in 1899, calling them 'back numbers' as economic carriers. The facts were on his side: the Morris Canal was only profitable from 1852 to 1876. It now competed against three railroads, the Central Railroad of New Jersey, the Delaware, Lackawanna and Western and the Lehigh Valley Railroad, each with a carrying capacity of 10,000,000 tons annually.

Thus, at the dawn of the twentieth century, the Morris Canal freighted little more than 120,000 tons of coal annually, which the Lehigh Valley Railroad diverted from its cars to canal boats at Phillipsburg. Although the Morris Canal had about 250 boats available in August 1900, the coal docks at Port

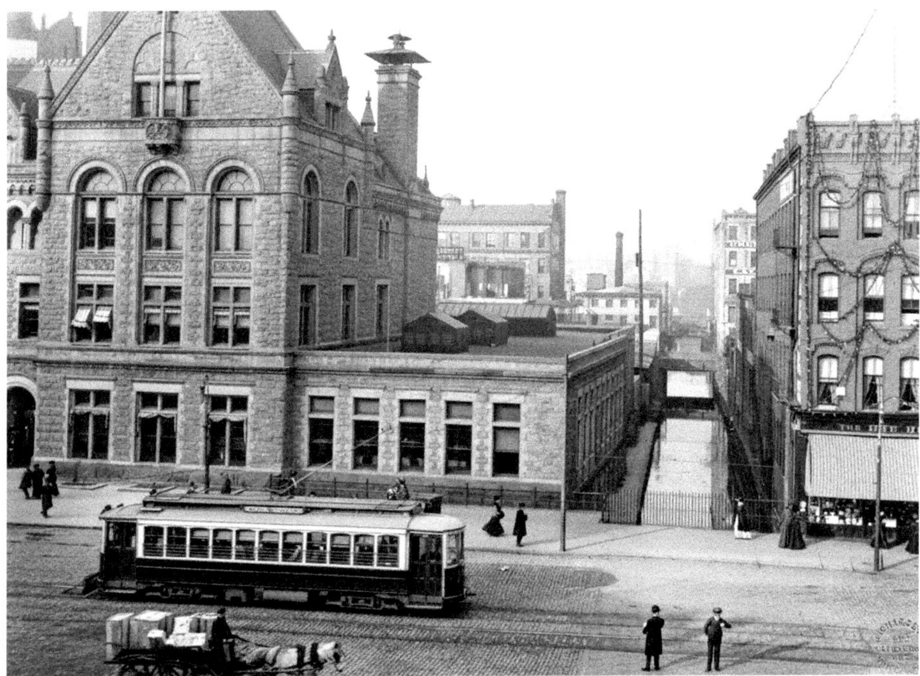

The Newark-Paterson trolley passes down Broad Street in front of the Romanesque-style Newark Post Office, which opened in 1898 and was razed in 1937. The one-story addition alongside the canal was built before 1910. The Bee Hive at 715 Broad Street was Newark's first department store, opening in 1870. Kresge's department store was built on its site in 1926. Raymond Boulevard now occupies the bed of the Morris Canal. (*Historic American Engineering Record, Library of Congress*)

Delaware in Phillipsburg only supplied ten to twelve boats daily.[29] Otherwise, the superannuated waterway largely served to carry stable manure to farmers. Locks and planes opened for business at 6 a.m. and closed at 7 p.m.[30] Boating was brisk in November 1901 as the company forwarded every ton of coal they could carry before a freeze; it was one of the longest seasons for navigation on record and 122,786 tons of freight were delivered. Canal officers announced construction of fifty new boats before spring.

A severe flood and coal strike in 1902, however, sounded the canal's death knell.[31] Heavy rains and meltwater occasioned a great flood on 1 March 1902, causing a great loss of property across northern New Jersey and in the Lehigh Valley, closing the western end of the Lehigh Canal. Thereafter, the Morris Canal operated only occasionally, running short hauls when necessary, and it was allowed to run down until it reached a state of irreversible dilapidation. Through its lease arrangement, however, the Morris Canal Company remained a pretty solid financial concern with $1,025,000 in consolidated stock and $1,175,000 in preferred stock with a par value of $100. At the annual meeting in April 1903, Eben Briggs Thomas, president of the Lehigh Valley Railroad Company, was re-elected president of the Morris Canal and Banking Company.

Speaking before the Newark Board of Trade on 24 November 1903, Thomas N. McCarter, president of the Public Service Corporation, suggested the canal bed be used for an electric railway. Roderick Byington, counsel for property owners about Lake Hopatcong, stated in the *Sunday Call,*

> [...] we would be willing to withdraw our opposition to the canal abandonment scheme, provided we received assurance that the waters of Lake Hopatcong would not be disturbed, and provided the Lehigh [Valley Railroad] would turn over to us the dam at the head of the Musconetcong River and the property adjacent to the dam.

A defeated abandonment proposal would have allowed the Lehigh Valley Railroad Company to draw down the lake waters by 10 feet, destroying its beauties along a 50-mile shoreline. Instead, Byington suggested state acquisition of the lake and dam for a public park.

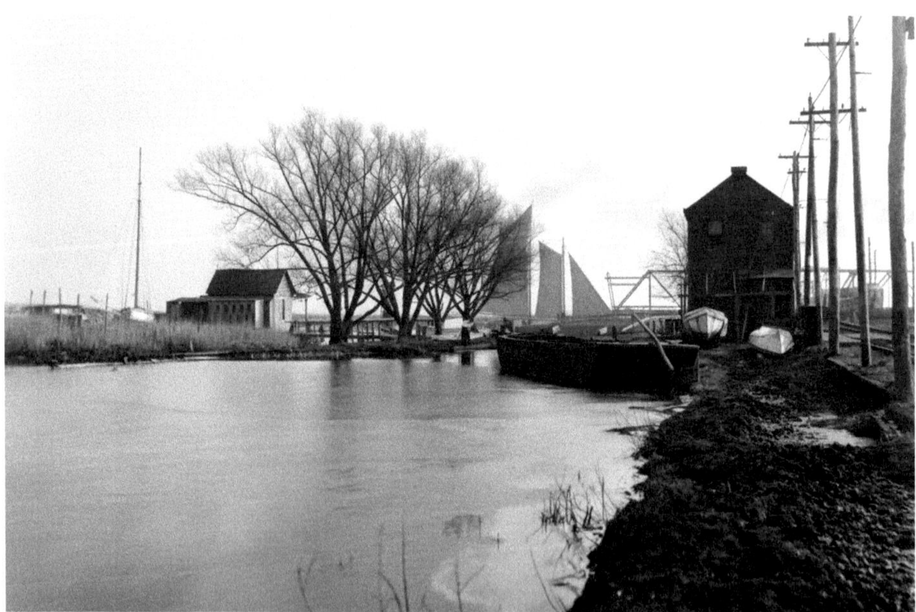

A scow docked at Lock No. 20 East near the mouth of the Passaic River on Newark Bay. The tracks and trolley cars of the Consolidated Traction Company, which opened an electric railway on the Newark Plank Road to Jersey City in 1894, are visible to the right. This line was leased to the North Jersey Traction Company in 1898 and to the Public Service Railway in 1908. The Plank Road became part of Lincoln Highway in 1913. (*Historic American Engineering Record, Library of Congress*)

The Lehigh Valley Railroad and the East Jersey Water Company lobbied to get the canal charter repealed. In 1903, the legislature appointed ex-Governors George T. Werts, John W. Griggs and Foster M. Voorhees to a Special Commission on the Morris Canal Abandonment. Governor Franklin Murphy sent their report to the legislature on 14 March 1904. According to their research, the route of the canal between Phillipsburg and Jersey City covered a little more than 106 miles, including feeders. Beyond the actual bed of the canal and its basins, the company owned reservoir properties, including 787 acres at Greenwood Lake; 460 acres at Lake Hopatcong; 351 acres at Stanhope; 300 acres at Cranberry Lake; 89 acres at Bear Swamp; and 10 acres at Green Pond. The Commission concluded the canal would never become profitable again, owing to the cheapness of railroad freight as compared to the slowness and seasonality of water carriage. It advised abandonment of the canal with provisions protecting the rights of stockholders; the rights of all persons holding any reversionary interest in any grants made to the canal company; and lastly, whatever rights the state might possess. It recommended legislative approval of a bill that would empower a three-man commission to sell the canal, in whole or in part, provided the Lehigh Valley Railroad Company consented to surrender its lease. It also recommended the proceeds of the sale be used, first, to pay off the canal company's bonded indebtedness of $556,000; secondly, to liquidate at an appraised value the $2,200,000 of outstanding stocks; and thirdly, that any excess amount received be put into the state treasury. The report highlighted the great damage that would result to landowners at Lake Hopatcong and Greenwood Lake, should the water rights of the Morris Canal be diverted.

A great deluge fell on 7 October 1903 and continued for three days. Although drought had dried the land, it could not absorb the enormous quantity of water. All northern New Jersey suffered and flood damage exceeded that of March 1902. The Pompton dam broke, wreaking havoc in the Passaic Valley. Property losses at Paterson were estimated at $3 million. At least 3,500 men were put out of work and hundreds of families left homeless. Owing to the sudden waterfall pouring down Garret Rock, it was necessary to cut the Morris Canal in four places. Business on the canal was suspended, owing to the impossibility of completing repairs before winter. Boats disposed of their coal cargoes at the most advantageous points. Gross earnings for 1904 and 1905 were, respectively, $96,231 and $86,155, while expenses amounted to $162,442 and $163,658.[32] Whereas 397 boats operated on the canal in 1890, the number dwindled to forty-seven in 1905. Navigation opened in May 1910 with only three boats.

The Lehigh Valley Railroad abandoned the idea of selling the canal's water rights to the East Jersey Water Company in 1911 and focused instead on gaining outright ownership of the canal basin on the Hudson River to avoid payment of taxes on a waterway it had forced into disuse—some estimates of the value of 1,600 feet of Jersey City waterfront soared as high as $20 million. In keeping with the Lehigh Valley Railroad's wish to end such 'an economic waste,' State Senator James F. Fielder, of Hudson County, introduced a bill on 27 February 1911, to repeal the Morris Canal charter and to dispose of the company's property. Republicans called Fielder's proposal 'an absolute shutout for every interest but the Lehigh Valley Railroad Company … which would get this enormously valuable property for virtually nothing.'[33] *The Hackensack Republican* described Senate Bill 141 as 'the most audacious bill for the aggrandizement of a railroad corporation and its affiliated interests that ever appeared in the New Jersey legislature.'[34] Even some of Fielder's fellow Democrats opposed surrendering the public interest to a railroad corporation, which was considered 'one of the members of the coal combine, which had wrecked all the benefits of the canal for his county, raised the price of coal $8 a ton, robbed Jersey City of an immense coal traffic and made living inordinately dear for the people.' Jersey City quickly demanded the Hudson waterfront property for its own use.

A group of recreationists and nature lovers formed the Morris Canal Parkway Association in 1911 to preserve the canal as a water parkway, at least west of Second River, under a plan prepared by engineer Cornelius C. Vermeule. They hailed the canal as 'a genuine paradise for canoeists, fishermen, swimmers, and skaters,' as a towpath trail for bicyclists and hikers, and as a source of recreation and breathing space for city dwellers.[35] They first attempted to amend the abandonment bill, but when that failed, they gathered 1,800 signatures to a petition. With so many conflicting interests, Fielder's bill was talked to death. As James F. Fielder was the Democratic candidate for Governor, the Republican press asked readers to predict, 'What kind of a bill will be introduced to get the powerful support of the governor?'[36]

After two years of deliberations, the Morris Canal Investigation Committee presented its findings to Governor Fielder in March 1914, recommending that the Jersey City basins and canal bed between the Hudson River and Fiddler's Elbow be deeded to the Lehigh Valley Railroad.[37] In return, the Lehigh Valley Railroad would pay $115,000 for the state's reversionary interest in the Big Basin at Jersey City. The section between Fiddler's Elbow and the Passaic River would remain a canal, with all rights to the canal west of Fiddler's Elbow being deeded to the state. Newark was to receive a preferential right to purchase the canal within its municipal limits. To please vested interests in the backcountry, the commissioners recommended the canal be maintained for navigation between Phillipsburg and Second River, a distance of 85.8 miles. The committee recommended construction of a boulevard alongside the canal, between Phillipsburg and Branch Brook Park in Newark, in preference to a water parkway. Otherwise, the canal right-of-way between Newark and

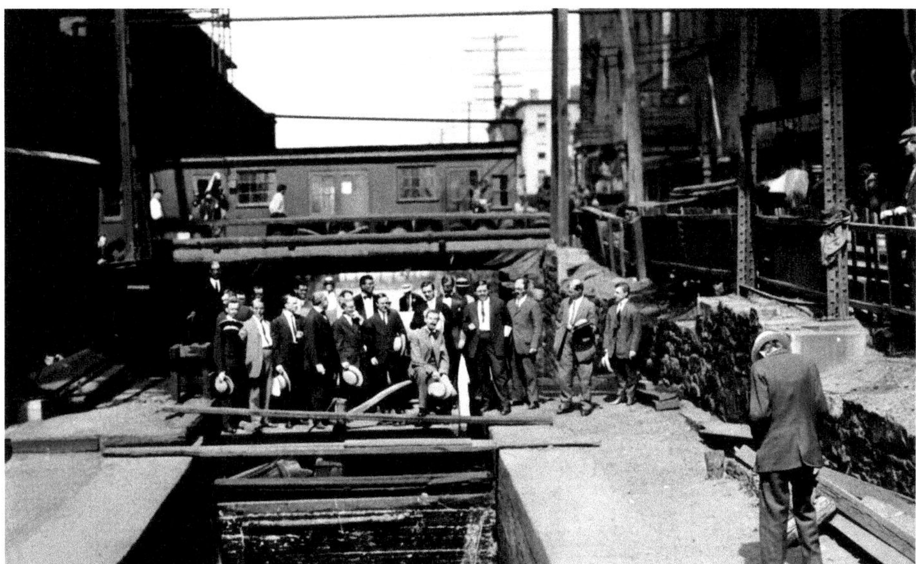

The Morris Canal Investigation Committee began its second tour of the canal for legislators and new committeemen in Jersey City on 1 July 1913. Carlton Godfrey, Speaker of the General Assembly, chaired the committee, which became known as the Godfrey Committee. (*Historic American Engineering Record, Library of Congress*)

Paterson might be reserved for an electric railway or other public purpose. The State of New Jersey would receive all water rights, except those affecting Newark and Jersey City, and the canal charter would continue under state control to perpetuate the Greenwood Lake dam and consequently a potential water supply worth at least $1 million.[38] Under this scheme, the state would receive not less than $1 million from the railroad and from the sale of canal lands; one-half of the money to be dedicated for construction of the proposed parkway and the other half reserved for boulevards in other parts of the state. Lastly, a new commission would have charge of the whole project. In its assessment of the aging waterway, the Morris Canal report concluded, 'This device of inclined planes in its time was considered a marvel of engineering skill. Today it is more curious than practical.'[39]

In response to an ongoing legal wrangle, the Morris Canal Investigation Committee endorsed a provision in the abandonment bill that stipulated the Lehigh Valley Railroad should renounce its claim to tax exemption as provided in the original charter of the Morris Canal and Banking Company and to any claim for reimbursement of taxes paid under protest. In making the state's original case, filed in 1907, attorney general Robert H. McCarter argued that tax exemption only applied for so long as canal property was 'used and occupied' for navigation purposes, which it no longer was. The State Supreme Court agreed in February 1908, upholding the state's right to tax the Big

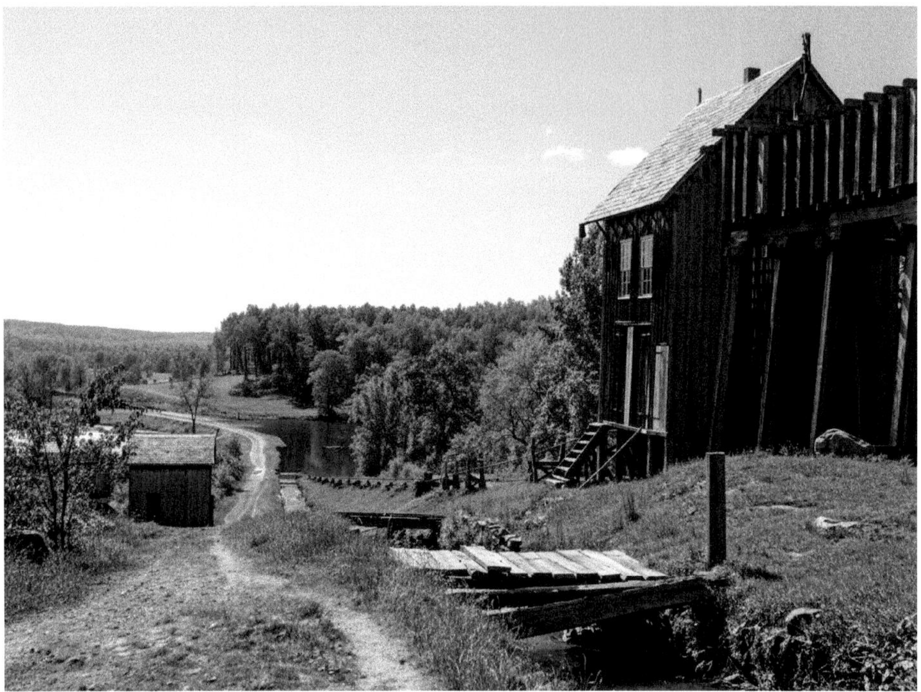

Standing near the powerhouse of Plane No. 2 East, above Ledgewood, NJ, the submerged plane car can be seen at the head of Plane No. 3 East below. Here as at Montville, two planes were situated close to one another. (*Library of Congress*)

Basin in Jersey City, then valued at $10 million, which the State of New Jersey owned, but which the Lehigh Valley Railroad leased. The Court of Errors and Appeals affirmed the decision of the lower court in November 1908, as did the Court of Chancery in February 1911. A few days before the ruling, the railroad company introduced its abandonment bill in the legislature.

The Lehigh Valley Railroad Company appealed to the United States Supreme Court, which postponed action in November 1914 after counsel for the state and for the railroad company agreed to try and resolve their dispute amicably. After more than seven years of legal contention, opening arguments were finally made before the US Supreme Court in October 1915. The stakes were high, since the state, if it lost its case, would have to repay more than $1 million in taxes and interest to the Lehigh Valley Railroad.[40] On 21 November 1915, the nation's highest court ruled in the state's favor.

The last trickle of commercial traffic on the canal dried up in 1916. Sunday strollers, canoeists, wandering photographers and sketch-artists became the only life along its towpath. Because railroads could not furnish cars and motive power sufficient to transport coal for domestic consumption during the First World War, many rural inhabitants got barely enough to run their kitchen stove. The

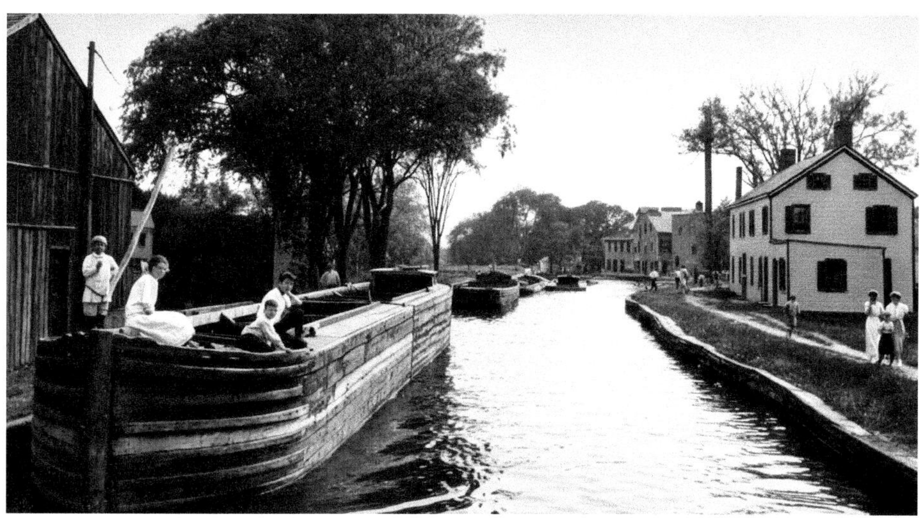

Bloomfield historian Richard Rockwell identifies this scene along the canal 'above Bloomfield' as the summit of Plane 11 East. The Combination Rubber Manufacturing Company and a canal store can be seen to the right (west). The building in the left foreground is a Morris Canal Company stable. (*Report of the Morris Canal Investigation Committee, Appointed under Joint Resolution of April 12, 1911, 1914*)

New Jersey fuel administrator encouraged country folk to burn wood, but it also proved difficult to get. The Lehigh Valley Railroad owned thirty canal boats in 1918, but only two actually operated, carrying coal from Jersey City to Bloomfield or occasionally to Paterson. Could the Morris Canal be summoned back from the grave to assist the war effort? *The Hackettstown Gazette* urged re-opening it, at least from Phillipsburg to Lake Hopatcong, to ease the wartime coal famine. Businessmen from Easton to Newark sought a resumption of navigation, but the Federal Railroad Administration doused all hope of awakening the old waterway, reporting in July 1918 that the Committee on Inland Waterways did not consider the Morris Canal a viable option to relieve rail congestion.

Contention over water rights ultimately sealed the canal's fate. The North Jersey District Water Supply Commission proposed construction of a dam at Midvale (Wanaque, NJ) in 1908 to create a reservoir, 6 miles long and a mile wide in places. The Morris Canal Company and the Lehigh Valley Railroad Company filed suit in February 1918 to halt construction of the proposed dam and a judge ruled in 1922 against depriving the canal of sufficient water from Greenwood Lake and the Wanaque River for its operation.[41] In 1921, Hudson Maxim, of Lake Hopatcong, widely known as the inventor of smokeless gunpowder, invited representatives of the Lehigh Valley Railroad, the City of Newark, Jersey City, the North Jersey District Water Supply Commission, and Morris and Warren Counties to a dinner at Day's Restaurant in Morristown.[42] A 'Get Together Committee' was chosen to discuss the touchy matter of canal

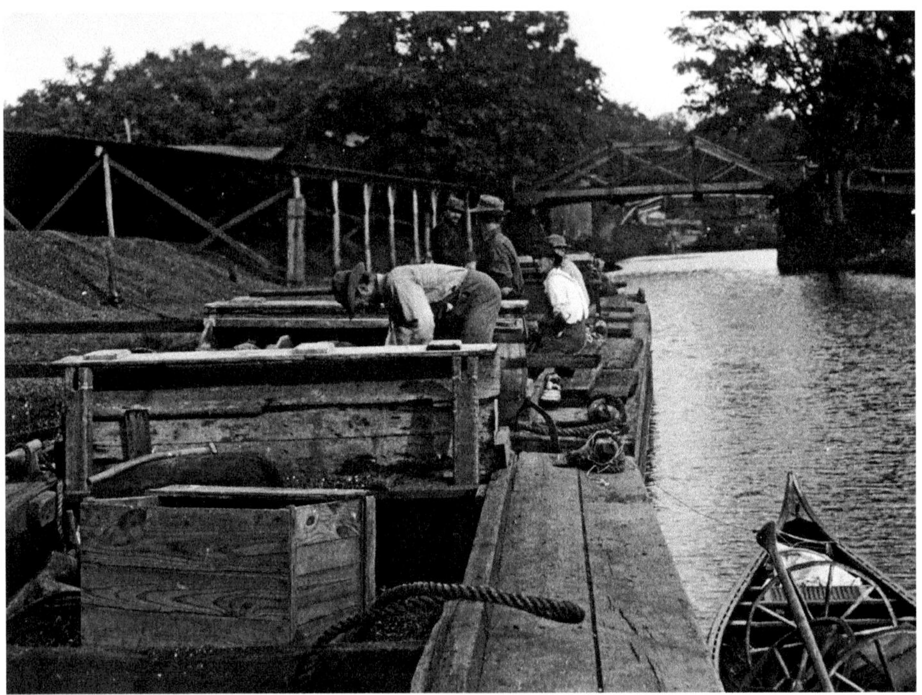

A canal boat is moored alongside the coal dock of the Powerville Felt Roofing Company, opposite the Powerville Hotel, in Boonton Township, NJ. (*Historic American Engineering Record, Library of Congress*)

abandonment.[43] Later, a subcommittee drafted an abandonment bill.[44] At that point, the Lehigh Valley Railroad spent less than $200,000 annually to maintain the canal in a rundown, unused condition. Consequently, on 11 March 1922, the New Jersey legislature passed the Roegner Bill, empowering a three-member state commission to negotiate with the Lehigh Valley Railroad Company.[45]

Employees of the Morris Canal gazed upon their last paychecks in March 1924. Although the Morris Canal Company continued as a corporation, holding property as trustee for the state, the Board of Conservation and Economic Development became its directors. On 7 April 1924, Cornelius C. Vermeule, of East Orange, was appointed consulting engineer for the abandonment project. He resigned in 1926 and his son, Major Cornelius C. Vermeule Jr, of Short Hills, succeeded him. Drainage of the canal and re-routing streams, which entered it at various points, was the most difficult problem to solve. Spillway dams of modern construction replaced eleven old dams, including those at Lake Hopatcong, Lake Musconetcong, Saxton Falls and Greenwood Lake. Work included removal of dangerous highway bridges. At Lake Hopatcong, a fountain was built to feed the lake's overflow into the Musconetcong River. A turbine from one of the planes was set up in a concrete shelter house with a descriptive tablet. An old millstone was also preserved.

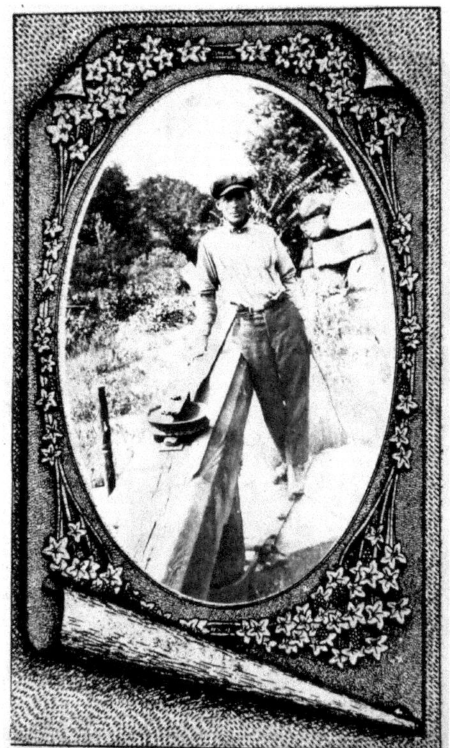

Albert James Sherer was born in
Netcong, NJ, on 16 November 1891.
He was the lock and plane tender
at Waterloo in 1920, living with
his mother Elizabeth Burdge and
younger brother Harry, who was
a car inspector on the railroad.

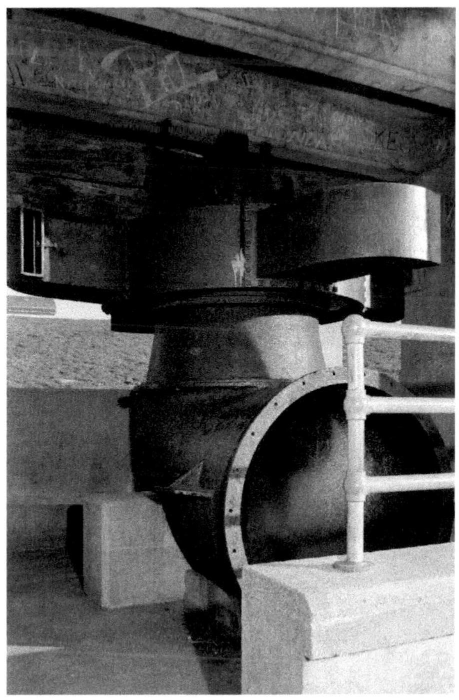

View of Scotch turbine mounted
at Lake Hopatcong State Park, NJ.
(*Historic American Engineering
Record, Library of Congress*)

Canal abandonment necessitated construction work in 459 different locations over a distance of 102 miles. Funds received from the sale of canal property covered $1,730,466 in costs. Municipalities, including Paterson and Newark, purchased the abandoned right-of-way and planned public improvements. Paterson gained immediately by the erection of a new railroad station. Cornelius C. Vermeule Jr finished the work of abandonment in June 1929, publishing an eighty-page illustrated booklet.

Thus the Morris Canal drained from view, leaving future generations to search for its ghost and wonder—here and there, now and then, wherever traces of its memory persisted—about a slow but steady-paced world gone by. In hindsight, it might have survived longer against railroad competition had it been sufficiently enlarged for boats of greater tonnage; but its seasonality and hoofed speed ultimately consigned its winding ways to history. So rapid was the pace of change that, in less than a century, a great novelty of its time aged to a discarded anachronism. But, in consolation, so did its lethal competitors, the railroads. For, in this continuing and often confusing Age of Ingenuity, something better always seems to come along.

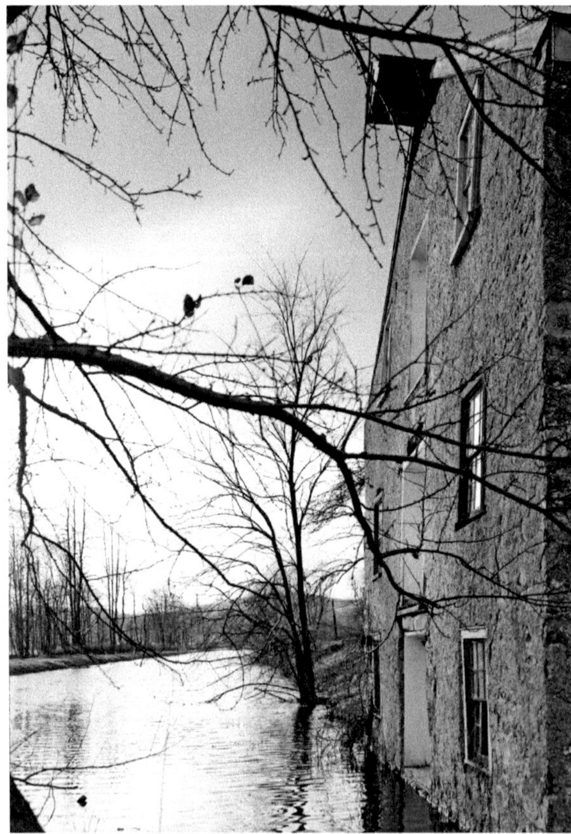

Alvin Linn Cassedy operated the canal store at Waterloo, NJ, between 1891 and 1916. He became the village's postmaster in 1898. (*Library of Congress*)

ᴇNDNOTES

1. The Coal Rush

1 Vethake, *A Dictionary, Practical, Theoretical, and Historical, of Commerce and Commercial Navigation*, Vol. 1 (Philadelphia: Thomas Wardle, 1840), p. 353.

2 Hermelin, *Report About The Mines In The United States of America, 1783* (Philadelphia: John Morton Memorial Museum, 1931), pp. 47-48.

3 *Ibid.*, pp. 59-60.

4 *Journal of Commerce*, quoted in *Niles' Weekly Register*, Vol. 45, 31 August 1833 (Baltimore: Franklin Press, 1834), p. 4.

5 Oak firewood increased from between $1.75 and $2.00 per cord to $6.00 per cord in 1815. *Niles' Weekly Register, From September 1815 to March 1816*, Vol. 9 (Baltimore: The Franklin Press, 1816), p. 95.

6 *Ibid.*

7 Rupp, *History of Northampton, Lehigh, Monroe, Carbon and Schuylkill Counties, Pa.* (Harrisburg: Hickok & Cantine, 1845), p. 306. Jesse Fell used anthracite in his nailery as early as 1788. By his description in 1826, he made his first coal grate, 10 inches in depth and 10 inches in height, of small iron rods. 'High Lights in Anthracite Trade History—1', *The Coal Trade Journal*, Vol. 50 (1919), pp. 569-570.

8 Blake and Lauris, *The Family Encyclopedia of Useful Knowledge and General Literature* (Philadelphia: Carey & Hart, 1849), pp. 428-430. Blacksmith Obadiah Gore and his brother Daniel first used anthracite in 1770. *The Coal Trade Journal*, No. 23, Vol. 50, 1919, pp. 569-570.

9 *Ibid.*, p. 570.

10 Daddow and Bannan, *Coal, Iron, and Oil; or, the Practical American Miner. A Plain and Popular Work on Our Mines and Mineral Resources, and a Text-Book or Guide to their Economical Development* (Pottsville, Pa: Benjamin Bannan, 1866), pp. 114, 120; Ruoff, *Biographical and*

Portrait Cyclopedia of Schuylkill County, Pennsylvania (Philadelphia: Rush, West and Company, 1893), p. 29.

11 'Coal, and the Coal-Mines of Pennsylvania', *Harper's New Monthly Magazine, June to November 1857*, Vol. 15 (New York: Harper Brothers, 1857), pp. 451-469.

12 These arks were 'square boxes … from sixteen to eighteen feet wide, and twenty to twenty-five feet long. They were steered with long oars like a raft. Boats of this description were used on the Lehigh till the end of the year 1831, in which year forty thousand nine hundred and sixty-six tons were sent down, which required so many boats to be built, that, if they had all been joined in one length, they would have extended more than thirteen miles. The boats made but one trip, and were then broken up in the city, and the planks sold for lumber, the spikes, hinges and other iron work, being returned to Mauch Chunk by land, a distance of eighty miles. The hands employed in running these boats walked back for two or three years, when rough wagons were placed on the roads by some of the tavern keepers, to carry them at reduced fares.' *Mauch Chunk and Vicinity With A Description Of The Famous Switch-Back Railroad* (Mauch Chunk: Boyle, Reed & Gihon, 1872), pp. 68-69.

13 His marriage to Frances, daughter of Brigadier-General William Malcolm (1732–1792), likely propelled his career. William Malcolm served in the NY provincial congress in 1776. He became major of the Second Battalion, New York City Militia, in 1775, and colonel of the Second Regiment, NY Volunteer Infantry, in 1776. When these state troops were absorbed into the Continental Line, Malcolm became Colonel of the Additional Regiment, Continental Infantry. He acted as Deputy Adjutant-General of the Northern Department from June to October 1778, and retired on 9 May 1779. He was Colonel of the First Regiment, NY Levies, in 1780–81, and Brigadier-General of New York City and County Militia, 1787–1792. Gen. Malcolm led the military escort at Washington's first inaugural in New York City, wearing a kilt.

14 Charles Snowden signed articles of association for the Society of the English Library of Reading, Pennsylvania, in 1808. 'Uplift of Reading Free Public Library', *The Reading Eagle*, 12 April 1914, p. 20.

15 Wharton and Morris, 'Hoffman against Coster and Others', *Reports of Cases Adjudged in the Supreme Court of Pennsylvania in the Eastern District*, Vol. 2 (Philadelphia: T. & J. Johnson & Co., 1884), pp. 453-476.

16 Rupp, p. 191.

17 Hazard, ed., 'History of the Discovery and Use of Anthracite Coal', *The Register of Pennsylvania, January to July 1829*, Vol. 3 (Philadelphia: W. F. Geddes, 1829), pp. 301-303.

18 Vethake, p. 367.

19 *The Sussex Register*, 20 February 1817.

20 'Delaware and Raritan Canal', *Niles' Weekly Register, From March to September 1817*, Vol. 12 (Baltimore: The Franklin Press, 1817), pp. 189-197.

21 *Ibid.*, p. 190.

22 Temin, *The Jacksonian Economy* (New York: W. W. Norton & Co., 1969), p. 46.

23 These two companies combined to form the Lehigh Coal and Navigation Company on 21 April 1820. 'High Lights in Anthracite Trade History—I', *The Coal Trade Journal*, Vol. 50, p. 570.

24 'Effects of Individual Enterprise, Extract of a letter from George F. Hauto, Esq., to a member of the legislature, relative to the progress made by Messrs. White, Hauto & Hazard in improving the navigation, &c. on the river Lehigh—dated Mauch Chunk, Northampton Co., Pa., Dec. 19, 1819', *The Republican Compiler*, 23 February 1820, p. 1.

25 'Lehigh Coal', *The New-York Evening Post*, 23 January 1824, p. 2.

26 'Inland Navigation', *The Republican Compiler*, 28 July 1824, p. 3.

27 *The Coal Trade Journal* (1919), pp. 307, 319.

28 Rupp, p. 372.

29 Cuvier, *Essay on the Theory of the Earth* (New York: Kirk & Mercein, 1818), p. 338. According to the *Laws of Pennsylvania, passed in the 1818/19 Session*, Charles Snowden of Schuylkill County was named in 'An act to incorporate a company to make a lock navigation on the west branch of the river Schuylkill.' Their purpose was to make a slack water navigation from the mouth of the West Branch of the Schuylkill at its junction with the East Branch, about 5 miles from Orwigsburg.

30 Colonel Joseph G. Swift was named Chief Engineer of the US Army in July 1812 at twenty-eight years of age. He was promoted to Brigadier-General in March 1814 and assigned to plan the defense and fortification of New York City. Named Superintendent of the US Military Academy at West Point in January 1817, he established the headquarters of the Army Corps of Engineers in Washington, DC, in April 1818. Swift was insulted when President James Madison appointed Simon Bernard, a military engineer in Napoleon's Army, as Assistant Engineer with the rank of Brigadier-General in the American Army. He resigned his military commission on 12 November 1818, and accepted appointment as surveyor and inspector of the revenue for the port of New York.

31 Swift gives the name 'Samuel Mitlin'. This may be the same Samuel Mifflin who was president of the Union Canal Company in 1811. He died in 1829. Cadwallader Evans Jr advocated construction of a canal along the Schuylkill River, connecting Philadelphia to the coal regions, in 1813. A director of the Second Bank of the United States, he died in 1841.

32 *Acts of the Forty-Fourth General Assembly, Second Sitting* (Trenton,

NJ: 1820), p. 55. The legislature named Samuel Breck and William J. Duane, of Philadelphia; Nathaniel Prime and Joseph G. Swift, of New York; John Rutherfurd and William S. Pennington, of Newark; John N. Simpson and Thomas Hill, of New Brunswick; and Garret D. Wall and Israel Taylor, of Trenton, as commissioners.

33 Swift, *The Memoirs of Gen. Joseph Gardner Swift, L.L.D., U. S. A., First Graduate of the United States Military Academy, West Point* (Worchester, Massachusetts: F. S. Blanchard & Co., 1890), p. 186. He and Nathaniel Prime advertised the opening of stock subscriptions in New York City 'for making a canal, or water communication [...] between the tide waters of the Delaware and Raritan rivers' on 19 April 1820.

34 *Ibid.*, p. 185.

35 *Ibid.*, p. 197.

36 *Ibid.*

37 *History of Schuylkill County, Pa* (New York: W. W. Munsell & Co., 1881), pp. 45, 262.

2. The Morris Canal and Banking Company

1 *Palladium of Liberty*, 28 December 1820.

2 According to his obituary in the *New York Times* on 7 June 1858, 'George P. Macculoch, Esq., a distinguished citizen of New Jersey, died in Morristown on Tuesday [1 June 1858], aged 83. He was born in Bombay, his father being a Scotch officer in the East India service. He was employed during the first Consulate of Napoleon, in various financial negotiations for the East India Company, and came to New York in 1806. He settled soon after at Morristown, where he has since resided. He was the projector of the Morris Canal, and took an active interest in public affairs.' At five years of age, and after the death of both parents, George Macculoch was brought from India to Edinburgh, Scotland, to be raised by his grandmother. After graduating from the University of Edinburgh, he moved to London and engaged in the East India trade with partner Francis Law. He immigrated to the United States in July 1806 with his wife Martha Louisa Edwina Sanderson and their two children, settling in Morristown. After suffering financial loss, he established a boys' academy in 1814.

3 When General Joseph G. Swift was placed in charge of New York City's defenses during the War of 1812, James Renwick was an aide-de-camp. Swift, *The Memoirs of Gen. Joseph Gardner Swift, L.L.D., U. S. A., First Graduate of the United States Military Academy, West Point* (Worchester, Massachusetts: F. S. Blanchard & Co., 1890), p. 135. James

Renwick was born in Liverpool, England, in 1792 and immigrated to New York City with his family in 1794. He entered the US Army in 1814 as topographical engineer with the rank of major and was commissioned colonel of engineers in the New York militia in 1817.

4 *The Biographical Encyclopædia of New Jersey of the Nineteenth Century* (Philadelphia: Galaxy Publishing Company, 1877), p. 286.

5 *Palladium of Liberty*, 27 June 1822.

6 'Delaware and Hudson Canal', 14 September 1822, *Niles' Weekly Register, From September 1822 to March 1823*, New Series, Vol. 11 or 23 (Baltimore: William Ogden Niles, 1823), pp. 26-27.

7 The Valley Bloomery was built about 1780 and rebuilt by Canfield & Losey in 1814 and by Jeremiah Baker in 1828. It stood on the Rockaway River about 7 miles west of Rockaway Station and within sight of the Morris & Essex track. This indicates its location on Baker Mill Pond in Wharton, NJ

8 'Delaware and Hudson Canal', *Niles' Weekly Register, From September 1822 to March 1823*, p. 27.

9 *Ibid.*

10 *The Biographical Encyclopædia of New Jersey of the Nineteenth Century*, p. 286. Nathaniel Saxton and Henry Dusenberry represented Hunterdon County; Morris Robinson and Gamaliel Bartlett represented Sussex County (then including Warren County); Lewis Condict and Mahlon Dickerson represented Morris County; Gerald Rutgers and Charles Kinsey represented Essex County; and John Rutherford and William Colfax represented Bergen County. *Palladium of Liberty*, 29 August 1822.

11 *The Sussex Register*, 1 March 1823.

12 *The Biographical Encyclopædia of New Jersey of the Nineteenth Century*, p. 287.

13 *Ibid.*

14 *Ibid.* In 1824, Congress created a Board of Engineers for Internal Improvements to generate surveys, plans and estimates for roads and canals. Those first named were General Simon Bernard, Lieutenant-Colonel Joseph G. Totten, chief engineer of the Army, and civil engineer John L. Sullivan.

15 *Ibid.* Ephraim Beach was born near Morristown in October 1783, the son of Jedediah Beach and Mary Post. Around 1793, his family moved to Springfield, NY. Ephraim Beach served as captain of the 112th Regiment, NY Militia, during the War of 1812. He married Ann Ogden Lindsley, of Morristown, on 13 September 1816. He became a surveyor in 1815, concentrating his practice on public works in 1820. He surveyed the Eastern Division of the Erie Canal, near Conajoharie, NY, between November 1822 and April 1823. His wife died on 29 December 1822, leaving daughter Zenas Lindsley Beach (born on 12 March 1819)

and newborn son Ephraim Ogden Beach (born on 11 December 1822). He was employed as chief engineer of the Schuylkill and Conestoga Navigation in November 1823, but was discharged from his duties on 11 November 1824. He assisted Canvass White in surveying the Delaware and Raritan Canal in 1825. He then became chief engineer of the Morris Canal. He married Eliza Crane on 7 September 1826 at Cranetown (Montclair, NJ), where son James Crane Beach was born on 21 July 1827. Their other offspring were: Anna Marie, Samuel Henry, Charles Edward, Robert J. and Frances Caroline. He surveyed the route of the proposed Susquehanna and Delaware Canal and Railroad in May 1831. He surveyed the New Jersey Railroad in 1832, but resigned as its chief engineer on 23 April 1835. He surveyed the route of the Morris and Essex Railroad and was then contracted to build the same on 20 January 1836. He also surveyed the route of the Great Au Sable Railroad in 1835. He surveyed the route of the Canajoharie and Catskill Railroad in 1831 and was hired as its chief engineer on 1 May 1836. Ephraim and his family then moved to Catskill, NY. He died there on 22 September 1857. See *Documents of the Assembly of the State of New-York, Fifty-Fifth Session, 1832*, Vol. 4 (Albany: E. Croswell, 1832), p. 76.

16 'Delaware and Hudson Canal', *Niles' Weekly Register, From September 1822 to March 1823*, p. 27.

17 Jones, ed., 'Report of the Committee of the Franklin Institute, on the Inclined Plane of Professor James Renwick', *The Franklin Journal and American Mechanics' Magazine* (Philadelphia: Judah Dobson, 1826), pp. 263, 321, 327. It would take twenty-five hours and forty-six minutes to pass 206 locks, which, added to the nineteen hours required to pass the levels, made a total of forty-four hours and forty-five minutes, or, at twelve hours a day, three days and two thirds, to pass from one end to the other. Renwick estimated his mix of locks and inclined planes would reduce passage over the proposed canal to twenty-eight hours and thirty-three-and-a-half minutes, or to two-and-a-half days.

18 *Ibid.*, p. 263. In November 1826, Renwick displayed a large model of an inclined plane at the annual exhibition of American manufactures and inventions. Born in Liverpool, England, on 30 May 1790, James Renwick came to New York with his father, who was a merchant. He graduated from Columbia College in 1807 and became an instructor there in 1812. Lieutenant Renwick served with the 82nd Regiment of NY Militia as a topographical engineer under chief engineer General Joseph G. Swift. He married Margaret Brevoort and had three sons—Henry Brevoort Renwick, James Renwick Jr and Edward S. Renwick—each of whom became successful in architecture or engineering. He was professor of natural and experimental philosophy from 1820 until 1854. He died in New York City on 12 January 1863.

19 *Ibid.*, p. 258. Renwick patented his design on 7 November 1823. See *The National Cyclopedia of American Biography*, Vol. 11 (New York: James T. White & Company, 1892), p. 101, and MacBean, *Biographical Register of Saint Andrew's Society of the State of New York*, Vol. 2, 1807–1856 (New York: Saint Andrew's Society, 1925), p. 26.

20 For historical precedents for the inclined planes, see Rees, 'Canal', *The Cyclopædia; or, Universal Dictionary of Arts Sciences, and Literature*, Vol. 6 (London: Longman, Hurst, Rees, Orme, & Brown, 1819).

21 *Ibid.*, and Plymley, *General View of the Agriculture of Shropshire* (London: Richard Phillips, 1803), pp. 291-294.

22 *The Franklin Journal and American Mechanics' Magazine* (November 1826), p. 258.

23 Dwight, *Travels in New-England and New York*, Vol. 1 (London: William Baynes and Son, 1823), pp. 286-288.

24 Trumbull, *History of Northampton, Massachusetts From Its Settlement In 1654*, Vol. 2 (Northampton, Mass.: Gazette Printing Co., 1902), pp. 576-582.

25 According to family genealogists, Benjamin Prescott died at Stillwater, NY, in 1826.

26 *The Franklin Journal and American Mechanics' Magazine* (December 1826), p. 328.

27 *Niles' Weekly Register, From September 1823 To March 1824*, p. 134. Clinton was invited as chairman of the Board of Commissioners of the Erie Canal. The report of General Bernard and Colonel Totten was presented to the General Assembly of New Jersey on 7 November 1823.

28 *Report of the Commissioners Appointed by the Legislature of the State of New-Jersey; For the Purpose of Exploring the Route of a Canal to Unite the River Delaware, near Easton, with the Passaic, near Newark* (Morristown: Jacob Mann, 1823), pp. 58-63. As first conceived, the Morris Canal was to be 75.49 miles in length, terminating at the head of navigation on the Passaic River. It was actually built to Newark, adding 15 miles, making its original length 90.5 miles. As built, it was 20 feet wide at bottom, not 16 as in the original cost estimate.

29 *Ibid.*, p. 134.

30 From 'Morris Canal, No. IV', *Newark Eagle*, reprinted in *The Sussex Register*, 5 April 1824.

31 *Charter of the Morris Canal and Banking Company, and the Several Acts of the Legislature in Relation Thereto* (New York: J. Narine, 1836). The legislature incorporated Jacob S. Thompson, of Sussex County; Silas Cook, of Morris County; John Dow, of Essex County; and Charles Board, of Bergen County, under the name of the Morris Canal and Banking Company.

32 From the *Elizabeth Town Gazette* and *Morris Town Palladium*, reprinted in *The Sussex Register*, 23 May 1825.

33 *The Sussex Register*, 8 August 1825.

34 *The New-York Evening Post*, 1 June 1825. George P. Macculloch served as presiding officer.

35 *Palladium of Liberty*, 21 July 1825; see *The Towpath Post, Journal of the Canal Society of New Jersey*, No. 4, Vol. 5 (Summer 1975).

36 *Report on the Origin and Increase of the Paterson Manufactories, and the Intended Diversion of Their Waters by the Morris Canal Company* (Paterson: Day & Burnett, 1828), p. 18.

37 *History of Morris County, New Jersey 1739–1882* (New York: W. W. Munsell & Co., 1882), p. 233.

38 Swift, *The Memoirs of Gen. Joseph Gardner Swift, L.L.D., U. S. A., First Graduate of the United States Military Academy, West Point* (Worchester, Massachusetts: F. S. Blanchard & Co., 1890), p. 198. Could 'Fay' be Edward F. Gay, assistant engineer to Captain Beach?

39 *The Sussex Register*, 19 December 1825.

40 'The Morris Canal', *Niles' Weekly Register, From September 1825 to March 1826*, 5 November 1825, pp. 158-159.

41 *Ibid.*, p. 158.

42 *Ibid.*

3. A Work in Progress

1 'Report of the Committee of the Franklin Institute, on the Inclined Plane of Professor James Renwick', *The Franklin Journal and American Mechanics' Magazine* (1826), pp. 258, 259. The review committee comprised civil engineer John Wilson, topographical engineer Hartman Bache, George W. Smith and Gerard Ralston.

2 *Ibid.*, p. 330. In his letter to the Franklin Institute in October 1826, Professor Renwick described 'two horizontal shafts, turning each other, in opposite directions, by means of spur-wheels.'

3 *Ibid.*, p. 262.

4 *Report of the Commissioners Appointed by the Legislature of the State of New-Jersey, For The Purpose of Exploring The Route of A Canal To United The River Delaware, Near Easton, With The Passaic, Near, Newark*, p. 5.

5 '[For the *American Railroad Journal*] Inclined Planes', 21 July 1832, *American Railroad Journal and Advocate of Internal Improvements, From July 1832 to January 1833*, Vol. 1, Part 2 (New York: D. K. Minor, 1833), p. 466.

6 *The Franklin Journal and American Mechanics' Magazine* (1826), p. 321.

7 *Niles' Weekly Register* (1826), 1 October 1825, p. 68.

8 Skinner, ed., 'Method of Raising and Lowering Boats, By William Knight, of Morristown, Morris County, N. Jersey', 5 June 1828, *The American Journal of Improvements in the Useful Arts and Mirror of the Patent Office in the United States*, No. 1, Vol. 1, January, February and March 1828 (Washington: William Greer, 1828), p. 305.

9 In 1792, Joshua Green patented the design of a double-inclined plane that employed boat cradles 'consisting of a frame of wood, and the bottom corded by strong ropes across each other like the common bedsteads, that the boat may not be strained....' Rees, 'Canal'.

10 Stevenson, *Sketch of the Civil Engineering of North America* (London: John Weale, 1859), p. 128.

11 *Niles' Weekly Register, From September 1825 to March 1826* (1826), 10 September 1825, p. 24.

12 Larned, com., 'Morris Canal (1836)', *The New Larned History for Ready Reference, Reading and Research*, Vol. 2 (Springfield, Massachusetts: C. A. Nichols Publishing Company, 1922), pp. 1392-1393. The committee of the Franklin Institute, which examined Renwick's model of an inclined plane in December 1826, suggested employing a primitive swivel-truck, developed for steam locomotives in Great Britain, to allow each pair of wheels to support the weight of the plane car by attaching each pair of wheels to a connecting beam, which would 'support the carriage by a pivot attached to its centre, on which it will traverse....' *Franklin Journal and American Mechanics' Magazine* (1826), p. 328.

13 From the *Morristown Palladium*, 1 September 1825, reprinted in *The Sussex Register*, 5 September 1825. Ezekiel Kitchell was born on 18 February 1777, a son of Stephen Kitchell and Hannah Darling, and baptized on 18 May 1777 at the Presbyterian Church in Hanover, NJ He married Mary Bishop and represented Morris County in the General Assembly in 1815–16. He traveled to Cuba several times. On 20 June 1831, Ezekiel Kitchell, a 'Mechanic', arrived in New York City from Havana. On 30 August 1845, Ezekiel Kitchell, aged about seventy years, arrived in Portland and Falmouth, Maine, from Cardenas, Cuba. He died in Cuba in 1848. Peter Freeman was likely born in Green Village on 30 January 1792, a son of Zopher Freeman and Mary Crowell. He married Phebe Condit on 10 September 1820 and died on 4 March 1854 at Newfoundland, NJ. He is buried in the First Presbyterian Churchyard in Morristown. Peter Freeman, of Morris County, NJ, filed an application to patent a 'Mode of Lessening Friction in Canal Boats' on 1 June 1825. In his own words, he discovered 'a new principle for obviating friction, intended to be applied to the use of cars upon the inclined plane that would lessen the expense

and establish the general use of inclined planes in preference to locks.' See also 10 September 1825, *Niles' Weekly Register, From September 1825 to March 1826* (1826), p. 24.

14 *Biographical and Genealogical History of Morris and Sussex Counties, New Jersey*, Vol. 1 (New York: The Lewis Publishing Company, 1899), pp. 43-44. Calvin Howell married Charlotte, a daughter of Captain Ezekiel Kitchell.

15 Renwick, *Applications of the Science of Mechanics to Practical Purposes* (New York: Harper & Brothers, 1840), p. 177.

16 *To the Stockholders of the Morris Canal and Banking Company, April 1, 1861* (New York: Latimer Bros. & Seymour, 1861), p. 16.

17 Reprinted in *The Sussex Register*, 10 July 1826; See Renwick, p. 177; *The Port Folio, Vol. I, or Hall's Second Series*, July to December 1826, Vol. 21 (Philadelphia: Harrison Hall, 1826), p. 175; *The Evening Post*, 1 July 1826.

18 *The Sussex Register*, 24 July 1826.

19 Renwick, p. 177. In 1840, Professor Renwick wrote, 'In the inclined planes now in use on the Morris Canal, the method of locks at the head of the plane is imitated; but as the trade is alternating, the power is derived from a water-wheel. Water-wheels are objectionable as a power for the inclined planes of a canal, because they require a continual supply of water, which, at heights of more than 40 feet, may exceed that necessary to fill a lock. A water counterpoise moving on a parallel inclined plane, where the quantity of water necessary to set the system in motion would continue the motion through any change of level whatever, is therefore preferable. This is the method which was proposed by the author in the original project of the Morris Canal.'

20 As the *Geneva Gazette, and General Advertiser* noted in reporting the grand jury indictments on 23 August 1826, 'The transactions of several rotten institutions are also undergoing an investigation.'

21 Joseph G. Swift was elected chairman of the Mechanics Life Insurance and Coal Company on 7 March 1822, with Henry Eckford as president. Swift was also surveyor of the port. He became a director of the Fulton Bank in 1825. Henry Eckford, who owned a shipyard on Stanton Street in Manhattan's Lower East Side, purchased the *National Advocate* to promote the presidency of John Quincy Adams and employed Swift to manage the paper. Eckford also recommended Swift for the vice-presidency of the Life and Fire Insurance Company. The Life and Fire Insurance Company owned the mortgage on property Swift purchased on Seventh Avenue between Thirty-first and Thirty-third Streets, for which he paid $7,000 in 1825, building his residence thereon. Eckford borrowed heavily from the Life and Fire Insurance Company to build four 64-gun frigates in Brazil for South

American governments, leading to its insolvency. After his conviction, he fled to Syria. Merchant William P. Rathbone, a Tammany Hall politician and alderman from the Eleventh Ward in 1825–26, lived on Stanton Street, across from Eckford's shipyard. He later moved to Bergen County, NJ.

22 *The Sussex Register*, 4 September 1826.

23 *The Sussex Register*, 13 November 1826.

24 *Ibid.*

25 *Ibid.*

26 William Bayard died on 18 September 1826.

27 Colden, *A Report to the Directors of the Morris Canal and Banking Company; Made by the President, May 1st, 1827* (New York: William Davis, Jr, 1827), p. 5. I am indebted to Robert R. Goller for sharing his research on the competition for the premium and the award to Ezekiel Kitchell.

28 *Palladium of Liberty*, 15 February 1827.

29 Domett, *A History of the Bank of New York 1784–1884* (New York: G. P. Putnam's Sons, 1884), p. 80.

30 Silliman, *The American Journal of Science and Arts*, Vol. 14, July 1828 (New Haven: Hezekiah Howe, 1828), p. 188.

31 The keystone of the arch was inscribed with the date 1829, indicating it took two years to complete.

32 *Report on the Origin and Increase of the Paterson Manufactories, and the Intended Diversion of Their Waters by the Morris Canal Company* (Paterson: Day & Burnett, 1828), p. 10.

33 'A Canal Advocate', *The Sussex Register*, 17 January 1828.

34 Saward, ed., *The Coal Trade Journal* (1900), p. 486. There were forty-eight locks and 360 feet of lockage on the Lehigh Canal between Mauch Chunk and Easton.

35 Work on the upper section commenced in 1835.

36 This mine railroad, later known as the 'Switchback', originally consisted of an iron band (instead of a rail) spiked to 4-by-6-inch wooden stringers. A steam-powered inclined plane was later built on a return track. By 1900, the Switchback only carried summer tourists. See *The Coal Trade Journal* (1900), p. 486.

37 Bernhard, *Travels Through North America During The Years 1825 and 1826*, Vol. 1 (Philadelphia: Carey, Lea & Carey, 1828), p. 189.

38 Isaac A. Chapman in a letter to *The Village Record* on 29 October 1826, reprinted in *The Sussex Register*.

39 *The Sussex Register*, 22 March 1827. Blackwell and McFarlan, iron merchants in Coenties Slip, NY, purchased the forges, rolling-and-slitting mills, and nail factory of Canfield & Losey at Dover in 1817. Daniel Ayres became a partner in May 1820. In 1830, the firm became McFarlan & Ayres. Henry McFarlan Jr succeeded Blackwell and McFarlan in the

operation of the nail factory, metal-chain and cable shops at Dover from 1830 to 1869.

40 *To the Stockholders of the Morris Canal and Banking Company, April 1, 1861*, p. 16. Robert P. Bell was listed as a dry-goods merchant in New York City in 1826. He was a director of the Morris Canal and Banking Company between 1826 and 1832. He operated the Stanhope gristmill from 1834 until an incendiary fire destroyed it in 1837. His daughter Charlotte married Andrew A. Smalley on 26 September 1837.

41 'Inclined Plane at Boonton Falls', *Niles' Weekly Register*, 23 August 1828, p. 411.

42 These two locks were originally numbered 16 and 17 East.

43 *The Torch Light and Public Advertiser*, 30 December 1830, p. 1.

44 Carhart, com., and Nelson, ed., *Genealogy of the Morris Family* (New York: The A. S. Barnes Company, 1911), p. 88. Ephraim Morris, son of Stephen and Katherine (Smith) Morris, was born on 27 August 1800. He assisted his father in the operation of a sawmill and invented a log cutter for dyewood. He married Martha Vandel in 1818 and they had four children: John, Mary, Augustus and Stephen. He served as general manager of the Morris Canal from 1832 to 1843. He later formed the Morris & Cummings Dredging Company. He died on 9 June 1865.

45 Jones, 'American Patents', *Journal of the Franklin Institute of the State of Pennsylvania*, New Series, Vol. 5 (Philadelphia: Franklin Institute, 1830), p. 30.

46 *To the Stockholders of the Morris Canal and Banking Company, April 1, 1861*, p. 16.

47 On 17 October 1829, *Niles' Weekly Register* published a description of the inclined plane at Bloomfield from the *Middletown* [Connecticut] *Sentinel*. The article, entitled, 'The Inclined Plane On the Morris Canal, at Bloomfield, NJ', was also reprinted in *The Sussex Register*.

48 Drawings submitted with Ephraim Morris's patent application appear to show the boat cradle suspended by such vertical rods from the plane car.

49 *To the Stockholders of the Morris Canal and Banking Company, April 1, 1861*, p. 16.

50 Hazard, ed., 'From the *N. Y. Com. Advertiser*. The Morris Canal—Inclined Plane', *The Register of Pennsylvania, January to July 1829*, Vol. 3 (Philadelphia: W. F. Geddes, 1829), p. 99.

51 Domett, p. 80.

52 The legislature authorized the company to borrow necessary sums of money and mortgage the canal as a security on 28 January 1830.

53 'Letter to the Editor of the Railroad Journal' from D. B. Douglass, of Brooklyn, N. Y., *American Railroad Journal and Advocate of Internal Improvements, July 1832 to January 1833* (1833), 18 August 1832, p. 532.

54 '[For the *American Railroad Journal*] Inclined Planes', *American Railroad Journal* (1833), 21 July 1832, p. 516.

55 Gordon, The *History and Gazetteer of New Jersey* (Trenton: Daniel Fenton, 1834), p. 24.

56 '[For the *American Railroad Journal*] Inclined Planes', *American Railroad Journal* (1833), 21 July 1832, p. 516.

57 David Bates Douglass was born in Pompton, NJ, on 21 March 1790. After graduating from Yale University in 1813, he was appointed Second Lieutenant in the army corps of engineers as commander of sappers and miners at West Point. During the War of 1812, he commanded a company on the northern frontier and participated in the Battle of Niagara. According to *Appleton's Cyclopædia of American Biography*, 'He was assistant professor of natural and experimental philosophy at West Point in 1819–20, with the rank of captain. As astronomical surveyor he fulfilled several important commissions; later he became professor of mathematics, and in 1823 of civil and military engineering. On March 1, 1831, he resigned his professorship and his commission in the army, and became chief engineer of the Morris Canal. His introduction of inclined planes in place of locks for canal navigation proved a success on the completion of the canal in 1832.' He died as professor of mathematics at Hobart College, in Geneva, NY, on 19 October 1849. He is buried in Greenwood Cemetery. Grant and Fiske, ed., *Appleton's Cyclopædia of American Biography*, Vol. 2 (New York: D. Appleton and Company, 1888), p. 217.

58 'The Inclined Plane on the Morris Canal, at Bloomfield, N. J. from the *Middletown* [Connecticut] *Sentinel*', *Niles' Weekly Register*, 17 October 1829.

59 William Scott, William Jackson, Thomas Munn, Joseph Dickerson Jr, Matthew Kitchell, David B. Hurd, Peter P. Brown, Zenas Hurd and John H. Stansborough.

60 'Statistics are from a report of the Congressional Committee on the Tariff Convention', October 1831.

61 *To the Stockholders of the Morris Canal and Banking Company, April 1, 1861*, p. 17.

62 Whitford, *Supplement to the Annual Report of the State Engineer and Surveyor of the State of New York For the Fiscal Year Ending September 30, 1905, History of the Canal System of the State of New York, Together with Brief Histories of the Canals of the United States and Canada*, Vol. 1 (Albany: Brandow Printing Company, 1906), pp. 513, 516, 518, 520, 523, 527, 531.

63 Gamst, ed., and Diephouse, trans., *Franz Anton Ritter Von Gerstner, Early American Railroads*, Vol. 1 (Stanford, California: Stanford University Press, 1997), p. 515.

64 'Canal', *The Encyclopædia Britannica, A Dictionary of Arts, Sciences, and General Literature*, Vol. 4 (Chicago: The Werner Company, 1895), p. 785.

65 Minor, ed., *American Railroad Journal and Iron Manufacturer's and Mining Gazette*, Vol. 21 (Philadelphia: J. H. Schultz, 1848), 25 June 1848, p. 390.

66 The obituary of William's son and namesake in *The Sun* (New York City) on 27 November 1891, reads: 'William H. Pragnell, long master boat builder for the Delaware and Hudson Canal Company, died last week at his home in Honesdale, Pa, aged 73 years. Early in life he resided at Dover, NJ, where his father built the first boat that ran on the waters of the Morris Canal, and named it the Dover. He leaves a sister, Mrs William A. Dickerson, of Dover, and six children living at Honesdale.'

67 Stevenson, *Sketch of the Civil Engineering of North America* (London: John Weale, 1859), p. 128.

68 *The National Cyclopedia of American Biography*, Vol. 7 (New York: James T. White & Co., 1897), p. 4.

69 Stuart, *Lives and Works of Civil and Military Engineers of America* (New York: D. Van Nostrand, 1871), pp. 206-207.

70 'The Inclined Plane, From the *New York American* of Dec. 16', *Niles' Weekly Register, From March 1831 to September 1831* (1831), 30 April 1831, pp. 159-160.

71 Stuart, pp. 198-207.

72 This packet boat, named for Cadwallader Colden's wife Maria Provoost, was built in Bloomfield and traveled regularly between Newark and Mead's Basin in 1829.

73 *The Mechanics' Magazine, Museum, Register, Journal and Gazette*, Vol. 15 (London: M. Salmon, 1831), 28 May 1831, p. 203. Article reprinted from the *Sentinel* in *The Disseminator of Useful Knowledge*, published in New Harmony, Indiana.

74 Hazard, ed., *The Register of Pennsylvania, January to July 1831*, Vol. 7 (Philadelphia: Wm. F. Geddes, 1831), p. 62.

75 *The Pittsburgh Gazette*, 22 July 1831, p. 3.

76 'The Inclined Planes of the Morris Canal', *American Engineer and Railroad Journal*, New Series, Vol. 68 (New York: M. N. Forney, 1894), p. 555.

77 Walch, *Notes on Some of the Chief Navigable Rivers and Canals in the United States and Canada, Made for the Government of Madras, During a Tour in 1876* (Madras: W. H. Moore, Lawrence Asylum Press, 1877), p. 4.

78 '[For the *American Railroad Journal*] Inclined Planes', *American Railroad Journal and Advocate of Internal Improvements, July 1832 to January 1833* (1833), pp. 516-517.

79 'Report of the Joint Committee of the Directors and Stockholders of the Morris Canal & Banking Company', *American Railroad Journal and Advocate of Internal Improvements, July 1832 to January 1833* (1833), 23 August 1832, pp. 626-627.

80 *Ibid.*

81 Joseph Jackson was born in 8 March 1774. He first married Elizabeth Platt Ogden in 1802. Their son Stephen Joseph Jackson was born in 1805. He next married Electa Beach, widow of Silas Dickerson, on 8 May 1808. He died at Rockaway, NJ, on 28 January 1855. The children mentioned in the story were likely twins Mary and David Robbin, born in 1830. *History of Morris County, New Jersey 1739–1882*, p. 179. Historian Robert R. Goller pointed out to me that an earlier but largely imaginative version of this story is found in Lyon, *Historical Discourse on Boonton* (Newark: The Daily Journal, 1873), p. 24.

82 *The New-York Evening Post*, 12 May 1832, p. 2.

83 '[For the *American Railroad Journal*] Inclined Planes', *American Railroad Journal and Advocate of Internal Improvements, July 1832 to January 1833* (1833), p. 466. The writer identified himself only as 'H'.

84 'Report of the Joint Committee of the Directors and Stockholders of the Morris Canal & Banking Company', *American Railroad Journal and Advocate of Internal Improvements, July 1832 to January 1833* (1833), p. 626-627.

85 The ton used in the company's calculations was the equivalent of 2,240 lb.

86 Shaw, *History of Essex and Hudson Counties, New Jersey* (Philadelphia: Everts & Peck, 1884), p. 191. The *Newark Sentinel* of 22 November 1831, announced the arrival of the first boats from Mauch Chunk, Easton and other places along the line of the canal.

87 Minor, ed., *Railroad Journal and Advocate of Internal Improvements, From January to December 1832*, p. 341.

88 *To the Stockholders of the Morris Canal and Banking Company, April 1, 1861*, p. 17.

89 *The Pittsburgh Gazette*, 10 May 1833, p. 3.

90 *Ibid.*, p. 24.

91 Gordon, p. 23.

92 *Ibid.*, p. 27.

93 *Ibid.*, p. 26.

94 *Ibid.*, p. 24.

95 Minor, ed., *American Railroad Journal and Advocate of Internal Improvements, January to July 1834*, pp. 273, 356, 404.

96 The Delaware Division Canal extended 59.75 miles between the feeder dam at Easton, Pa, and the tidal basin at Bristol. Twenty-five miles were opened to navigation in 1830, but construction on the remainder proved defective

and had to be redone. See 'Canal Commissioners' Report', *Republican Compiler*, 18 January 1831, p. 2. Water was admitted into the whole length of the canal in December 1831 and it was navigable by July 1833.

97 The post office at Port Colden, Warren County, NJ, was named to honor Cadwallader Colden in the year he died. James B. Murray was listed as a trustee of the Greenwich Savings Bank of New York and as Portuguese consul in New York City in *Williams's New-York Annual Register, 1835*. He served as New York City alderman from the Fifteenth Ward. He was a real estate investor and developer and a noted theater patron. Port Murray in Warren County, NJ, was named in his honor shortly after his death in 1866.

98 Shaw, p. 191.

99 'Morris Canal', *The Daily Pittsburgh Gazette*, 4 August 1834, p. 2.

100 *The Boston Morning Post*, 14 August 1833, p. 2.

101 'Wall Street in Wartime', *Harper's New Monthly Magazine, December 1864 to May 1865*, Vol. 30 (1865), p. 619. In April 1865, *Harper's New Monthly Magazine* described this as the 'first great corner on record....' Traders thought the stock overvalued and sold it short, allowing 'a shrewd clique' to purchase all available offerings and lock it in a trunk. As their contracts matured, those who sold it short discovered no stock could be had, except at an exorbitant price. There was no precedent on Wall Street for such an action and bears accused the 'cornerers' of conspiracy, but the bulls responded, 'by inquiring why their antagonists had sold that which they did not possess and apparently could not procure.' Acting as referee, the Board of Brokers, 'new to such points, actually decided in favor of the shorts, pronouncing a verdict which virtually relieved them from the necessity of fulfilling their contracts, on the ground that the corner was a conspiracy.'

102 'The History of Wall Street Corners', *The Bankers' Magazine and Statistical Register, From July 1881, to July 1882,* Third Series, Vol. 36 or 16 (New York: Benjamin Homans, 1882), pp. 308-309.

103 'Morris Canal Stock sold on Saturday at 165', *The Evening Post*, 13 January 1835.

104 *Niles' Weekly Register, From March 1835 to September 1835* (1835), 16 May 1835, p. 190.

105 *The Evening Post*, 12 May 1835, p. 2.

106 Minor, ed., 'Canal Intelligence', *American Railroad Journal and Advocate of Internal Improvements, January to July 1835* (1835), p. 420.

107 Minor, ed., *American Railroad Journal and Advocate of Internal Improvements, January to July 1835* (1835), p. 470.

108 Roswell B. Mason was employed as an engineer on the Eastern Division of the Erie Canal and came with Ephraim Beach to work on the Morris

Canal. He was appointed resident engineer of the Morris Canal in May 1833 and replaced Ephraim Beach as chief engineer in March 1836.

109 'The Inclined Planes of the Morris Canal', *American Engineer and Railroad Journal* (1894), p. 555. See *To the Stockholders of the Morris Canal and Banking Company, April 1, 1861*, p. 17.

110 Historian Robert R. Goller informs me the description of an inclined plane from the *Civil Engineer and Architect's Journal* (1842), quoted here, was lifted from French civil engineer Michel Chevalier's *Histoire et Description des Voies de Communication aux États-Unis* and specifically describes Inclined Plane 9 West. Chevalier personally observed and studied the Morris Canal plane, located 4⅓ miles from Phillipsburg, in 1835.

111 *Civil Engineer and Architect's Journal, Scientific and Railway Gazette* (1842), p. 105.

112 *Ibid.*

113 The act of 5 March 1836, named twenty-three directors to the board: Louis McLane, John S. Crary, James Parker, George Griswold, John Haggerty, Garret D. Wall, Samuel R. Brooks, Washington Irving, John S. Darcy, Henry Yates, Peter M. Ryerson, Christian B. Zabriskie, Edwin Lord, Joseph L. Joseph, Isaac H. Williamson, Daniel Jackson, Jonathan Goodhue, John Travers, Henry W. Hicks, James B. Murray, John Moss, Stephen Whitney and Philemon Dickerson.

114 Minor and Schaeffer 'Notice To Contractors', *American Railroad Journal and Advocate of Internal Improvements*, 10 December 1836, p. 495.

115 'Accident on the Morris Canal', *The Sussex Register*, 18 July 1836.

116 Minor and Schaeffer, *American Railroad Journal, and Advocate of Internal Improvements*, (1837), 10 December 1836, p. 778.

117 'Statement of Hon. Caleb B. Smith', *Letter of Charles Butler, Esq., to the Legislature of Indiana in relation to the Public Debt* (Indianapolis: Morrison & Spann, 1846), p. 45.

118 *Ibid.*, pp. 41-43.

119 'Morris Canal & Banking Company—Report for 1848', *American Railroad Journal and Iron Manufacturer's and Mining Gazette* (1848), 17 June 1848, pp. 389-391.

120 Eleven states defaulted on their debts between 1838 and 1840, namely, Florida, Mississippi, Arkansas, Alabama, Louisiana, Georgia, Illinois, Indiana, Michigan, Maryland and Pennsylvania.

121 *Letter of Charles Butler, Esq., to the Legislature of Indiana in relation to the Public Debt*, p. 41.

122 'Special message concerning the five million loan', *Documents Accompanying the Journal of the Senate of the State of Michigan at the Annual Session of 1841*, Vol. 1 (Detroit: George Dawson, 1841), pp. 266-311.

123 *Documents Accompanying the Journal of the Senate of the State of Michigan at the Annual Session of 1840*, Vol. 2 (Detroit: George Dawson, 1840), p. 498.

124 *Documents Accompanying the Journal of the Senate of the State of Michigan at the Annual Session of 1840*, Vol. 1, pp. 105-106.

125 Minor and Schaeffer, 'From the *Williamsport Free Press*, Nov. 17, Northumberland and Erie Railroad Convention', *American Railroad Journal, and Advocate of Internal Improvements*, 10 December 1836, p. 776.

126 Minor and Schaeffer, *American Railroad Journal and Advocate of Internal Improvements* (1838), p. 593. The first shipments of Beaver Meadow coal occurred in 1837.

127 *Report of the President and Directors of the Morris Canal & Banking Company to the Stockholders, March 1837* (1837), pp. 7-8. The State of Pennsylvania incorporated the Little Schuylkill and Susquehanna Railroad in 1836 to build a railway from Williamsport to the Beaver Meadow Railroad. The Lehigh Coal and Navigation Company completed a railway from White Haven in 1843.

128 *Ibid.*, pp. 5-6. See also *Franz Anton Ritter Von Gerstner, Early American Railroads*, Vol. 1, p. 515.

129 Poor, *History of the Railroads and Canals of the United States of America, Exhibiting their Progress, Cost, Revenues, Expenditures & Present Condition*, Second Quarto Series, Vol. 1 (New York: John R. Schultz & Co., 1860), p. 429.

130 'To Canal Contractors', *The Evening Post*, 21 April 1834, p. 6.

131 Minor and Schaeffer, 'Morris Canal', *American Railroad Journal and Advocate of Internal Improvements* (1837), 26 August 1837, p. 529.

132 'Morris Canal', *The Evening Post*, 1 December 1836, p. 2; 'Morris Canal', *The Pittsburgh Gazette*, 5 December 1836,

133 *Report of the President and Directors of the Morris Canal & Banking Company to the Stockholders, March 1837*, p. 4.

134 Tanner, *Brief Description of the Canals and Railroads of Pennsylvania and New Jersey* (Philadelphia: H. S. Tanner, 1834), pp. 28, 29. As historian Robert R. Goller notes, the Morris Canal started with twenty-five lift locks, the number of which was reduced when a lift lock at Drakesville (Ledgewood) was eliminated by lengthening Inclined Plane No. 3 East. Two lift locks near the Passaic River in Newark were combined into the so-called Deep Lock (No. 17 East).

135 Thomas V. Johnson married Jonathan Cory's daughter Sarah Frances in 1835.

136 Potts, *The New Jersey Register for the Year Eighteen Hundred and Thirty-Seven*, Vol. 1 (Trenton: William D'Hart, 1837), p. 216.

4. Troubled Waters

1 Southard worked as an attorney for the Morris Canal Company both before and after his tenure as president.

2 Elmer, *Collections of the New Jersey Historical Society, Vol. VII, The Constitution and Government of the Province and State of New Jersey, with Biographical Sketches of the Governors from 1776 to 1845, and Reminiscences of the Bench and Bar, During More Than Half A Century* (Newark, NJ: Martin R. Dennis and Company, 1872), pp. 201-234.

3 *Ibid.*, p. 228.

4 *The Sussex Register*, 27 November 1838. The suit was settled in 1840. Robert P. Bell was appointed a county judge in March 1839. He sold his Stanhope real estate in April 1840. Suit was brought against him in Morris County circuit court in December 1840 for two promissory notes, which he acknowledged in 1838, but which he subsequently claimed were forgeries. He died in Jersey City on 4 June 1849, at sixty-one years of age.

5 *The Sussex Register* reported on 1 February 1839, that citizens of Morris County were opposing an increase in the privileges of the Morris Canal and Banking Company. Macculloch succeeded in his cause with assistance from son-in-law Senator Jacob W. Miller.

6 Elmer, pp. 232-233.

7 Gouge, *The Journal of Banking from July 1841 to July 1842* (Philadelphia: J. Van Court, 1842), p. 138.

8 *Letter of Charles Butler, Esq., to the Legislature of Indiana in relation to the Public Debt*, p. 48.

9 Hunt, 'Art. I. Debts and Finances of the States of the Union: With Reference to their General Condition and Prosperity, Chapter VI, The Western States—Indiana', *The Merchants' Magazine and Commercial Review, From July to December 1849*, Vol. 21 (New York: Freeman Hunt, 1849), p. 151.

10 *Letter of Charles Butler, Esq., to the Legislature of Indiana in relation to the Public Debt*, pp. 41-44.

11 The Morris Canal and Banking Company sold $907,000 in Michigan bonds to the Farmers Loan and Trust Company on 4 October 1838; $200,000 worth to George Griswold, president of the Bank of the United States in New York, on 4 July 1838; $80,000 worth to James Buchanan; $60,000 worth to Powell Bank of Newburgh, NY; $45,000 to the Bank of Kinderhook; $40,000 to the Merchants and Farmers' Bank of Ithaca, NY; $20,000 worth to the Pine Plains Bank; $5,000 worth to the Fort Plains Bank; $5,000 to the US War Department; and $50,000 to John Wilson, of London, England. See 'Debts and Finance of the State of the

Union', *Documents Accompanying the Journal of the Senate of the State of Michigan at the Annual Session of 1840*, Vol. 2, p. 372. The Morris Canal and Banking Company informed the Michigan governor that they could not sell the remainder on the same terms, but could dispose of them if the state consented to receive promissory notes of the Bank of the United States for three quarters of the amount and the guarantee of the Morris Canal and Banking Company for the remaining quarter of the amount, bearing 6-percent interest, payable in quarterly installments extending over about four years. Taking possession of the state bonds, these banks raised money on them in England by way of a loan as upon any other security. See 'Money-Market and City Intelligence', *The Times* of London, England, 15 June 1849, p. 6.

12 *Documents Accompanying the Journal of the Senate of the State of Michigan at the Annual Session of 1840*, Vol. 2, p. 497.

13 'The Debt of Michigan', *Boston Morning Post*, 19 June 1842, p. 1.

14 *Boston Morning Post*, 26 August 1840, p. 2.

15 Henry Jordan and Company successfully experimented with heated air at Oxford Furnace in June–July 1835, reducing the height of the furnace and strengthening its walls to withstand higher temperatures. He adopted the German method of pre-heating air from the bellows by blowing it into cast iron boxes and through tubes, set in the masonry near the hottest part of the furnace. This allowed for a more efficient use of charcoal and was not employed to burn anthracite.

16 Henry, *History of the Lehigh Valley* (Easton: Bixler & Corwin, 1859), pp. 165, 346. Francis C. Lathrop, of Trenton, was a civil engineer who specialized in bridge design.

17 'Anthracite Iron', *American Railroad Journal and Mechanics' Magazine* (1840), p. 320.

18 'High Lights in Anthracite Trade History—I', p. 570, and 'High Lights in Anthracite Trade History—II', p. 644, *The Coal Trade Journal*, Vol. 50. The use of anthracite to smelt iron surpassed charcoal in 1855 and remained the principal fuel for blast furnaces until displaced by coke or bituminous coal in 1875. After the iron mines of the Lake Superior region opened, bituminous coal steadily superseded the use of anthracite in manufacturing industries until, by 1920, bituminous coal production was more than five times as great as that of anthracite.

19 *Ibid.*, p. 224.

20 Tenney, *The Mining Magazine: Devoted to Mines, Mining Operations, Metallurgy, &c., &c.*, Vol. 8 (New York: John F. Trow, 1857), p. 435.

21 The Morris and Sussex Manufacturing Company was incorporated on 28 February 1835 to raise $75,000 to purchase real estate and erect three blast furnaces to smelt iron ore with anthracite. The legislature

authorized an alteration in the corporate name to the Stanhope Iron Company and an increase in the capital stock to $250,000 on 25 February 1841. *Acts of the Sixty-Fifth General Assembly of the State of New Jersey* (1841), pp. 38-39. On 20 March 1845, the legislature authorized Edwin Post, William Nelson Wood, Jacob Lowrance and Charles Lewis to incorporate the Sussex Iron Company and to issue $350,000 in capital stock. *Acts of the Sixty-Sixth General Assembly of the State of New Jersey* (1845), pp. 133-137. William Nelson Wood was born in Morristown on 22 December 1805, and died on 25 July 1865. He graduated Princeton in 1828 and later served as judge in the Court of Errors and Appeals.

22   Andrew A. Smalley married Charlotte A. Bell, daughter of Robert P. Bell, on 26 September 1837.

23   *The Sussex Register*, 18 August 1840.

24   'Treasurer's report on $5,000,000 loan', *Joint Documents of the State of Michigan at the Annual Session of 1841*, Vol. 1 (1841), p. 269.

25   *Ibid.*, pp. 271-276. Properties and obligations received as securities by the State of Michigan included: an assignment of mortgage, executed by the Mount Hope Mining Company, to the Morris Canal on a mineral tract of 800 acres and mineral rights on an adjacent 800 acres, worth $50,000; a bond and mortgage executed by the Morris Canal for property purchased of Nathaniel Saxton in Warren and Morris Counties, containing 1,152 acres, worth $20,000; a bond and mortgage executed by the Morris Canal and Banking Company to the State of Michigan on their two farms in Pequannock, Morris County, containing 315 acres with saw mill, two good dwelling houses and other improvements, worth $10,000; an assignment of bond and mortgage on lands situated in Luzerne County, Pa, on the headwaters of the Lehigh River, for $20,000, executed by J. Scarinus, J. T. Pierson and Stiles Williams, which had a balance due of $10,000; a bond and mortgage executed by the Morris Canal and Banking Company on their banking house and two lots of land on the corners of Grand, Greene and Sussex Streets in Jersey City, worth $20,000; a deed of conveyance from George Griswold to the State of Michigan for the banking house lot at 45 William Street in New York City, worth $100,000; a deed of conveyance, executed by the Little Schuylkill & Susquehanna Railroad Company, for a tract of land purchased from Charles S. Coxe, of Philadelphia, containing 100 acres, on the headwaters of the Little Schuylkill, worth $8,000; an assignment of residue of debts, bills receivable, stocks, bonds and securities held by the American Exchange Bank in liquidation of a stock transaction, dated March 1, 1839, worth $20,000; obligations of the Morris and Sussex Manufacturing Company to deliver iron in New York worth $177,000;

an obligation of Biddle, Chamber & Company, of Danville, Pa, to deliver iron in New York, worth $27,500; and an assignment on judgment on Long Island Railroad's rolling stock for $40,000. Theodore Romeyn, of Detroit, brought the availability of the Michigan bonds to the attention of the Morris Canal and Banking Company during a visit to New York.

26 *Ibid.*, p. 270.

27 *The Jeffersonian Republican*, 24 February 1841, p. 2. According to Poor's *History of the Railroads and Canals of the United States of America*, Vol. 1, p. 411: 'During the years 1840 and 1841, the lift locks were enlarged to ninety-eight by twelve feet. Immediately after the locks were enlarged the company failed, and its effects were placed in the hands of receivers, by whom the canal was leased for a small annual rent until the close of the season of 1844.'

28 It fully re-opened on 28 October 1841.

29 Gouge, p. 138.

30 *Ibid.*, p. 287.

31 'Another Explosion', *Public Ledger*, 21 October 1841, p. 4.

32 Gouge, p. 2.

33 *Public Ledger*, 21 October 1841, p. 2

34 *New-York Tribune*, 2 February 1842, p. 3.

35 *American Railroad Journal and Mechanics' Magazine* (1842), p. 32. Lewis Slate Coryell was born at Lambertville, Hunterdon County, NJ, on 20 December 1788, a son of Joseph and Eleanor Coryell. He apprenticed as a house-carpenter in 1803 and later opened a carpentry business at Morrisville, Pa. He married Mary W. Vansant, of New Hope, on 21 August 1813. Earning a reputation as 'a civil engineer of great skill,' he established Union Mills, a grist-and-saw mill on the Delaware River at New Hope, in partnership with Joseph D. Murray in 1817. Described as 'an early advocate of internal improvements,' he was appointed in 1822 as 'one of the commissioners to improve the rafting and boating channels of the Delaware, and the work was placed under his charge.' According to tax records, he moved to Solebury Township, Bucks County, Pa, around 1826. He was named county auditor in 1828. Lewis S. Coryell and Joseph D. Murray contracted to build 'the [Delaware Division] canal through New Hope, about a mile, including all the locks and aqueducts, in 1829–30, and also the canal locks at Trenton and Bordentown, of stone from the Yardleyville quarries, which they owned.' The firm dissolved in 1836 with Mr. Murray's retirement. Coryell was appointed postmaster at New Hope in July 1837. He joined with other businessmen to form the Hanover Coal Company in 1839 'for the purpose of mining coal, and the transportation of the same, within the counties of Luzerne and Northampton.' Lewis S. Coryell died on 30 January 1865, and is

buried at New Hope. See Battle, *History of Bucks County, Pennsylvania* (Philadelphia: A. Warner & Co., 1887), pp. 526, 529, 689.

36 Minor and Schaeffer, *American Railroad Journal and Mechanics' Magazine* (1843). George Sylvester Mills, son of Eden Mills and Rosanna Pettibone Wilcox, was born in Norfolk, Connecticut, on 16 December 1795. He married Elizabeth Ryerson, of Morris County, NJ, in 1819. His children, Elizabeth and Samuel, were born in New York in 1827 and 1830. He died a widower at Newark on 18 December 1876. Apparently only the youngest of his five children, Samuel Ryerson Mills, an invalid who worked as his father's store clerk, survived him, living until 1893. Lorenzo A. Sykes was born in Springfield, NY, on 4 January 1806. By his own testimony, he was 'by profession a civil engineer; that he has followed that profession since 1826....' While working as assistant engineer on the Morris Canal, he married Eliza Ann Wurts, daughter of Dr George Wurts and Abigail Pettit, of Montville, NJ, in 1831. He became assistant engineer on the New Jersey Railroad, succeeding Ephraim Beach as chief engineer in April 1835. He and his wife resided in Newark, NJ, in 1840. Having entered the employ of the Delaware and Hudson Canal Company in 1849 as their principal coal dealer, he was listed as a New York City resident in 1850. He succeeded his wife's uncle, Maurice Wurts, as general agent and superintendent of the Delaware and Hudson Canal and moved to Rondout, NY, in 1857. He served on the original board of directors of the First National Bank of Rondout in 1863. Retiring in 1866, he and his family toured Europe before settling in East Orange, NJ, where he died on 8 December 1878. His death certificate lists his occupation as 'Civil Engineer'. His daughter, Caroline, married Robert H. Atwater.

37 Reprinted from the *Newark Daily Advertiser* in *American Railroad Journal, and Mechanics' Magazine* (June 1843), p. 189.

38 The Morris & Essex Railroad opened between Morristown and Newark on 1 January 1838, and soon began running three daily trains.

39 'The Money Markets', *Public Ledger*, 17 October 1844, p. 2.

40 The new directors were: Joseph W. Alsop, Joseph Bishop, Samuel P. Brooks, John J. Bryant, Chester Clark, Jonathan J. Coddington, Zebedee Cook Jr, Frederick T. Frelinghuysen, John C. Green, George Griswold, J. Woodward Haven, Jacob Little (declined and replaced by Theodore Delton), Henry McFarlan, Peter McMattin, John Rankin, James J. Scofield, Elijah Scott, John Strader Jr, Thomas Tileston, Daniel Tyler, Joseph B. Varnum, Benjamin Williamson, and John A. Willink. George Griswold, of New York, and Richard Alsop, of Philadelphia, established the Bank of the United States in New York with $200,000 in capital in 1838. Banker Joseph Woodward Haven married Griswold's daughter

Cornelia. Daughter Matilda Elizabeth Griswold married Frederick T. Frelinghuysen.

41 On 1 January 1853, Dudley B. Fuller formed a partnership with J. Couper Lord and the firm of D. B. Fuller & Company continued business under the name of Fuller & Lord.

42 *The Evening Post*, 24 April 1845, p. 2.

43 'Morris Canal & Banking Company—Report for 1848', *American Railroad Journal and Iron Manufacturer's and Mining Gazette* (1849), 17 June 1848, p. 390.

44 *Ibid.*

45 *Ibid.*, p. 406.

46 'Riot on the Morris Canal', *Public Ledger*, 17 May 1845, p. 2.

47 *The Proceedings of the American Society of Civil Engineers*, Vol. 19, January to December 1893 (New York: Published by the Society, 1893), p. 98. William H. Talcott, son of Captain William Talcott and Dorothy Blish, was born in Hebron, Connecticut, on 7 April 1809. He died on 8 December 1868.

48 'Report of the President of the Morris Canal and Banking Company to the Board of Directors, August 12, 1845', *The Evening Post*, 18 August 1845, p. 2. The Morris Canal and Banking Company claimed it was using water impounded in its new Long Pond (Greenwood Lake) reservoir without diminishing the flow of the Passaic River.

49 Minor, ed., *American Railroad Journal and Iron Manufacturer's and Mining Gazette, From January to December 1848* (1849), 17 June 1848, p. 390.

50 'Outlet Lock on the Delaware Division', *American Railroad Journal and General Advertiser* (1846), 9 May 1846, p. 299.

51 'Cooper, Peter', *Appleton's Annual Cyclopædia and Register of Important Events of the Year 1883*, p. 256.

52 The heirs were Henry Chew, of Baltimore, Maryland, administrator of Benjamin Chew Sr, of Philadelphia; Henry Chew, William W. Chew and James M. Mason, executors of Benjamin Chew, late of Clivedon, Germantown; Lawrence S. Lardner, administrator of Lynford Lardner; Richard Lardner, John Lardner and Lawrence S. Lardner, of Philadelphia; Mary A. Auchmutty, Richard Livingston and Catherine Livingston, of New York City; and Richard Wells, administrator of Henry Hill.

53 Minor, ed., *American Railroad Journal and Iron Manufacturer's and Mining Gazette, From January to December 1848* (1849), p. 705.

54 A son named John was born to Thomas Hewitt and Cynthia Cannon in Newton Township on 22 September 1851.

55 *The New Jersey Herald*, 12 January 1850.

56 *American Railroad Journal and General Advertiser, From January to*

December 1847 (1848), p. 487.

57 Minor, ed., 'Morris Canal & Banking Company—Report for 1848', *American Railroad Journal and Iron Manufacturer's and Mining Gazette, From January to December 1848* (1849), 17 June 1848, pp. 389-391; 24 June 1848, pp. 404-408; 1 July 1848, pp. 424-425.

58 *Ibid.*, p. 405; see also, Jones, *The Economic History of the Anthracite-Tidewater Canals* (Philadelphia: The University of Pennsylvania, 1908), p. 114.

59 *Minute Book of the Morris Canal Company*, 6 August 1847, pp. 101-102.

60 Minor, ed., *American Railroad Journal and Iron Manufacturer's and Mining Gazette, From January to December 1848* (1849), p. 425.

61 *Ibid.*, p. 391.

62 *Ibid.*, p. 405.

63 *Ibid.*

64 Poor, ed., *American Railroad Journal*, Vol. 8 or 25, p. 327.

65 *The New Jersey Herald*, 16 November 1850.

66 Poor, ed., *American Railroad Journal*, Vol. 8 or 25, p. 327.

67 Walch, pp. 2-3.

68 Jones, C. L., p. 114.

69 Poor, ed., *American Railroad Journal*, Vol. 6 or 23, p. 314.

70 *Ibid.*

71 *The Sussex Register*, 30 May 1850.

72 *Minute Book of the Morris Canal Company*, 11 July 1850.

73 Contractors Goulden and Van Dyke were hired to rebuild Planes Nos. 3 and 4 West; Solen Chapin was hired to re-do Planes Nos. 9, 10 and 11 West.

74 Minor, ed., *American Railroad Journal and Iron Manufacturer's and Mining Gazette, From January to December 1848* (1849), p. 405.

75 *Ibid.*

5. A Paying Proposition

1 *The New Jersey Herald*, 1 May 1852.

2 Poor, ed., *American Railroad Journal*, Vol. 9 or 26, pp. 714-715.

3 *Ibid.*, p. 714.

4 Whitelaw and Stirrat, of Paisley, Scotland, invented the 'Scotch Mill', which they patented in the United States in 1843. *Transactions of the American Society of Civil Engineers*, Vol. 85 (New York: American Society of Civil Engineers, 1922), p. 1338.

5 Poor, ed., *American Railroad Journal*, Vol. 9 or 26, p. 715.

6 *Ibid.*

7 *Journal of the Franklin Institute* (1848), p. 323.

8 *Journal of the Fourth Senate of the State of New Jersey, Being the Seventy-Second Session of the Legislature* (1848), p. 500.

9 The Central Railroad of New Jersey opened between Elizabeth, NJ, and Easton, Pa, in 1852. In that same year, the Delaware, Lackawanna and Western began breaking coal into market sizes, i.e., egg, stove, chestnut and pea. See 'High Lights in Anthracite Trade History—I', *The Coal Trade Journal*, Vol. 50, p. 570.

10 *Fourth Annual Report of the Board of Managers of the Delaware, Lackawanna & Western Rail-Road Co. to the Stockholders, January 1857* (New York: George F. Nesbitt & Co., 1857), p. 36.

11 *Ibid.*, p. 38.

12 Poor, ed., *American Railroad Journal*, Vol. 16 or 33, p. 769.

13 Schultz, ed., *American Railroad Journal*, Vol. 21 or 37, p. 849.

14 Poor, ed., *American Railroad Journal*, Vol. 13 or 30, p. 666.

15 *Ibid.*, p. 733.

16 *The New Jersey Herald*, 9 April 1859.

17 Colburn, *Engineering, An Illustrated Weekly Journal, From July to December 1868*, Vol. 6 (London: Office for Advertisements and Publication, 1868), p. 11. The ferryboat was a flat, measuring 10 by 50 feet, with two leeboards on its upstream side that could be raised or lowered to present more surface to the action of the current. Wire ropes traveled through guide sheaves mounted on the tailpieces of the axle bearers of two grooved wheels, set 15 feet apart, which traveled on a wire rope suspended 20 feet above the river. A windlass on the ferryboat tightened one wire rope, while slackening the other, directing the boat towards the riverbank nearest the tightening rope.

18 'Internal Improvements-Morris Canal, No. 2' from the *Commercial Advertiser*, reprinted in *The Sussex Register*, 17 September 1827.

19 Poor, ed., *American Railroad Journal*, Vol. 16 or 33, pp. 390-391.

20 *To the Stockholders of the Morris Canal and Banking Company, April 1, 1861*, p. 15.

21 Walch, pp. 8-12.

22 *Ibid.*, p. 20.

23 Saward, ed., *The Coal Trade Journal*, No. 32, Vol. 39 (New York: The Coal Trade Journal, 1900), 8 August 1900, p. 510.

24 Dodge, *Encyclopedia, Vermont Biography* (Burlington, Vermont: Ullery Publishing Company, 1912), p. 327. The scale was based upon a design patented on 15 January 1856.

25 'On the Line of the Morris Canal', *Public Ledger*, 23 July 1860, p. 1.

26 Each keg weighed 100 lb. The nail works not only smelted about three quarters of the iron it used from the ore, but it also manufactured kegs from felled timber.

27 Chapin, 'Among the Nail-Makers', *Harper's New Monthly Magazine*, Vol. 21, June to November 1860 (New York: Harper & Brothers, 1860), pp. 145-164.

28 'The Money Market', *The Public Ledger*, 24 July 1860.

29 Receipts for 1861 showed a decrease of $58,864 and a decrease in expenses of $869, making the decrease in net earnings $57,994.

30 Schultz, ed., *American Railroad Journal*, Vol. 18 or 35, p. 326.

31 *To the Stockholders of the Morris Canal and Banking Company, April 1, 1861*, p. 14. Masons used lime mortar instead of hydraulic cement when they enlarged the lock chambers in 1841, which washed out over time as the lime dissolved, endangering the stability of the masonry.

32 *Ibid.*, p. 16.

33 *Ibid.* Lift locks Nos. 2, 3 and 4 West and Nos. 2, 3, 11 and 12 East were lengthened, as were the guard lock at Saxton Falls and the tide lock at Jersey City.

34 Schultz, ed., *American Railroad Journal*, Vol. 18 or 35, p. 326.

35 *To the Stockholders of the Morris Canal and Banking Company, April 1, 1861*, p. 16. Presumably, eliminating Locks Nos. 3, 4, 5, 6 and 7 East (representing combined changes in elevation of 44 feet) and relocating and increasing the elevation of Plane No. 5 East from 66 to 110 feet.

36 *Ibid.*

37 *The New Jersey Herald*, 22 March 1862.

38 Starting in 1862, labor organizers in the anthracite coal fields (first popularly styled the *Buckshots*, but later known as the *Molly Maquires*) fought for better conditions and pay. The Workingmen's Benevolent Association was organized during a strike for the eight-hour workday in July 1868. A strike against a reduction of pay in 1869 resulted in the adoption of a sliding pay scale in the Lehigh and Schuylkill coalfields, being based on the prices received for Lehigh coal at tidewater and for Schuylkill coal at Port Carbon. When non-union miners were employed near Scranton in 1871, the resulting violence left three men dead. Another reduction of wages in 1875 caused further strife. By this time, immigrants from southern Europe, especially Slavs and Italians, steadily supplanted miners from the British Isles (then including Ireland) and Germany. The labor movement was largely suppressed on 21 June 1877, when five *Molly Maquires* were hung at Mauch Chunk. See 'High Lights in Anthracite Trade History—II', *The Coal Trade Journal*, Vol. 50, p. 644.

39 *The New Jersey Herald*, 3 May 1862.

40 'The Flood in the Lehigh Valley', *Friends' Intelligencer*, 14 June 1862, p. 224.

41 The upper section of the Lehigh Canal, extending 25 miles above Mauch Chunk to White Haven, was never rebuilt, ceding its traffic to the

railroad.

42 Schultz, ed., *American Railroad Journal*, Vol. 19 or 36, p. 448.

43 Schultz, ed., *American Railroad Journal*, Vol. 20 or 37, p. 445.

44 John Dod Ward, civil engineer and foundry owner, was born in Morristown, N.J., on 6 January 1795, to Silas Ward and Phebe Dod. Ward relocated from Vermont to superintend construction of a section of the Morris Canal. His wife, Laura Roburds, was Canadian. He died on 19 May 1873 in Jersey City.

45 Schultz, ed., *American Railroad Journal*, Vol. 21 or 38, pp. 849-850.

46 *The Sussex Independent*, 2 August 1918.

47 *The New-York Times*, 4 September 1865, p. 2.

48 For the fiscal year ending on 28 February 1866, receipts amounted to $600,584, compared with expenses of $272,865, leaving $327,719 in net earnings. After paying interest on bonds, a balance of $117,851 remained. Freight amounted to 716,587 tons—7,340 tons less than the previous year. The canal shipped 428,180 tons of coal; 174,838 tons of ore; and 18,407 tons of iron. Due to striking miners, shipments of coal fell 26,732 tons below that of the previous year.

49 'Morris Canal Explorations', *The New Jersey Herald*, 2 August 1866.

50 Coal shipments from Port Delaware, delivered by railroad, increased by 52 percent, from 74,502 tons in 1865 to 112,790 tons in 1866; coal shipments from Port Washington increased by 13 percent, from 124,204 tons to 141,034 tons over the same period. At the same time, the amount of coal received from the Lehigh Canal at Port Delaware shrank by 6 percent, from 217,933 tons to 205,351 tons.

51 Saward, ed., *The Coal Trade Journal*, No. 32, Vol. 39, p. 499. When the tonnage of canal boats increased to 70 tons, the dock could load about forty-five boats daily.

52 Schultz, ed., *American Railroad Journal*, Vol. 23 or 40, p. 457.

53 On 15 November 1865, two cars loaded with coal at Mauch Chunk became the first shipment to pass over the Morris and Essex Railroad between the mines and tidewater at Hoboken, NJ. On 24 December 1865, the Morris and Essex Railroad opened to Phillipsburg with coal trains running regularly.

54 Schultz, ed., *American Railroad Journal*, Vol. 24 or 41, p. 534.

55 *Ibid.* Of this amount, 142,925 tons crossed the Delaware River into the Lehigh Valley and 61,958 tons were delivered to the Warren Railroad at Port Washington, leaving 83,667 tons to be distributed along the line of the canal.

56 *Ibid.*

57 *Ibid.*

58 *The Proceedings of the American Society of Civil Engineers, January to December 1893*, p. 98.

59 Schultz, ed., *American Railroad Journal*, Vol. 25 or 42, p. 454.

60 Schultz, ed., *American Railroad Journal*, Vol. 26 or 43, p. 511. When the Lehigh Valley Railroad renumbered the locks, it became Lock No. 14 East.
61 *Ibid.*, p. 511.
62 *Ibid.*, p. 1121.
63 Schultz, ed., *American Railroad Journal*, Vol. 27 or 44, p. 544.
64 *The New Jersey Herald*, 23 March 1871.
65 *The Brooklyn Daily Eagle*, 22 March 1871, p. 2.
66 Schultz, ed., *American Railroad Journal*, Vol. 27 or 44, p. 544.
67 *Ibid.*

6. Back Number

1 'The Morris Canal, The People who Work on it and How They Live' from the *New York Evening Post*, reprinted in *The Sussex Independent*, of Deckertown, NJ, 17 November 1871.
2 *Ibid.*
3 *Ibid.*
4 'Canal Boat Life', *The Chatham Record*, 14 February 1889.
5 *Ibid.*, p. 1.
6 *Ibid.*
7 *Ibid.*
8 *Ibid.*
9 *Ibid.*
10 *Ibid.*
11 *Ibid.*
12 'High Lights in Anthracite Trade History—II', *The Coal Trade Journal*, Vol. 50, p. 644.
13 *The Manufacturer and Builder*, No. 6, Vol. 6, June 1872 (New York: Western and Company, 1872) p. 121.
14 Schultz, ed., *American Railroad Journal*, Vol. 29 or 46, p. 200.
15 Schultz, ed., *American Railroad Journal*, Vol. 30 or 47, p. 123.
16 *Ibid.*, p. 258.
17 Saward, ed., *The Coal Trade Journal*, No. 32, Vol. 39, p. 510.
18 'New-Jersey', *The New York Times*, 22 March 1873, p. 12.
19 'The Cause of Hard Times', *The New Jersey Herald*, 9 February 1876.
20 *The New Jersey Herald*, 19 January 1876.
21 'New-Jersey Water, Proposed Supply from the Morris Canal', *The New York Times*, 21 August 1874, p. 2.
22 *First Annual Report of the State Board of Assessors of the State of New Jersey for the Year 1884*, p. 400.
23 Werts, Griggs and Voorhees, *Report of the Commissioners Appointed*

Under Concurrent Resolution of March 31, 1903, To Investigate and Report Upon the Abandonment of Navigation of the Morris Canal (Trenton, NJ: 1905), p. 31.

24 Vermeule, C. C., *Report on Water-Supply, Geological Survey of New Jersey, Vol. III of the Final Report of the State Geologist* (Trenton: John L. Murphy Publishing Co., 1894), p. 180.

25 Maxim, *Morris Canal Abandonment Problems* (New York: The McConnell Printing Co., 1913), p. 20.

26 'A Hotbed of Contagion', *New York Herald*, 7 July 1871. As early as July 1871, sewers from poor tenements in Jersey City emptied into the canal, rather than extending under it to the river, creating both a stench and a health hazard. It also became a receptacle for dead dogs, cats, horses and hogs.

27 Saward, ed., *The Coal Trade Journal*, No. 32, Vol. 39, p. 511. The Morris Canal and Banking Company allowed the Centre Market building to be built over the canal between Broad and Market Streets in 1852.

28 'High Lights in Anthracite Trade History—II', *The Coal Trade Journal*, Vol. 50, p. 644.

29 Saward, ed., *The Coal Trade Journal*, No. 32, Vol. 39, p. 499.

30 *Ibid.*

31 John Mitchell organized the United Mine Workers of America in 1899. The new union called a general strike on 15 May 1902, cutting supplies of coal. President Theodore Roosevelt resolved the crisis on 23 October 1902 through creation of the Anthracite Coal Strike Commission, which, although denying the union recognition, did result in the formation of the Anthracite Board of Conciliation to settle disputes between workers and owners. Accepting President Roosevelt's offer of arbitration, a miners' union convention at Wilkes-Barre called off the strike on 21 October 1902, instructing members to resume work in two days. The Morris Canal carried 27,392 tons of cargo in 1902.

32 *Preliminary Report of the Inland Waterways Commission* (Washington, DC: Government Printing Office, 1908), p. 264.

33 'Fielder and the Morris Canal', *The Hackensack Republican*, 16 October 1913.

34 *Ibid.*

35 'Trying To Make The Old Morris Canal A State Park', *The New York Times*, 17 March 1912, p. 13. The Morris Canal Parkway Association had 2,000 members in March 1912. Its officers were: president Julian R. Tinkham, Upper Montclair; vice-president Colonel Samuel Phillips; Dundee Lake; secretary Aldis Squire, Bloomfield; and treasurer Paul Van Daeli, New York City.

36 *Ibid.*

37 Between the Hackensack and Hudson Rivers, the Morris Canal went south along Newark Bay to circumvent Bergen Hill, reaching the boundary between Jersey City and Bayonne, where it made a sharp bend near present Interchange 14A of the New Jersey Turnpike before returning north along the shores of Upper New York Bay to its outlet basin. This sharp bend was known as Fiddler's Elbow. Carlton Godfrey, Speaker of the General Assembly, chaired the committee, which was also known as the Godfrey Committee.

38 'Morris Canal Big Enterprise of 1820', reprinted from *The Morristown Jerseyman* in 'The Morris Canal Big Entreprise of 1820', *The New Jersey Herald*, 1 August 1918.

39 *Bulletin of the Atlantic Deeper Waterways Association*, No. 2, Vol. 7, January 1915 (Philadelphia: The Atlantic Deeper Waterways Association, 1915), p. 12.

40 'Morris Canal Taxation', *Trenton Evening Times*, 30 October 1915, p. 6.

41 Vermeule, C. C. Jr, *Morris Canal and Banking Company. Final Report of Consulting and Directing Engineer, June 29, 1929* (East Orange, NJ: Abbey Printing Company, 1929), p. 65.

42 'Morris Canal Bill Critics Answered', *The Sussex Register*, 30 March 1922.

43 The Get Together Committee consisted of Edgar H. Bolles, Lehigh Valley Railroad; Jerome T. Congleton, corporation counsel for Newark; Spaulding Frazer, assistant city counsel, Newark; Elmer King, of Netcong; Hudson Maxim, of Lake Hopatcong; John Milton, corporation counsel for Jersey City; Senator William H. Parry, of Newark; Frank H. Sommer, counsel, North Jersey District Water Supply Commission; W. H. Walters, of Warren County.

44 The subcommittee included: Jerome T. Congleton, Elmer King, Hudson Maxim, Judge Fred G. Stickel Jr, Frank H. Sommer, George L. Record, W. H. Walters and ex-officio chairman E. B. Mott.

45 'Morris Canal Bill, Dry Ratification, Pass Legislature', *The Sussex Register*, 16 March 1922. Judge William H. Spear, Frank H. Sommer and Louis A. Focht were appointed commissioners.

BIBLIOGRAPHY

Press

Boston Morning Post
The Chatham Record (Pittsboro, North Carolina)
The Daily Pittsburgh Gazette
The Evening Post (New York)
Geneva Gazette, and General Advertiser (Geneva, NJ)
The Hackensack Republican (Hackensack, NJ)
The Jeffersonian Republican (Stroudsburg, PA)
The New Jersey Herald (Newton, NJ)
The New York Evening Post
New York Herald
The New York Times
New-York Tribune
Palladium of Liberty (Morristown, NJ)
Paterson Guardian
The Pittsburgh Gazette (Pittsburgh, PA)
Public Ledger (Philadelphia, PA)
The Reading Eagle (Reading, PA)
The Sun (New York)
The Sussex Independent (Deckertown, NJ)
The Sussex Register (Newton, NJ)
The Times (London, England)
Trenton Evening Times (Trenton, NJ)

Periodicals

American Engineer and Railroad Journal, New Series, Vols. 68 and 8 (New York: M. N. Forney, 1894)

The American Magazine of Useful and Entertaining Knowledge, Vol. 1 (Boston: John L. Sibley, William D. Ticknor, 1834)

American Railroad Journal and Iron Manufacturer's and Mining Gazette, Vol. 21 (Philadelphia: J. H. Schultz, 1848)

The Bankers' Magazine and Statistical Register, From July 1881, to July 1882, Third Series, Vol. 36 or 16 (New York: Benjamin Homans, 1882)

Bulletin of the Atlantic Deeper Waterways Association, No. 2, Vol. 7, January 1915 (Philadelphia: The Atlantic Deeper Waterways Association, 1915)

Chapin, J. R., 'Among the Nail-Makers', *Harper's New Monthly Magazine*, Vol. 21, June to November 1860 (New York: Harper & Brothers, 1860)

Civil Engineer and Architect's Journal, Scientific and Railway Gazette, Vol. 5 (1840) (London: R. Groombridge, 1842)

The Coal Trade Journal, No. 21, Vol. 50, 14 May 1919 (New York); No. 23, Vol. 50, 1919 (New York)

Colburn, Z., *Engineering, An Illustrated Weekly Journal, From July to December 1868*, Vol. 6 (London: Office for Advertisements and Publication, 1868)

The Family Magazine or Monthly Abstract of General Knowledge, Vol. 5 (New York: J. S. Redfield, 1838)

Friends' Intelligencer (Philadelphia: Charles H. Davis)

The Franklin Journal and American Mechanics' Magazine; Devoted to the Useful Arts, Internal Improvements, and General Science, No. 5, Vol. 2, November 1826 (Philadelphia: Judah Dobson, 1826)

Goller, R., *The Towpath Post, Journal of the Canal Society of New Jersey*, No. 1, Vol. 6 (Autumn 1975)

Harper's New Monthly Magazine, June to November 1857, Vol. 15 (New York: Harper Brothers, 1857); *December 1864 to May 1865*, Vol. 30 (New York: Harper & Brothers, 1865)

Hazard, S., ed., *The Register of Pennsylvania, January to July 1829*, Vol. 3 (Philadelphia: W. F. Geddes, 1829); *July to January 1830*, Vol. 4 (Philadelphia: Wm. F. Geddes, 1830); *January to July 1831*, Vol. 7 (Philadelphia: Wm. F. Geddes, 1831)

Hunt, F., ed., *The Merchants' Magazine and Commercial Review, From July to December 1849*, Vol. 21 (New York: Freeman Hunt, 1849)

Jones, T. P., ed., *The Franklin Journal and American Mechanics' Magazine* (Philadelphia: Judah Dobson, 1826)

—*Journal of the Franklin Institute of the State of Pennsylvania*, New Series, Vol. 5 (Philadelphia: Franklin Institute, 1830)

Larned, J. N., com., *The New Larned History for Ready Reference, Reading and Research*, Vol. 2 (Springfield, Massachusetts: C. A. Nichols Publishing Company, 1922)

The Manufacturer and Builder, No. 6, Vol. 6 (New York: Western and Company, 1872)

The Mechanics' Magazine, Museum, Register, Journal and Gazette, Vol. 15 (London: M. Salmon, 1831)

Minor, D. K., ed., *American Railroad Journal and Advocate of Internal Improvements, From January to December 1832*, Nos. 1-52, Vol. 1 (New York: D. K. Minor, 1833); From July 1832 to January 1833, Vol. 1, Part 2 (New York: D. K. Minor, 1833); January to July 1834, Vol. 3, Part 1 (New York: D. K. Minor, 1834); January to July 1835, Vol. 4, Part 1 (New York: D. K. Minor, 1835)

—*American Railroad Journal and General Advertiser,* Second Quarto Series, Vol. 2 or 19 (Philadelphia: D. K. Minor, 1846); From January to December 1847, Second Quarto Series, Vol. 3 or 10 (Philadelphia: D. K. Minor, 1848)

—*American Railroad Journal and Iron Manufacturer's and Mining Gazette,* From January to December 1848, Second Quarto Series, Vol. 4 or 21 (Philadelphia: D. K. Minor, 1849)

Minor, D. K. and Schaeffer, G. C., ed., *American Railroad Journal*, and *Advocate of Internal Improvements*, No. 49, Vol. 5 (New York: G. Mitchell, 10 December 1836); Vol. 6 (New York: G. Mitchell, 1837 and 1838)

—*American Railroad Journal and Mechanics' Magazine*, New Series, No. 1, Vol. 10, and Whole Series, No. 421, Vol. 16, January 1843 (New York: George C. Schaeffer and D. K. Minor, 1843); Third Series, No. 6, Vol. 1, and Whole Series, No. 425, Vol. 16, June 1843 (New York: George C. Schaeffer and D. K. Minor, 1843)

Niles, H., ed., *Niles' Weekly Register*, From September 1815 to March 1816, Vol. 9 (Baltimore: The Franklin Press, 1816)

—From March to September 1817, Vol. 12 (Baltimore: The Franklin Press, 1817)

—From September 1822 to March 1823, New Series, Vol. 11 or 23 (Baltimore: William Ogden Niles, 1823)

—From September 1823 to March 1824, Third Series, Vol. 1 or 25 (Baltimore: Franklin Press, 1824)

—From September 1825 to March 1826, Third Series, Vol. 5 or 29 (Baltimore: Franklin Press, 1826)

—Third Series, No. 26, Vol. 10, and Whole Series No. 884, Vol. 34 (Baltimore: Franklin Press, 23 August 1828)

—Fourth Series, No. 8, Vols. 1 and 37 (Baltimore: Franklin Press, 17 October 1829)

—From March 1831 to September 1831, Fourth Series, Vol. 4 or 40, 30 April 1831 (Baltimore: Franklin Press, 1831)

—Fourth Series, No. 1, Vol. 9, and Whole Series, No. 1, Vol. 45, 31 August 1833 (Baltimore: Franklin Press, 1834)

—From March 1835 to September 1835, Fourth Series, Vol. 12 or 48 (Baltimore: H. Niles, 1835)

Poor, H. V., ed., *American Railroad Journal*, Second Quarto Series, Vol. 6 or 23 (New York: J. H. Schultz, 1850)

—Vol. 8 or 25 (New York: J. H. Schultz, 1852)

—Vol. 9 or 26 (New York: J. H. Schultz, 1853)

—Vol. 13 or 30 (New York: J. H. Schultz, 1857)

—Vol. 16 or 33 (New York: J. H. Schultz, 1860)

—*History of the Railroads and Canals of the United States of America, Exhibiting their Progress, Cost, Revenues, Expenditures & Present Condition*, Vol. 1 (New York: John R. Schultz & Co., 1860)

The Republican Compiler, No. 19, Vol. 13 (Gettysburg, PA: 18 January 1831)

Saward, F. E., ed., *The Coal Trade Journal*, No. 32, Vol. 39 (New York: The Coal Trade Journal, 1900)

Schaeffer, G. C., ed., *American Railroad Journal and Mechanics' Magazine*, New Series, Vol. 15 and 9 (New York: George C. Schaeffer, 1842)

Schaeffer, G. C. and Hedge, E., ed., *American Railroad Journal and Mechanics' Magazine*, New Series, Vol. 5 or 11 (New York: George C. Schaeffer and Egbert Hedge, 1840)

Scientific American, New Series, No. 20, Vol. 46 (New York: 20 May 1882)

Schultz, J. H., ed., *American Railroad Journal*, Second Quarto Series, Vol. 18 or 35 (New York: J. H. Schultz, 1862); Vol. 19 or 36 (New York: J. H. Schultz, 1863); Vol. 20 or 37 (New York: John H. Schultz, 1864); Vol. 21 or 38 (New York: John H. Schultz, 1865); Vol. 23 or 40 (New York: John H. Schultz, 1867); Vol. 24 or 41 (New York: John H. Schultz, 1868); Vol. 25 or 42 (New York: John H. Schultz, 1869); Vol. 26 or 43 (New York: John H. Schultz, 1870); Vol. 27 or 44 (New York: John H. Schultz, 1871); Vol. 29 or 46 (New York: John H. Schultz, 1873); Vol. 30 or 47 (New York: John H. Schultz, 1874)

Silliman, B., ed., *The American Journal of Science and Arts*, Vol. 14, July 1828 (New Haven: Hezekiah Howe, 1828)

Skinner, I. L., ed., *The American Journal of Improvements in the Useful Arts and Mirror of the Patent Office in the United States*, No. 1, Vol. 1, January, February and March 1828 (Washington: William Greer, 1828)

Tenney, W. J., ed., *The Mining Magazine: Devoted to Mines, Mining Operations, Metallurgy, &c., &c.*, Vol. 8 (New York: John F. Trow, 1857)

The Republican Compiler, No. 24, Vol. 2, 23 February 1820 (Gettysburg, PA); No. 47, Vol. 6, 28 July 1824 (Gettysburg, PA)

The Torch Light and Public Advertiser, No. 10, Vol. 17, 30 December 1830 (Hagerstown, Maryland)

The Towpath Post, Journal of the Canal Society of New Jersey, No. 4, Vol. 5 (Summer 1975)

Youmans, W. J., ed., *The Popular Science Monthly, November 1890 to April 1891*, Vol. 38 (New York: D. Appleman and Company, 1891)

Published Works

Aaseng, Nathan, *Business Builders in Real Estate* (Minneapolis, MN: The Oliver Press, 2002)

Acts of the Forty-Fourth General Assembly, Second Sitting (Trenton, NJ: 1820)

Acts of the Sixty-Fifth General Assembly of the State of New Jersey (Trenton: Phillips and Boswell, 1841)

Acts of the Sixty-Sixth General Assembly of the State of New Jersey (Somerville: S. L. B. Baldwin, 1845)

Appleton's Annual Cyclopædia and Register of Important Events of the Year 1883, New Series, Vol. 8, and Whole Series, Vol. 23 (New York: D. Appleton and Company, 1885)

Atkinson's Casket, Gems of Literature, Wit and Sentiment (Philadelphia: Samuel C. Atkinson, 1836)

Bacon, E. M., *The Connecticut River and the Valley of the Connecticut* (New York: G. P. Putnam's Sons, 1906)

Barber, J. W. and Howe, H., *Historical Collections of the State of New Jersey* (New York: S. Tuttle, 1844)

Battle, J. H., ed., *History of Bucks County, Pennsylvania* (Philadelphia: A. Warner & Co., 1887)

Bernhard, Duke of Saxe-Weimar Eisenach, *Travels Through North America During The Years 1825 and 1826*, Vol. 1 (Philadelphia: Carey, Lea & Carey, 1828)

Biographical and Genealogical History of Morris and Sussex Counties, New Jersey, Vol. 1 (New York: The Lewis Publishing Company, 1899)

The Biographical Encyclopædia of New Jersey of the Nineteenth Century (Philadelphia: Galaxy Publishing Company, 1877)

Blake, D. D. and Lauris, J., *The Family Encyclopedia of Useful Knowledge and General Literature* (Philadelphia: Carey & Hart, 1849)

Bryant, W. C., ed., *Picturesque America: Or, The Land We Live In* (New York: D. Appleton and Company, 1872)

Carhart, L. A., com., and Nelson, C. A., ed., *Genealogy of the Morris Family* (New York: The A. S. Barnes Company, 1911)

Charter of the Morris Canal and Banking Company, and the Several Acts of the Legislature in Relation Thereto (New York: J. Narine, 1836)

Chevalier, M., *Histoire et Description des Voies de Communication aux États-Unis*, Tome II, (Paris, Librairie de Charles Gosselin, 1841)

Colden, Cadwallader D., *A Report to the Directors of the Morris Canal and Banking Company; Made by the President, May 1st, 1827* (New York: William Davis, Jr, 1827)

Condict, U. W., *The History of Easton, Penn'a From The Earliest Times To The Present, 1739–1885*, (Easton, PA: George W. West, 1885)

Cuvier, G. M., *Essay on the Theory of the Earth* (New York: Kirk & Mercein, 1818)

Daddow, S. H. and Bannan, B., *Coal, Iron, and Oil; or, the Practical American Miner. A Plain and Popular Work on Our Mines and Mineral Resources, and a Text-Book or Guide to their Economical Development* (Pottsville, PA: Benjamin Bannan, 1866)

Documents Accompanying the Journal of the Senate of the State of Michigan at the Annual Session of 1840, Vol. 1-2 (Detroit: George Dawson, 1840)

Documents Accompanying the Journal of the Senate of the State of Michigan at the Annual Session of 1841, Vol. 1 (Detroit: George Dawson, 1841)

Documents of the Assembly of the State of New-York, Fifty-Fifth Session, 1832, Vol. 4 (Albany: E. Croswell, 1832)

Dodge, Prentiss C., ed., *Encyclopedia, Vermont Biography* (Burlington, Vermont: Ullery Publishing Company, 1912)

Domett, H. W., *A History of the Bank of New York 1784–1884* (New York: G. P. Putnam's Sons, 1884)

Dwight, T., *Travels in New-England and New York*, Vol. 1 (London: William Baynes and Son, 1823)

Elmer, L. Q. C., *Collections of the New Jersey Historical Society, Vol. VII, The Constitution and Government of the Province and State of New Jersey, with Biographical Sketches of the Governors from 1776 to 1845, and Reminiscences of the Bench and Bar, During More Than Half A Century* (Newark, NJ: Martin R. Dennis and Company, 1872)

The Encyclopædia Britannica, A Dictionary of Arts, Sciences, and General Literature, Vol. 4 (Chicago: The Werner Company, 1895)

First Annual Report of the State Board of Assessors of the State of New Jersey for the Year 1884 (Trenton: John L. Murphy, 1884)

Fourth Annual Report of the Board of Managers of the Delaware, Lackawanna & Western Rail-Road Co. to the Stockholders, January 1857 (New York: George F. Nesbitt & Co., 1857)

Gamst, F. C., ed., and Diephouse, D. J., trans., *Franz Anton Ritter Von Gerstner, Early American Railroads*, Vol. 1 (Stanford, California: Stanford University Press, 1997)

Gordon, T., *The History and Gazetteer of New Jersey* (Trenton: Daniel Fenton, 1834)

Gouge, W. M., *The Journal of Banking from July 1841 to July 1842* (Philadelphia: J. Van Court, 1842)

Wilson, J. G. and Fiske, J., ed., *Appleton's Cyclopædia of American Biography*, Vol. 2 (New York: D. Appleton and Company, 1888)

Henry, M. S., *History of the Lehigh Valley* (Easton: Bixler & Corwin, 1859)

Hermelin, S. G., *Report About The Mines In The United States of America, 1783* (Philadelphia: John Morton Memorial Museum, 1931)

History of Morris County, New Jersey 1739–1882 (New York: W. W. Munsell & Co., 1882)

History of Schuylkill County, PA (New York: W. W. Munsell & Co., 1881)

Joint Documents of the State of Michigan at the Annual Session of 1841, Vol. 1 (Detroit: George Dawson, 1841)

Jones, C. L., *The Economic History of the Anthracite-Tidewater Canals* (Philadelphia: The University of Pennsylvania, 1908)

Journal of the Fourth Senate of the State of New Jersey, Being the Seventy-Second Session of the Legislature (Flemington: Henry C. Buffington, 1848)

Journal of the Franklin Institute, Third Series, Vol. 15, and Whole Series, Vol. 45 (Philadelphia: Franklin Institute, 1848)

Letter of Charles Butler, Esq., to the Legislature of Indiana in relation to the Public Debt (Indianapolis: Morrison & Spann, 1846)

Lossing, B. J., ed., *Harper's Encyclopedia of United States History*, Vol. 8 (New York: Harper and Brothers, 1912)

Lyon, I. S., *Historical Discourse on Boonton* (Newark: The Daily Journal, 1873)

MacBean, W. M., *Biographical Register of Saint Andrew's Society of the State of New York*, Vol. 2, 1807–1856 (New York: Saint Andrew's Society, 1925)

Mauch Chunk and Vicinity With A Description Of The Famous Switch-Back Railroad (Mauch Chunk: Boyle, Reed & Gihon, 1872)

Maxim, Hudson, *Morris Canal Abandonment Problems* (New York: The McConnell Printing Co., 1913)

Minute Book of the Morris Canal Company

Moat, L. S., ed., *Frank Leslie's Illustrated History of the Civil War* (New York: Mrs. F. Leslie, 1895)

The National Cyclopedia of American Biography, Vol. 11 (New York: James T. White & Company, 1892); Vol. 7 (New York: James T. White & Co., 1897)

Northrop, H. D., *The Student's History of the United States*, Vol. 2 (Boston: New England Home Educational Society, 1901)

Plymley, J., *General View of the Agriculture of Shropshire* (London: Richard Phillips, 1803)

The Port Folio, Vol. I, or Hall's Second Series, July to December 1826, Vol. 21 (Philadelphia: Harrison Hall, 1826)

Potts, J. C., *The New Jersey Register for the Year Eighteen Hundred and Thirty-Seven*, Vol. 1 (Trenton: William D'Hart, 1837)

Preliminary Report of the Inland Waterways Commission (Washington, DC: Government Printing Office, 1908)

The Proceedings of the American Society of Civil Engineers, Vol. 19, January to December 1893 (New York: Published by the Society, 1893)

Renwick, J., *Applications of the Science of Mechanics to Practical Purposes* (New York: Harper & Brothers, 1840)

Report of the Commissioners Appointed by the Legislature of the State of New-Jersey, For The Purpose of Exploring The Route of A Canal To United The River Delaware, Near Easton, With The Passaic, Near, Newark (Morristown: Jacob Mann, 1823)

Report of the Morris Canal Investigation Committee, Appointed under Joint Resolution of April 12, 1911 (New York: Isaac H. Blanchard Company, 1914)

Report on the Origin and Increase of the Paterson Manufactories, and the Intended Diversion of Their Waters by the Morris Canal Company (Paterson: Day & Burnett, 1828)

Report of the President and Directors of the Morris Canal & Banking Company to the Stockholders, March 1837 (New York: James Van Norden, 1837)

Rees, A., *The Cyclopædia; or, Universal Dictionary of Arts Sciences, and Literature*, Vol. 6 (London: Longman, Hurst, Rees, Orme, & Brown, 1819)

Ruoff, H. W., ed., *Biographical and Portrait Cyclopedia of Schuylkill County, Pennsylvania* (Philadelphia: Rush, West and Company, 1893)

Rupp, L. Daniel, com., *History of Northampton, Lehigh, Monroe, Carbon and Schuylkill Counties, PA.* (Harrisburg: Hickok & Cantine, 1845)

Schultz, G. W., *Antique Iron Works and Machines of the Water Power Age* (Bowers, PA: Geo. W. Schultz, 1927)

Second Annual Report of the Geological Survey of the State of New Jersey for the Year 1855 (Trenton: The True American Office, 1856)

Shaw, W. H., com., *History of Essex and Hudson Counties, New Jersey* (Philadelphia: Everts & Peck, 1884)

Stevenson, D., *Sketch of the Civil Engineering of North America* (London: John Weale, 1859)

Stillman, B., ed., *The American Journal of Science and Arts*, Vol. 14, July 1828 (New Haven: Hezekiah Howe, 1828)

Stuart, C. B., *Lives and Works of Civil and Military Engineers of America* (New York: D. Van Nostrand, 1871)

Swift, J. G., *The Memoirs of Gen. Joseph Gardner Swift, L.L.D., U. S. A., First Graduate of the United States Military Academy, West Point* (Worchester, Massachusetts: F. S. Blanchard & Co., 1890)

Talcott, S. V., com., *Talcott Pedigree in England and America From 1558 to 1876* (Albany: Weed, Parsons and Company, 1876)

Tanner, H. S., *Brief Description of the Canals and Railroads of Pennsylvania and New Jersey* (Philadelphia: H. S. Tanner, 1834)

Temin, P., *The Jacksonian Economy* (New York: W. W. Norton & Co., 1969)

Thomas, R., *Pictorial History of the United States of America* (Hartford: E. Strong, 1846)

To the Stockholders of the Morris Canal and Banking Company, April 1, 1861 (New York: Latimer Bros. & Seymour, 1861)

Transactions of the American Society of Civil Engineers, Vol. 85 (New York: American Society of Civil Engineers, 1922)

Trollope, F., *Domestic Manners of the Americans* (New York: Vintage Books, 1949)

Trumbull, J. R., *History of Northampton, Massachusetts From Its Settlement In 1654*, Vol. 2 (Northampton, Mass.: Gazette Printing Co., 1902)

Vethake, H., ed., *A Dictionary, Practical, Theoretical, and Historical, of Commerce and Commercial Navigation*, Vol. 1 (Philadelphia: Thomas Wardle, 1840)

Vermeule, C. C., *Report on Water-Supply, Geological Survey of New Jersey, Vol. III of the Final Report of the State Geologist* (Trenton: John L. Murphy Publishing Co., 1894)

Vermeule, Jr, C. C., *Morris Canal and Banking Company. Final Report of Consulting and Directing Engineer, June 29, 1929* (East Orange, NJ: Abbey Printing Company, 1929)

Walch, G. T., *Notes on Some of the Chief Navigable Rivers and Canals in the United States and Canada, Made for the Government of Madras, During a Tour in 1876* (Madras: W. H. Moore, Lawrence Asylum Press, 1877)

Walker, A. M., *Historic Hadley: A Story about the Making of a Famous Massachusetts Town* (New York: The Grafton Press, 1906)

Weaver, E. A., *The Forks of the Delaware Illustrated* (Easton, PA.: The Eschenbach Printing House, 1900)

Werts, G. T., Griggs, J. W., and Voorhees, F. M., *Report of the Commissioners Appointed Under Concurrent Resolution of March 31, 1903, To Investigate and Report Upon the Abandonment of Navigation of the Morris Canal* (Trenton, NJ: 1905)

Wharton, T. I. and Morris, I. T, *Reports of Cases Adjudged in the Supreme Court of Pennsylvania in the Eastern District*, Vol. 2 (Philadelphia: T. & J. Johnson & Co., 1884)

Whitford, N. E., *Supplement to the Annual Report of the State Engineer and Surveyor of the State of New York For the Fiscal Year Ending September 30, 1905, History of the Canal System of the State of New York, Together with Brief Histories of the Canals of the United States and Canada*, Vol. 1 (Albany: Brandow Printing Company, 1906)

Wilson, James Grant and Fiske, John, ed., *Appleton's Cyclopædia of American Biography*, Vol. 2 (New York: D. Appleton and Company, 1888)

Wilson, W., *A History of the American People*, Vol. 4 (New York: Wm. H. Wise & Co., 1931)